CONFRONTING
VALUES IN
POLICY ANALYSIS

──────── BOOKS IN THIS SERIES ────────

Volume 14. Sage Yearbooks in Politics and Public Policy

CONFRONTING VALUES IN POLICY ANALYSIS

The Politics of Criteria

FRANK FISCHER
and
JOHN FORESTER
Editors

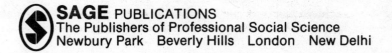

SAGE PUBLICATIONS
The Publishers of Professional Social Science
Newbury Park   Beverly Hills   London   New Delhi

For information address:

SAGE Publications, Inc.
2111 West Hillcrest Drive
Newbury Park, California 91320

SAGE Publications Inc.   SAGE Publications Ltd.
275 South Beverly Drive   28 Banner Street
Beverly Hills   London EC1Y 8QE
California 90212   England

SAGE PUBLICATIONS India Pvt. Ltd.
M-32 Market
Greater Kailash I
New Delhi 110 048 India

Printed in the United States of America

Library of Congress Cataloging-in-Publication Data

Main entry under title:

Confronting values in policy analysis

(Sage yearbook in politics and public policy ; v. 14)
Includes index.
1. Policy sciences. 2. Social policy. I. Fischer,
Frank, 1942-   . II. Forester, John, 1948-
III. Series.
H97.P77 1986   361.6   86-6647
ISBN 0-8039-2616-2
ISBN 0-8039-2617-0 (pbk.)

CONTENTS

SERIES EDITOR'S INTRODUCTION

This is the fourteenth volume in the series of Yearbooks in Politics and Public Policy published by Sage Publications in cooperation with the Policy Studies Organization. This volume is on *Confronting Values in Policy Analysis: The Politics of Criteria,* edited by Frank Fischer and John Forester. It is the first volume in the series that deals with normative or ethical issues in public policy analysis. Other volumes in the series have dealt with the substance, process, or methodology of public policy analysis. This volume is thus overdue in a series that prides itself on covering broad, cross-cutting public policy issues.

The main social values that are dealt with in this book are those that relate to the goals that a society, polity, or economy seeks to achieve and that policy analysts or evaluators should bear in mind when systematically evaluating alternative public policies. Social values exist on various levels of generality. At the highest level, one might say that the goal of public policy is to maximize societal benefits minus societal costs. In a sense that is true by definition, given that societal benefits minus societal costs can be defined as what a society seeks to maximize. Benefits and costs in this context can be either monetary or nonmonetary and either quantitative or qualitative.

At the next highest level, one might say that the goals of a society are to have public policies that are effective, efficient, and equitable. Effectiveness refers to achieving or maximizing the specific goals toward which the policies are directed. Efficiency refers to being able to achieve those goals with a minimum of cost or at least within a budget constraint. Equity refers to seeing that no groups, places, or individuals receive less than a minimum quantity of benefits or are assessed more than a maximum quantity of costs. Equity can also refer to apportioning the benefits and costs in proportion to criteria such as need and merit.

Closely related to those "three E's" that are associated with economics are the "three P's," which are associated with political science. They are the social values of political participation, predictability, and procedural due process. Political participation refers at a minimum to majority rule while allowing minorities to try to convert the majority to their viewpoints. It can also refer to a variety of devices for facilitating input from the general public into governmental decision making. Predictability refers to the minimum idea that governmental laws and other rules will not be changed retroactively to behavior that has already occurred. It can also refer to having rules that are reasonably clear and that are changed only after giving reasonable notice to those who are likely to be affected. Procedural due process refers at a minimum to procedures designed to enable those who are accused of wrongdoing to be notified of the accusation, to be able to present witnesses on their behalf, to be able to question the accusing witnesses, and to have a decision maker who is not also an accuser.

At the next level of generality, we could talk about liberal and conservative values. Liberal values are those oriented toward (1) having the government play a more positive role in dealing with social problems, (2) promoting more equality of opportunity if not income and wealth, and (3) having consumers and workers play a more important role in economic decision making. Conservative values are those oriented toward (1) having the marketplace play a more positive role in dealing with social problems, (2) justifying inequalities based on merit or sometimes ancestry, and (3) having managers and owners play a more important role in economic decision making.

At a lower level of generality, although still high, one can talk about such goals as low unemployment, low inflation, consumer protection, lively business competition, cooperative labor-management relations, environmental protection, acceptable housing, low poverty, non-discrimination along ethnic or gender lines, compliance with the law, energy conservation, a healthy public, easy communication and transportation, and international peace. Those social values can be subdivided further, but then one would be getting into public policy substance and out of the realm of public policy theory and social values.

Another set of values that tends to be covered when discussing social values in policy analysis are the criteria for resolving dilemmas faced by policy analysts or evaluators when they decide among controversial alternative roles to perform in the interests of society. One set of such dilemmas of professional ethics relates to the ends policy analysts should seek to pursue. One end relates to purposes. The key dilemma here is the extent to which policy analysts have an obligation to go beyond the purpose of merely describing the impact of one or more public policies and discussing the public policies that ought to be adopted for optimizing societal goals or subgoals. Another end or goal-oriented dilemma is the extent to which policy analysts can ethically pursue the values of groups such as political parties or interest groups and the values of individuals such as incumbent politicians, as well as what seem to be the values of society. Another concern for ends or effects is the extent to which policy analysts have an ethical and possibly legal obligation to go out of their way to foresee foreseeable consequences, as contrasted to truly unforeseeable consequences.

In addition to ethical dilemmas that relate to purposes, goals, and effects, there is a set of ethical dilemmas that relate to appropriate methods for policy analysts to use. One such dilemma relates to how far policy analysts have to go in seeking valid conclusions, even when requiring elaborate research may be wasteful of resources. At a minimum, policy analysts should have an obligation to show what it would take to bring a second- or a third-place alternative up to first place. Another dilemma relates to the obligation to share data that may be helpful to the public interest but that may conflict with maximizing the interests of one's firm or oneself. Another methodological dilemma relates to the extent to which human subjects need to be fully informed of the purposes behind quasi-experimental research even when doing so may bias the nature of their participation.

Issues of social values in policy analysis like these are discussed in this book. The issues include both matters of societal values and professional ethics. They include a concern for goal-oriented and methods-oriented dilemmas. The chapters operate on various levels of generality from integrating principles in the beginning to case studies at the end. The chapters are authored by leading scholars in the realm of political and administrative theory. This book is likely to be a substantial contribution to the literature of public policy studies.

—*Stuart S. Nagel*
Urbana, Illinois

VOLUME EDITORS' INTRODUCTION

Policy analysis is an important enterprise. Millions of dollars are spent each year on policy research. Policy analysts work in governmental agencies, policy think tanks, academic departments, private consulting firms, the staffs of interest group associations, and legislatures. Indeed, access to political power today can depend on one's ability to command the resources of policy expertise

The need for such expertise is growing—witness the expansion of academic training in policy analysis. One of the fastest-growing specializations in the social sciences over the past fifteen years, policy analysis is now well-established in such disciplines as political science, economics, public administration, and urban planning. Such training has a number of important intellectual roots. To set the stage for the essays that follow, we shall briefly discuss several essential aspects of the development of contemporary policy analysis.

The idea of policy research is not new. In one form or another it has been carried out as long as policymakers have been making decisions. But as a discipline and a profession, policy analysis is a relatively new endeavor. It dates, in rough terms, from the end of World War II and was a response, in large part, to the changing structure of American government. As postwar government grew and its problems became increasingly complex, the need for policy guidance and expertise grew too—and has continued to press for attention ever since.

The modern policy analysis movement dedicated itself to the development of an "applied social science." Advocates sought the ideal of a discipline that could be both scientifically rigorous and practical at the same time. In practice this took the form of a discipline operating within the intellectual confines of an epistemology limited essentially to technical or instrumental rationality. Policy analysts, as a result, have often been trained primarily to serve as social engineers engaged in the calculation of efficient means to stipulated ends. About the ends themselves policy analysts have often had little to offer. Indeed, practitioners of policy analysis have largely presented themselves as ethically neutral if not altogether value free.

However, as policy analysis has come to play a larger role in policymaking processes, the limits of the discipline's emphasis on efficiency and value neutrality have become increasingly apparent. Such issues have arisen in numerous ways. Perhaps the most significant events triggering these normative concerns were the experiences of the Great Society and the Vietnam war. In each case policy experts had been involved in all phases of the policymaking process. Yet far from simply being objective and independent analysts, policy experts were deeply involved in helping to shape and resolve the basic political issues that defined the period. In this light, the idea of value neutrality was seen to be a wholly inadequate description, if not a misleading ideology, of the policy advisor's conduct.

Moreover, in this period vast amounts of money were spent to evaluate public policies and programs. For Great Society antipoverty programs, for example, Congress attached funds for program evaluation to much of the legislation, a practice later expanded by the Nixon administration. The result was a substantial expenditure of funds for policy research, which in turn gave rise to a small-scale industry both inside and outside government.

In the universities the response was dramatic. Possessing the requisite personnel and always in search of funds, one major university after another developed a policy research institute or center. As policy research began to attract national attention and research grants became easier to obtain, graduate students from various disciplines flocked to the policy orientation. In the process countless numbers of policy analysis dissertations were completed, and new policy journals appeared to define and record the progress of this new field. As one writer put it, the word "policy" soon seemed to be attached to almost everything in the university. In short, policy-oriented programs had become synonymous with the search for a new, more pragmatic and realistic social and political relevance. Such relevance, however, often eluded the various academic attempts to capture it. Indeed, it was not long before the principal consumers of policy analysis—politicians and government administrators—began to express doubts about the relevance of many policy research findings. As the head of one major governmental agency put it, everybody is for policy analysis, but few have come to expect much from it.

What was the problem? Often, it seemed, the dominant empirical methodologies that were so central to policy analysis could not address underlying normative, "value" problems that plagued American society. In the turbulent period characterized by civil rights protests, urban riots, environmental demonstrations, marches against the Vietnam war, and more, America was seen by many to suffer from a "crisis of values." Confronted by normative conflicts of such major proportions—often raising questions about the very nature of the good life and how we ought to live together—an empirical discipline geared wholly to the criterion of efficiency (or its variant, "effectiveness") seldom seemed to address the issues, let alone provide the answers. Thus in the minds of many people the question began to shift from efficiency per se to "efficiency for what?" If no single criterion, such as efficiency, could suffice any longer to order policy choice, the fundamental questions now came to involve situations of hardly commensurable—indeed, conflicting—values and decision criteria. How are policy decisions in such situations to be formulated and judged? The discipline, in short, was forced to face a troublesome reality: Decision criteria are always political. How, then, shall the politics of criteria be explored? The essays collected here explore these questions by probing the normative foundations of policy analysis in contemporary practice.

In the 1970s these concerns led to a good deal of intellectual soul-searching in the policy-oriented social sciences. Several approaches emerged to address these problems. One emphasized the search for "usable knowledge" and added fuel to the fires of a growing special-ization, namely the study of "knowledge utilization." Essentially, research in this area involved the pursuit of a more relevant policy knowledge, defined primarily as knowledge that addresses the needs of its constituents or consumers. This approach was primarily empirical and in most cases tended to limit its focus to the needs of a particular consumer: government policymakers.

A second approach—the focus of this particular anthology—took a different path. For many theorists, the issue of relevance had to be understood in a broader framework of normative (or evaluative) discourse. How were the value dimensions of policy analysis to be addressed? To rescue the discipline from irrelevance, analysts had to incorporate a wide range of evaluative criteria into their analyses. This involved confronting the value implications of policy analysis on their own terms. Toward this end, writers such as Duncan MacRae, Martin Rein, and Frank Fischer argued that the solution was to be found in the integration of empirical and normative modes of analysis.

Renewed interest in normative discourse led to various theoretical and methodological explorations in the field of policy analysis. As this volume demonstrates, such work has attracted authors from related fields as well: social and political philosophy, anthropology, medical ethics, and city planning, among others. The result has often been a stimulating cross-fertilization between theoretical and practical disciplines.

But bringing values—or, more precisely, normative arguments—into the equation has proven to be no easy feat. For an empirically oriented discipline designed around the principle of value neutrality, the introduction of normative questions poses a number of complex epistemological issues, many of which were already long-standing problems in the broader philosophy of social science. Because of its inherent effort to bridge the realms of theory and practice, policy analysis is built upon an interesting mix of empirical and normative concerns. On one hand it is empirical but not rigorously scientific in the classical sense of the term. On the other hand it is fundamentally concerned with the realization of norms and values, but it is not ethics per se. Policy analysis lies squarely (if uncomfortably) between science and ethics. The essays collected here explore this unique character of the policy analysis enterprise.

This volume has five parts. Part I sets out emerging ethical issues. Part II describes the practice of policy analysis and its institutional context: the administrative state. Part III assesses basic theoretical and methodological issues involved in the normative work of policy analysts. Part IV explores central questions of ethical responsibility. Part V provides a rich set of cases illustrating and setting out the basic themes of the book as a whole. Consider briefly now each essay in turn.

Beginning Part I, Charles Anderson describes policy analysis as an intellectual enterprise designed to assist those who assume responsibilities for public choice. As an applied social science, the discipline has roots in classical traditions of thought, but it is concerned fundamentally neither with scientific discovery nor with the justification of thought systems. Its unique mission, as recounted in textbook after textbook, is the improvement of policymaking. Although such an objective seems quite straightforward, Anderson shows that it rests on a number of sophisticated and often controversial political and epistemological assumptions. Indeed, as audacious as it seems, the intent of policy analysis can be described as nothing short of an attempt to reduce the great imponderables of politics to a set of rules about good practices. Anderson maintains that political philosophy, long concerned with such questions, can make an important contribution to policy analysis. He suggests that four classical modes of political discourse—advocacy, explanation, criticism, and deliberative judgment—bear directly on policy decision-making, and each, in fact, is closely associated with a particular policy methodology. The goal of the policy analyst, Anderson suggests, should be to establish and maintain a balance between the contributions of these four modes of policy discourse. In effect, the policy analyst must become a vigilant "partisan of the neglected perspective."

Asking "Can Policy Analysis Be Ethical?" Douglas Amy addresses the normative roles of policy analysts by focusing upon the institutional context in which these roles are performed. Amy detects an inverse relationship between the growing academic interest in ethical policy analysis and its prospects for use in the real world of bureaucratic practice. Although scholars write at length about the need for ethical analysis, analytical practitioners seem increasingly to shy away from it. Amy traces the problem to the bureaucratic context of policy analysis and its hierarchical norms of conduct. To illustrate, he sketches a number of bureaucratic constraints that discourage the incorporation of ethics into policy analysis: for example, the dominance of the technocratic ethos, the psychology of "groupthink," the pervasive influence of bureaucratic politics, and more. Finally, Amy suggests how these constraints might be mitigated if not overcome.

Part II focuses more specifically on the normative context of policy analysis. John Byrne assesses the role of a policy science methodology—cost-benefit analysis—and examines its implications for the larger political system in which it is applied. Cost-benefit analysis, elevated to the status of a primary analytical test for all policy decisions by the Reagan administration, is a methodology designed to discipline policymakers to allocate scarce resources (both public and private) to their highest valued uses. Cost-benefit advocates argue that it helps decision makers confront two major problems of modern government: how to arrive at rational definitions of complex social problems, and how to supply these problems with nonpolitical—or "rational"—solutions.

Analyzing the arguments of the key advocates of cost-benefit analysis, Byrne shows, contrary to their rhetoric, that the technique actually introduces a number of hidden "normative costs" that do not receive sufficient attention. The most important one concerns the nature of governance itself. Essentially, Byrne argues, cost-benefit analysis replaces democratic politics with a technocratic model of administrative decision making. Cost-benefit analysis can thus be seen less as a value-neutral technique and more as an instrument of the administrative state.

Frank Fischer's essay also concerns the relation of policy analysis to the state. Fischer challenges the neoconservative argument that liberal policy expertise has emerged as a new political phenomenon now threatening the future of representative government. Such policy experts, according to the neoconservatives, must be seen as part of a "new class" striving for political power. This power, according to them, is reflected in the leading roles that policy experts have played in the formulation of public policy. The Great Society period of the 1960s is typically cited as the most dramatic example of this phenomenon.

Fischer examines developments of the Great Society period and reveals the neoconservative thesis to be a misleading simplification of a complex pattern of events. The new role of policy expertise, he argues, is less the product of a new and unrepresentative elite conniving for power than the result of the emerging ideological and technical realities of postindustrial politics. Furthermore, he contends that the conservative response to this phenomenon has served to support the technocratic trends that conservatives otherwise purport to challenge. Here he addresses the conservative effort to counter liberal expertise with the development of a "counterintelligentsia." Manifest in the rise of conservative think tanks and a new emphasis on policy techniques more compatible with conservative objectives, the result is a significant politicization of policy analysis.

To begin Part III's discussion of normative theory and related methodological issues, Bruce Jennings offers a far-reaching reformulation of the interpretive foundations of policy analysis. Arguing that "policy analysis today is in search of both a self-identity and a profession," Jennings sets out to provide a powerful account of policy analysis as counsel, an account that provides both a practical identity and an ethical and epistemological basis for the profession.

Policy analysis as counsel takes shape as two alternative models, those of Science and Advocacy, reveal their flaws. Jennings traces the historical roots of these models and does so quite sympathetically, even if ultimately he remains unconvinced of their adequacy. On its own terms, the Science model of policy analysis cannot satisfy its stringent requirements of separating radically issues of fact from value and the knowing subject from the known object. In turn, the Advocacy model seems ultimately to threaten us with the truth of the more muscular advocate. Jennings thus proposes a model of policy analysis as counsel in which ordinary language interpretation provides a public basis upon which policy debates and assessments can take place. Interpretation as an approach to knowledge neither makes the unrealistic demands of the Science model nor leads, Jennings maintains, to an ethical relativism. Indeed, an interpretive turn in contemporary policy analysis might itself encourage more communitarian and democratic, participatory and dialogical, relationships among policymakers, policy analysts, and citizens alike.

In the next essay John Forester explores a transcript of a project review meeting in which a real estate developer and a metropolitan city planner review the developer's plans for two new office buildings. This empirical study of a planning analyst at work shows clearly the interpretive character of analysis that Jennings had introduced. The transcript reveals several strategic normative judgments that planning and policy analysts must routinely make.

Forester argues that the transcript shows a particular type of interpretation at work: Analysts not only predict but they work to anticipate and shape project outcomes as well. Such anticipation has a practical structure. Before an analysis can be presented, arguments must be prepared and managed, and before that the functional, normative, and cultural settings in which implementation is to occur must be enivisioned. But how can such management of arguments take place? What are the practical and theoretical requirements of envisioning future settings? Based on the empirical transcript, Forester's essay seeks to answer these questions, providing an account of planning and policy analysis that is intrinsically interpretive and inescapably normative as well.

Concluding Part III, Timothy Luke asks, "What can rational choice theory contribute to the practice of normative reasoning in the policy sciences?" Luke wishes to answer this question in order to clarify basic methodological problems of the policy sciences. Today an increasing number of rational choice theorists are coming to question the traditional gulf separating the realms of "facts" and "values," Luke argues. What are we to make of proposals to use scientific analysis to "test" the value positions of normative political theorists? Luke distinguishes the character of "is" and "ought" judgments along the lines of their logical structure, their epistemological and ontological character, and their practical intention. Considering the weaker claims of choice theorists to inform conditionally normative judgments, Luke argues that here rational choice theory may indeed make a modest contribution to policy craft—a contribution reminiscent of Max Weber.

Part IV explores the ethical responsibilities involved in the work of policy analysts. Rosemarie Tong focuses on the moral constraints imposed by the bureaucratic context of policy analysis. A philosopher by profession, Tong's purpose is to assess policy analysts' practice in terms of contemporary ethical arguments about responsibility, particularly as they have been applied to existing professional practices. Her analysis begins with a discussion of Michael Walzer's seminal analysis of the problem of "dirty hands" in public service, and she poses the solutions offered by the two most influential ethical lines of argument: utilitarian and rights-based theories. Both theories provide important perspectives on the problem, but, Tong argues, neither adequately grapples with the hierarchical and collection character of most policy decisions. Thus the problem in policy analysis often turns out to be less a matter of analyzing the responsibility of an action than merely identifying those responsible. Rather than "dirty hands," the problem is usually better characterized as one of "no hands."

Borrowing from Alasdair MacIntyre, Tong argues that the remedy to the problem must begin with a sharper distinction between practices and institutions. From this distinction, she maintains, we can begin to develop criteria that will assist us better in thinking about the ways in which the institutional structures of policy analysis might be reshaped to make them more compatible with the requirements of ethical responsibility.

Leonard Cole's essay examines the tension between the promised benefits of policy experimentation and the rights of subjects who may be involved. Clarifying the ethical dimensions of such policy research, Cole examines informed consent as a complex criterion that may be used to protect human subjects. Reviewing the history of concern with such issues—from the Nuremburg Code to recent presidential commissions—the essay proceeds to examine an area of research in which such ethical considerations seem in substantial danger of being ignored: current biological warfare tests that may expose vast civilian populations to chemicals and bacteria.

Assessing U.S. Army proposals for such tests that are being litigated in the mid-1980s and that promise to set precedents for many years to come, Cole concludes that inadequate protections exist to safeguard citizens who may be exposed. An Army spokesperson glibly suggested, the essay reports, that exposed populations were not to be considered as experimental subjects. The ethics of such research, of course, can hardly be addressed by being dismissed via definitional fiat. The strength of Cole's analysis lies not merely in his examination of the biological warfare tests but in the clarity of his discussion of the pervasive normative and ethical issues that are involved.

Part V presents three case studies that vividly illustrate the politics involved as normative criteria are employed in policy analysis. The first concerns a case of urban development.

The planning controversies surrounding the proposed redevelopment of Times Square in New York City provide Susan Fainstein with poignant and compelling examples of the thoroughly politicized nature of urban policymaking and urban policy analysis. Noting the oft-cited tensions between the criteria of efficiency and equity, Fainstein's analysis leaves such litanies behind by considering squarely the ambiguities of criteria that may be used to evaluate such a redevelopment proposal. The Times Square controversy not only involves efficiency criteria such as job creation and economic multiplier effects and equity criteria such as the protection of a low-income residential area; it calls into question the political meaning, not just the value, of efficiency itself.

Fainstein reviews the arguments of the central participants in the controversy and argues that the weighing of such arguments is necessarily political in two senses. What weights are given to the many conflicting and hardly commensurable criteria involved is as political a question as is the balance of pressure and power that will shape the decision-making agenda itself.

Steven Maynard-Moody and Donald Stull then provide an interpretive account of a comprehensive reorganization in a major state agency, the Kansas Department of Health and Environment. What can we learn, Maynard-Moody and Stull ask, by considering policymaking not simply as an instrumental process of reaching ends but as a symbolic process of shaping popular (and organizational) perceptions, expectations, and loyalties? If policies have significant symbolic aspects, in some cases no doubt overshadowing their supposedly means-ends character, what is implied for the practice and methods of policy analysis? By quoting interviewees, the authors are able to depict the agency's reorganization as a shift not so much in the productive capacity or performance of the organization as in the dominant political subculture of that agency. The reorganization politically shifted the policy criteria used to govern the department. Their study suggests how much planners and policy analysts risk missing if, in the pursuit of instrumental results, they fail to recognize the very real symbolic and cultural significance of policymaking and particular policy proposals.

But what of methods? Assessing in detail the experience of the Occupational Safety and Health Administration (OSHA), Charles Noble examines the difficulties of economic, cost-benefit approaches to policy analysis—approaches whose cogency depends upon ranges of assumptions, the political shape of which radically effects resulting cost-benefit calculations. Reviewing strengths and weaknesses of economic reviews of protective regulations, this chapter recognizes the centrality of questions of efficiency, but it refuses to abandon policy review by democratic choice.

Noble argues that the use of cost-benefit criteria focuses policy-makers' attention on issues of isolated individuals' market choice and thus shifts it subtly away from more public and democratic political processes of choice concerning the proper (perhaps necessarily unequal) distribution of risk in society. Reviewing the OSHA labeling and coke oven standard controversies, Noble argues that economic review of such policies not only involves serious methodological flaws but also presents us with disturbing political and institutional consequences: the undue centralization of policy oversight by the White House and the Office of Management and Budget.

The chapters in this anthology provide complementary views, then, of the practice of policy analysis. Treating both empirical case material and long-standing issues of social and political theory, these chapters present both the complexity and the challenge of addressing normative value questions in the conduct of contemporary policy analysis. In the face of such complexity, to call policy analysis an "art" or a "science" or "politics" itself risks substituting a label for thought. Policy analysis is the work of being politically rational and practical at the same time, at once ethically sensitive and pragmatic. Without attention to the abiding normative questions in this field, the study of policy analysis will become only a collection of the rationalizations of those in power. These essays, in contrast, written for this volume by policy scholars from a variety of disciplines, seek to articulate a new purpose for students of policy analysis: the pressing need to recognize and explore, carefully and systematically, the deeply normative character of policy analysis, and thus the necessity to engage the abiding politics of policy criteria.

—*Frank Fischer*
John Forester

PART I

Principles and Practices

1

POLITICAL PHILOSOPHY, PRACTICAL REASON, AND POLICY ANALYSIS

CHARLES W. ANDERSON

University of Wisconsin—Madison

Policy analysis would seem to be a distinctive kind of intellectual enterprise. Its aim is neither scientific discovery nor the elaboration and justification of systems of thought, which are the purposes of most classic disciplines. Rather, the avowed intent of policy science is the improvement of policymaking. The theme has been repeated in countless books and program statements. And although the goal may be pursued through the critical study of government programs or the processes by which they are made, the most persistent aim is to recommend some conception of technique, a mode of analysis or style of thinking that, if consistently employed by public officials, would presumably result in better public decisions.

The more one thinks of it, the more audacious this seems. The intent is nothing less than to reduce the great imponderables of politics to rules of good practice, as though one were discussing standard building procedures or the principles of range management. Nonetheless, this seems to be what policy analysis is about. Most of the classic works in the field, and certainly most texts, are statements of prescriptive methodology. Academic disputes have mainly to do with the adequacy of such systems of practical reason. In the end I think this is a defensible intellectual project, once we comprehend its implications. The modern policy sciences are perhaps no more than the lineal descendents of

Aristotle and Machiavelli, who also sought to define doctrines of practical political reason; and the ghosts of the English utilitarians, whose aspirations were similar, are still very much with us.

To be sure, the founders of the modern policy sciences tried to delimit the scope of the project, and thus avoid the more contentious issues, by focusing on the more prosaic and routine issues of public choice. Thus if politics could be distinguished from administration and policy analysis from the more fundamental controversies over public purpose, it might be possible to think of some aspects of governance as craftlike and to prescribe rules for their proper performance. However, this delimited conception of the aim of policy sciences has always met with objections. It has seemed an evasion of essential questions of public good and public interest or of class or factional advantage. The familiar persisting complaints against an image of policy science as "neutral competence," founded on a discipline of rational technique, may perhaps be summarized as follows:

(1) Policy analysis is not defensible as a doctrine of instrumental rationality, a fitting of efficient means to stipulated ends. The goals of policy are seldom made manifest in clear, unambiguous, or uncontestable terms. Analysis inevitably involves a clarification and ordering of values, and any policy analysis inevitably rests on some conception of desirable public purpose.

(2) The objectivity or neutrality of social science "knowledge" brought to bear on policy problems cannot be certified by the rules of scientific inquiry. Theoretical frameworks for the interpretation of social reality are potentially multiple and conflicting; the choice among them cannot be dictated exclusively by scientific criteria; and all such frameworks have normative implications.

(3) The classic distinction between politics and administration cannot be sustained. Administrators have broad discretion in interpreting political mandates and translating them into policy. Further, public officials as initiators of policy and as policy critics are inevitably parties to the broader process of public debate.

(4) Policy analysis, divorced from a broader conception of political discourse on fundamental public purposes, too often yields organizational inertia or patchwork expedients that tend to buttress existing institutions and practices. An expediential conception of policy analysis is at odds with the critical, constitutive character of genuine political deliberation.

(5) Fundamental ethical dilemmas inevitably arise in political activity, and a conception of policy analysis that ignores the moral dimensions of public choice and public service is an inadequate pedagogy.

In light of such criticisms of orthodox doctrine, it is now argued that the policy sciences should deal more explicitly with the normative dimensions of public choice and that policy analysis should be more consciously informed by political and moral philosophy. Once again, the question is posed as one of method or technique. The issue becomes, "How should the analyst deal with the problem of value judgment?"

Herein I want to consider the relationship of political philosophy to policy analysis, asking particularly what recent appeals for greater theoretical self-consciousness and more explicit attention to the normative dimensions of decision making imply for the field's peculiar vocation as formulator, critic, and teacher of disciplines of applied political reason. I begin with some general orienting observations on the so-called natural relationship of political theory and policy analysis. I go on to consider some of the implications of the current efforts to base techniques for normative policy analysis on the approaches of contemporary philosophic inquiry. I conclude by sketching a conception of normative discourse and practical political judgment that I think comes closer to expressing how issues of principle arise and are properly resolved in the course of public debate in liberal democratic societies.

POLICY ANALYSIS AS
APPLIED POLITICAL PHILOSOPHY

In some respects the question of how political and moral philosophy contributes to policy analysis hardly requires asking. All conceptions of policy analysis are derived from some political theory. Policy analysis in essence is no more than applied political philosophy, an idea of technique or method founded on some classic model of the norms of inquiry and rightful authority. Cost-benefit analysis is, of course, simply applied utilitarianism. Systems analysis, in trying to make explicit complex interdependencies and relationships, seems to reflect an organic view of purposive collective endeavors and solidarities perhaps, ultimately, of Hegelian origin.[1] In a somewhat broader context, Lenin, Trotsky, Guevara, and Mao can be taken as providing policy-analytic versions of Marxism. Similarly, many of the corporatist policy innovations of contemporary Europe—German codetermination for example—have their foundations in Continental conservative thought.

Disputes about the proper aim and method of policy science inevitably reflect larger philosophical issues. In our society such arguments take place within the broad framework of liberal democratic thought. The controversy generally is between approaches grounded in the tradition of formal, rationalist liberalism and those that have their foundations in the legacy of American philosophical pragmatism.

To some extent these arguments reflect the dominant partisan ideologies of twentieth-century American politics. Policy analysis often seems to be the sometimes opportunistic, often belated handmaiden of emerging social trends and dominant configurations of power. Thus what we might now call "classical" policy analysis, with its emphasis on social problem solving, the creative design of public programs, social criticism and incremental reformism, an activist state and public administration, echoes the basic tenets of American Progressivism, culminating (temporarily perhaps) in the New Deal and the Great Society, a long-evolving political ideology itself grounded in pragmatic philosophy. In recent years policy analysis has tended more toward the critique of positive public programs, an emphasis on economizing rationality, incentive structures, the virtues of marketlike arrangements and Lockean conceptions of individual rights, more attuned to the resurgent classic liberalism of the late 1970s and 1980s.

In another respect the controversies over doctrine in the policy sciences reflect differences in the historical development and para-digmatic structure of the social science disciplines. Economics tends to be the preservator and protagonist of the rigorous, axiomatic methods and models of classic liberalism. It espouses doctrines of rational individual choice, the logic of efficiency in unencumbered markets, and formal utilitarian calculation. Political science, in contrast to a greater extent than we sometimes realize, is the intellectual legatee of the "revolt against formalism" of American pragmatic thought.[2]

Political scientists, far more than economists, continue to share pragmatism's skeptical temper: its belief that experience is more important than logic; its intellectual pluralism, accepting the multiplicity and potential incompatibility of theoretical frameworks; its social, group-oriented sense of human action and purpose; its disbelief that liberalism could be reduced to a rationally unassailable set of first principles; its distaste for abstract formalism and its insistence on discovering how institutions "work in practice" to the end of the contrivance of piecemeal reform. Harold Lasswell perhaps exemplifies the historic vision of policy science as it is understood in political science, and his conception of policy science as systematic social inquiry brought to bear on public problems and of policy interventions as social experiments, constantly revised and reconsidered in a progressively perfected democratic polity, perfectly reflects Dewey's image of the polity as a "community of inquiry," like an idealized scientific society. The debates of policy science largely concern the implications of rival conceptions of applied, or practical, liberal democratic reason, and the distinctive methods of policy analysis taught by political science emerged primarily as a matter of taking exception to the rational formalism of economics. Thus, Herbert Simon and Charles E. Lindblom argued against the cognitive possibility of idealized utilitarianism, represented as the comprehensive cost-benefit analysis, as a workable conception of practical reason.[3] In place of this, they elaborated alternative conceptions of technique, "satisficing rationality" and "disjointed incrementalism" respectively. Richard Goodin recently argued that Braybrooke and Lindblom's strategy of incrementalism was a matter of "trying to do policy analysis without theory."[4] In this, he was totally mistaken. *A Strategy of Decision* is a remarkably articulate and coherent statement of the pragmatic philosophy of Pierce, James, Royce, and Dewey formulated as a doctrine of decision making.

Because policy analysis is inevitably derived from political philosophy, it is possible to have as many forms of policy analysis as there are systems of political thought. Policy analysis is inevitably relativistic and contextual. It seldom tries to justify its foundations. These it takes as a given and an act of commitment. Arguments among schools of policy analysis ordinarily occur within a shared philosophic context and have to do both with the applicability of a conception of method and its authenticity in representing some system of values. This is as true of disputes between the various forms of applied Marxism as it is of rivalries over questions of method in our own society.

In the United States debates about the proper concerns and procedures of policy analysis inevitably take place within the context of liberal democratic thought. And within the liberal rationalist tradition ethical action is always presumed to be that which can be subsumed under universal, impartial principles.

SHOULD POLICY ANALYSIS CULMINATE IN A STATEMENT OF PRINCIPLES?

It may seem commonplace to say that morally rightful or politically justifiable decisions should be made on principle. We naturally oppose principled judgments to those of expediency or interest. However, the idea that public decisions should be shown to rest on and serve principle is, in the modern world at least, a distinctive characteristic of liberal thought. Neither Marxists nor organic conservatives think about the problem in quite that way. Acting on principle is not the same as acting out of sympathy, compassion, respect for tradition or authority, or an understanding of the dynamic forces of history.

In the liberal scheme of things, acting on principles is taken to be a necessary safeguard against arbitrariness of judgment. To the extent that we act consistently, binding ourselves to treat all similar cases by the same general rules, our decisions are at least not whimsical or random. To act in this manner is to participate in the development of rational order, the creation of a predictable human environment in which people can fashion life plans with some degree of confidence in their outcome.

The persistent aim of liberal philosophy has been to derive principles of individual right and legitimate public purpose from a basic agnosticism concerning conceptions of the good and ultimate human purpose. The difficulty is that the method of liberal philosophy does not result in a unique set of principles. It is possible to order the guiding values of liberalism in a variety of ways, and the meaning of such fundamental concepts as right, freedom, equality, public interest, and the like seems always to be contestable. It is possible to create systems of liberalism but liberalism has never been reduced to definitive system.

The great problem, then, for a conception of policy analysis that would culminate in a statement of defensible principles is to describe how the analyst should arrive at such a statement given the manifest heterodoxy of liberal thought. Most of the intimations of technique for normative policy analysis that have begun to appear in the literature in fact have a highly introspective, heuristic quality. They recommend an exploration of the mind. The analyst must *find*, or *discover*, the ground of values from which analysis will proceed and which, in the end, will justify policy choice. There is, I think, a latent pragmatic skepticism and a persistence of historic commitments to value neutrality underlying such conceptions of method. Policy science provides a procedure of analysis but one that is taken to be logically indeterminate among outcomes. Seldom does method connote doctrine. The task of recommending theories of justice, or arguing conceptions of the legitimate role of the state, is left to political philosophers—or perhaps to economists, who, as members of a profession not notable for philosophical introspection or epistemological doubt, have few qualms about asserting Pareto optimality or the virtues of the unobstructed market as the proper foundations for policy choice.

Nevertheless, the implications of the methods currently being argued are in fact quite varied. At one extreme, the requirements of normatively informed policy analysis appear to be quite modest. Some writers (Douglas Yates is a good example) hold to the basic Weberian prescription that public officials should be clear and explicit about the principles that inform their analyses. These should not be treated as givens or hidden under a veil of scientific competence or neutrality. Basically, what Yates has in mind is a kind of "truth in analysis" proviso. Policy analysis inevitably rests on value judgments. In making clear the contested trade-offs among values in a given situation, and their own commitments, analysts identify themselves as protagonists in the public debate, as indeed they should.[5]

For some this might seem sufficient. Yet as Braybrooke and Lindblom reminded us long ago, a simple statement of "naive preferences"—saying, for example, merely that one favors increased equality—does not take us very far.[6] Some effort, it seems, should be made to order the principles of evaluation and to justify them, to show why they should be regarded as definitive in resolving an issue of public concern.

Thus it is more common to urge the analyst to undertake an exercise in "value clarification." This too may mean a variety of things, but it often seems to have to do with the principle of ethical generalization, a kind of rough-and-ready Kantianism.[7] The analyst is asked to examine the implications of adhering to a certain ethical maxim in a wide variety of situations. "Lying is wrong," but there may be circumstances in which lying seems a moral imperative. Similarly, would one uphold the ideal of free market choice in the face of irreversible environmental deterioration, or pursue equality to the point that no one had the incentive to lift a plow again? By seeking out "hard cases" in which a general rule becomes doubtful, we are presumably led to qualify the "naive" principle, to bound it in relation to other principles and circumstances that would require an "exception to the rule." The goal of this procedure seems to be the formulation of a coherent schema of principles, one that could be upheld consistently as a formula for public choice.

As a method of policy analysis, this procedure would seem to have much in common with John Rawls's notion of reflective equilibrium.[8] As Rawls describes it, reflective equilibrium is the procedure of moving from a series of considered moral intuitions to the principles or theories that seem to govern these intuitions. One moves back and forth between intuitions and principles, modifying either the general principles so as to fit the intuitions or the intuitions to fit the principles. The goal is to develop a theory that could be applied routinely and consistently across cases.

Rawls's conception of reflective equilibrium seems to have influenced several recent attempts to define appropriate normative method for the policy sciences.[9] Thus David Paris and James Reynolds see policy inquiry culminating in the statement of "rational ideologies," coherent systems of principles that can guide, inform, and justify policy choice.[10] Frank Fischer, though following a very different road in getting there, argues that in the end we must be prepared to *vindicate* the value judgments that underlie public choice—to show, at a second level of reflective analysis, their pertinence to a "valued way of life."[11] Similarly, Duncan MacRae envisions the policy sciences engaged in a process of moral discourse, along lines compatible with their commitment to the rules of scientific procedure, to the end of generating normative principles that are general, consistent, and clear. Like Rawls, MacRae's strategy is intended to provide rational systems, or theories, consistent with shared moral convictions.[12]

There is an interesting distinction to be drawn between MacRae's prescriptions for normative analysis and those of other authors, one well worth noting, for it tells us much about where such methods are presumed to lead. MacRae addresses the problem of policy science as an organized, collective, professional academic pursuit. He finds the normative doctrines underlying the several social science disciplines to be inconsistent and incomplete. He would have the policy sciences engage in systematic, critical normative discourse to the end of creating a more rational system of analysis. What MacRae is after, apparently, is a doctrine of practical reason, one that could be taught with authority resembling that accorded established bodies of scientific thought. To put the sharpest point possible on this, despite qualifications and equivocations, MacRae's proposed methodology for policy analysis seems intended to produce a rational ideology of liberalism, one that would reconcile the discrepancies not only among various social science disciplines but among the variants of liberal democratic thought. MacRae's ideal, like that of the scientific method on which he would build, is a methodology of self-conscious criticism that would lead to ever closer approximations to truth. The end is apparently to render policy science rational, with regard not only to means but to ends as well.

In contrast, other writers of prescriptive methodology seem to address themselves to individuals, to the problem of the analyst confronting a problem of normative choice. They concur that policy analysis should culminate in a coherent statement of principles. However, they do not appear to think (nor does Rawls) that the method of reflective equilibrium will lead in the end to a *unique* set of social principles. Such an analysis does not conclude in something like a Cartesian proof. Rather, it culminates in a *stand*. The purpose of the exercise seems to be that of achieving a broad, sustainable statement of one's commitments within the liberal political enterprise.

Thus understood, the idea of "acting on principle" as a dictum of policy analysis has some interesting implications. The problem of justification is not that of demonstrating that one's actions conform to some universal scheme of values that all rational beings would endorse, which was the classic goal of liberal philosophy. Rather, these methodological prescriptions seem to take for granted the intellectual pluralism of philosophic pragmatism, that it is possible to construct many rational theories within the liberal tradition. Hence the task of the analyst is not to show why a particular system of principles should be adopted as a ground of decision but merely to *account* for one's decisions in terms of some consistent scheme of principles.

This puts a different light on the whole purpose of philosophic reflection. The classic aim of liberal philosophy was to create a theory of political obligation, to show the conditions under which a free person would rationally consent to public authority, and thus to define the legitimate sphere of action of the state. However, the objectives of philosophical justification in policy analysis seems to be somewhat different. One should "act on principle" rather than on the basis of personal, factional, or institutional interest. However, it is not assumed that philosophical reflection will yield a "solution" to the problem of value judgment, that the analyst will somehow achieve a position of impartiality or objectivity distinct from that of other parties to the public debate.

Rather, the methodological imperative seems to be that the analyst identify with some general conception of the larger liberal political project. Policy analysis should be associated with a partisan effort to steer society toward an explicit conception of the regime. Perhaps the issue before us is no more than a request for a zoning variance in a small community. But in justifying one's response to such an issue on principle, one is saying in effect that one is either for a political order in

which people have maximum latitude to use their property as they see fit
or that one favors a regime in which property is progressively regulated
in the name of community interests.

It is true that we will either stand for something in the larger public
debate or be driven about like so many leaves in the wind. Those who say
that they will "judge each case on its merits" usually deceive both
themselves and others. Nonetheless, I doubt that we are persuaded that
wise political judgment necessarily results simply from acting consistently on principle, relentlessly following some rational method
oblivious to context and contingency, to situational opportunities and
constraints, and the differing perceptions of those who will be implicated
in and affected by our actions. The idea that policy analysis should be an
expression of rational ideology and that political discourse should be
argument among the proponents of such ideologies suggests a political
style that only an unabashed admirer of Fourth Republic France would
find wholly congenial.

Argument from principle is an important part of liberal politics, and
to raise the question of the principled justification of policy may be a
necessary corrective to a purely instrumental, "problem-solving" view of
policy analysis. However, formal philosophical reflection hardly provides a sufficient conception of method for policy analysis. Something
more needs to be said, and can be said, about the relation of political
theory to practical political reason. There are other recognizable bases
for normative judgment in politics whose implications we have yet to
explore.

OF THEORY AND PRACTICE

There are two ways in which we can apply theory to practice. In the
first sense we start from a theory, an ideal set of principles, and try to
derive specific policy proposals from it. This effort frequently leads to
disappointing results. Most principles do not yield unambiguous
prescriptions. Even such a straightforward maxim of fundamental
liberalism as John Stuart Mill's "harm principle" could be used to
support either a minimal nightwatchman state or massive governmental
intervention, depending on how we define what counts as an unwar-
ranted intrusion by one individual into the private realm of another.
Similarly, Rawls's two principles of justice could justify either a
program of "trickle-down" economics or a conscious program of social
redistribution.

In a second way of relating theory to practice, we begin from practice and apply theory to it. Philosophical pragmatists have frequently suggested that principles "emerge" out of the consideration of a particular problem of judgment. (So have Aristotelians, some Kantians and phenomenologists, but there is no real need for an elaborate philosophical disquisition on the point here.) By "practice" I mean simply an established way of doing things. Liberalism has long believed that the state should not be the architect of social order but that most social functions should be performed through collective undertakings emerging spontaneously within the political community. The organization of production, religion, science, learning, and the arts, and of family and community life should arise autonomously within a broad regime of freedom of expression, association and contract. This is the essential logic of pluralist society.

The problem of applying theory to practice is that of adjudging whether there is public interest in a specific form of association or collective project. Given the presumption in favor of autonomous collective action, the burden of argument falls on those who give good reasons for the suppression or control of practices or, alternatively, their protection and promotion through state action. Such argument can concern presumed harms to individual or common interests inherent in various projects or undertakings, or it can speak to a public interest in their diffusion or universalization by public means, as in the public support accorded such initially autonomous, private undertakings as education, science, social insurance, trade unions, and the like.

It is in applying liberal concepts of private right and public benefit to such pluralist projects and practices that public policy arises. And, in the ongoing discourse of liberal democratic society, most social enterprises are already heavily infused with prior determinations of public purpose relevant to the performance of such undertakings. Thus political discourse becomes a continuing *reappraisal* of how theory should be applied to practice, the focus shifting among concepts available within the liberal repertoire of values. One generation's determination to see air transport as a public utility, a practice that should be universally available, is replaced by another's decision to regard the proper distribution and incidence of airline service as a matter of aggregate social efficiency, to be determined by canons of profitability within the context of market competition.

It is this quality of real-world policy choice that makes it seem so unreasonable to try to subsume every decision under a categorical rule of public choice. We enter the policy arena not at the beginning but always in mid-current, acting always against a background of experience and precedent, structured expectations, the manifest workability of the going concern. We work within a legacy of policy and procedure that has itself passed scrutiny in repeated iterations of the "reflective equilibrium" of liberal civilization. Every existing policy, at the time of its adoption, was regarded as a legitimate expression of public authority.

Thus we *reevaluate* policy in terms of neglected considerations or different interpretations of principle. Or we debate whether existing policies are adequate to realize desired values. Understanding that social security was initially seen as a means of securing income security in old age based on individual contribution, we ask now whether social efficiency and distributive justice might not be served better by regarding it as a redistributive welfare program, a floor, or income maintenance scheme. And it is not altogether clear that we could determine, through philosophical reflection alone, which principle should prevail. The case for the status quo and thus, necessarily, the case for reform rests on very different conceptions of the public interest that is relevant to the particular practice.

This is a disaggregated view of the role of principled argument in policy discourse and practical political judgment. The object is not to arrive at principles that will be prescriptive for the regime as a whole, which may be the purpose of political philosophy, but to judge which principles should determine the relationship of the state to particular "going concerns," to the ongoing, highly differentiated, complex, inevitably "mixed enterprises" of pluralist society. There is no reason why such determinations should all be reducible to a single categorical rule. In some instances the appraisal of practice will turn on considerations of individual rights (Is abortion a question of individual choice in relation to the practice of medicine?); others, a matter of distributive justice (Should all have equal access to the practice of higher education?); yet others, a matter of social efficiency (Would sanitation services be more economically provided through private contract?). Although particular parties and administrations may try to move society generally toward some overall conception of the liberal project, emphasizing themes of market-based efficiency and autonomous choice or social redistribution, the specific application of these principles, they will soon learn, depends very much on the particular character of prevailing practices.

OF DISCOURSE AND DELIBERATION

The characteristic aim of theory in the policy sciences is to recommend a discipline of political judgment, a mode of practical reason that will presumably result in "better" public decisions. Academic disputation has much to do with the merits and shortcomings of various methodological prescriptions. Thus committed utilitarians, who try with increasing subtlety to show that all human concerns can be reduced to economic calculations of more and less, contest with the immanentist and ameliorative strategies of pragmatists, and these now with the neo-Kantian persuasion that rational policy prescriptions must be derived from a coherent system of principles. Each of these approaches to policy analysis is conventionally recommended as a unique path of "right reason" to the exclusion of the rest. The analyst, in following any of these methodological imprecations, is presumed to stand somewhat apart from the vagaries of ordinary political argument. Oddly, although all such theories recognize that public decision is a social process, the clear implication of their teaching seems to be that the indicated course of action can arise within the single mind of one who can make the underlying meaning of the situation clear.

The alternative is to see public decision arising, ideally, out of a situation of discourse, in which a variety of perceptions, interpretations, claims, and contentions are commonly deliberated. It is difficult to specify precisely what the idea of "discourse" means when it is evoked as a central ideal of inquiry and public decision. It is, on one hand, opposed to collective judgments reached merely through the aggregation of preferences without discussion of argument, the method taught by utilitarian economics, and, on the other, to "rational demonstration" in which the worth of statements is tested by explicit rules of proof. Discourse seems to connote an extended exchange of ideas in which both proposals for action and prospective tests of the merit of such proposals are simultaneously deliberated. In this sense the idea of discourse can be associated with a pragmatic conception of truth and the common good. Appeal is ultimately to the "community of inquirers" as Pierce and Dewey understood it.

However, it is possible to say something more about the nature of political discourse and its relation to the methods of policy analysis. To me discourse implies advocacy, explanation, criticism, and, in the end, deliberative judgment, and each of these forms of argument can be associated with a particular role in the process of discourse and with a characteristic method of policy analysis. Each of these modes of analysis can further be associated with a particular philosophical tradition.

Each of these ideas of practical reason is recommended independently in the literature of policy science as a unique conception of appropriate method. My own view is that there is an organic relationship among them, that each is essential and none is determinative in the process of political argument. Each has a distinctive bearing on the problem of practical political judgment, of defining how theory is to be applied to practice.

ENTREPRENEURIAL JUDGMENT: STARTING FROM PROJECTS

The task of advocacy in political discourse falls to the proponent of a new undertaking, project, or policy, a "better way of doing things." Politics has much to do with framing and organizing collective projects. The work of the entrepreneur, as Bertrand de Jouvenal puts it, is to "enlist the support of other wills" in an endeavor.[13]

Entrepreneurial judgment perhaps corresponds most closely to the classic model of rational choice. Thinking is instrumental, a matter of finding means appropriate to indicated ends. The economic entrepreneur must fashion a relationship of capital, labor, supply, and demand if the dream of a new productive activity is to become a going concern. The political entrepreneur must win the support of voters and power brokers, fashion a coalition, and develop the administrative means that will transform project into policy.

In the logic of the pluralist polity, it is assumed that the ever-tentative, ever-changing fabric of institutions and associations will arise from entrepreneurial initiative. The modes of production and exchange, the forms of religion, the disciplines of the arts and sciences are all to arise from the competitive efforts of innovators to win assent to their programs and designs. Such entrepreneurial activities are essentially political in form. They are an act of leadership. They create patterns of order, forms of community, and common purposiveness bound together by norms, rules, systems of punishment and reward, incipient lawfulness. The legitimacy of such projects in the larger polity rests on the principle of affiliation. The adherent is presumed always free to choose to do otherwise, to change one pattern of engagements for another, in a society of manifold possibilities.

The broader questions of political judgment, of rightful authority, of collective efficiency and essential fairness will eventually arise within the associations formed by entrepreneurial initiative. However, the larger community may also be called upon to take cognizance of the political relationships created by such purposive undertakings. Again, the policy issues may have to do with the regulation or suppression of such designs, or with their encouragement or diffusion through subsidy, incentive, corporatist arrangements, or the transformation of private association into public agency. The principle of such action may rest on the rights of those who are parties to the project, third-party interests, or diffuse social interests in the undertaking.

The initiative for such public involvement may be a part of entrepreneurial design itself. The economic entrepreneur may seek incentives or subsidies. The "policy entrepreneur" may see advantage in transforming a private project into a public function. (One thinks of Robert Moses, who converted a park system based on private philanthropy into a broad public undertaking.)

We normally think of the relationships of public policy and private initiative in broad, aggregate, universal terms. Thus we speak of incentives to productive investment, producer liability, or rights of employment, generically and categorically. Nevertheless, the actual pattern of public policy arises out of deliberation of the particular character of specific entrepreneurial initiatives. Thus the historical regime of regulated industries in the United States emerged out of no comprehensive plan or concept but in contemplation of specific technological innovations and patterns of industrial organization that emerged in transportation, telecommunications, and other fields. Similarly, within the general regime of religious pluralism and experimentation, the specific recruitment and financial initiatives of Reverend Moon raise particular issues of the relation of theory to practice, of the relation of public policy to entrepreneurial design.

Entrepreneurial advocacy is an essential ingredient of political discourse, but it is not the whole of it. Practical political reason cannot be taught as simple strategic calculation and the promotion of projects, nor can it be taught without it. Entrepreneurial reasoning is the valued source of innovation and change, of the critical creation of alternatives to orthodoxy and tradition within the liberal polity. Liberal politics is primarily reactive, and it is in assessing the appropriate public response to such concrete initiatives, finding cause to regulate them or seeing opportunities in them for larger public undertakings, that public policy arises.

In the end entrepreneurial judgment is but one form of political thinking and argument. In effect, it exhausts itself in its own success. For if it is successful, the entrepreneurial project becomes an established institution and a going concern. It becomes the prevailing orthodoxy. At this point the indicated mode of political judgment and the ground of justification change. We enter the realm of trusteeship, which is a distinctive form of political thinking.

JUDGMENTS OF TRUSTEESHIP: STARTING FROM PRACTICE

The dilemmas of decision making do not arise in a vacuum. We do not normally "make up" public problems. Rather, we are confronted with them, or charged with them, in the context of some specific role and responsibility. Judgments of trusteeship turn on conceptions of purpose and authority, duty and obligation. One weighs the options against considerations of the point of an undertaking and what one is expected or entitled to do. These too become the grounds of justification for the decision one eventually advocates.

In the literature of the policy sciences, this too is an indicated counsel of good judgment. One searches for solutions in the vicinity of the problem, seeking a satisfactory resolution of the requirements of organizational role and purpose.[14] Good judgment (and good governance) is a matter of adjusting relationships within a complex, ongoing system, to the end of sustaining the organic integrity and furthering the purposes of a particular going concern.[15]

The ideal of trusteeship has a strong foundation in Western political thought. Appeal to experience, history, and shared norms, customs, and usages is the counterpoise that Aristotelian and classic conservative notions of practical judgment offer to the rationalist tradition. The search in judgments of trusteeship, is for responses that "fit the situation," that represent a prudential sense for the preservation and furtherance of valued continuities.

If advocacy is the role of the entrepreneur in political discourse, then explanation is the rhetorical function of the trustee. In policy deliberation it is always wise to hear the rationale for established ways of doing things. Thus does one begin to understand the implications of applying theory to practice.

Against the liberal propensity to think in universal, categoric terms, the view of the trustee inevitably arises from the particular. The trustee speaks for "rules of good practice," for the nuances of settled and customary ways of achieving social purposes in the governance of *specific* industries, churches, and professions. In defense of the Amish desire to keep their children out of public schools, one can only refer to the history, traditions, and values of the Amish. To create an industrial policy for a modern capitalist economy, it is not enough to think in terms of macroeconomic incentives to investment and productivity. One must also know much of the distinctive *cultures* of steel and automobiles, wheat and milk, medicine and the building trades.

Liberal rationalism has always been suspicious of this mode of political thought and argument. It seems unreflective and uncritical. The larger consequences of action, the relation of specific performances to abstract norms and principles, is often unarticulated or anomalous. Yet this is how most of the world's work gets done, and it is this mode of valuation and judgment that lends coherence to most human undertakings. Those who would disregard trusteeship as a valid form of normative argument may risk the peril of Oakeshottian rationalism, the desire to analyze and reconstruct everything. Yet those who think only in the mode of trusteeship miss liberalism's sense for critical detachment, its capacity to transcend the immediate and the particular. Trusteeship plays a necessary role and provides an essential counsel in political deliberation. But it is not the whole of it.

RATIONAL CRITICISM:
STARTING FROM PRINCIPLES

From a certain point of view, to ground judgment on principle is a counsel of political prudence. This is how we achieve consistent, coherent political order. However, in ordinary political discourse the function of argument from principle is often social criticism. To apply principle to practice is normally to reveal some inadequacy and to create appeals for improvement. The reason for this is that liberal ideals are inherently radical in character. No collective undertaking, whether based on rational organization or tradition, custom and usage, can ever quite meet the highest standards.

Thus it is inherent in liberal thought that all social institutions and practices be regarded as forms of voluntary association, resting on willful consent and contract. To meet this test it must be shown that the parties to an undertaking are equals in all significant respects. Any disparities of power or opportunity, of information or access, raise questions about the legitimacy of the practice. Yet in the real world all markets fail in some respect, the conditions of free contract are never quite met, and intimations of dominance are always present.

Similarly, the simple test of economic efficiency is a standard of judgment that can always be used to raise questions about the initiatives of entrepreneurs or the counsels of trustees. In the utilitarian formuation, the measure of all practices is their contribution to aggregate social utility. If a way can be shown to perform a function more economically, prevailing practice is properly regarded as socially wasteful. It is a simple question of opportunity costs. Thus the economic analyst stands in constant judgment of all innovations and practices. No human project is ever quite optimal.

For the procedural democrat, social undertakings can be legitimate only if they rest on the autonomous choices of individuals, equally considered, as full participants in the discourse of governance in any institution. Yet the human projects that do not reflect some element of entrepreneurship or hierarchically defended orthodoxy are few and far between, and those spontaneous undertakings that arise from a true "politics of friends" usually do not sustain that form for very long.

In policymaking arguments from principle can take two forms. In the first the case is made for the application of a universal norm to all projects and enterprises, the gradual achievement of consistency and coherence throughout the polity. Thus if the state cannot assign status on the basis of race or gender, neither should any other collective undertaking. However, arguments from principle may have a more delimited, contextual quality. It is possible to argue the cost-effectiveness of a program of tax incremental financing without committing oneself to a consistent utilitarianism. Or one might deliberate the distributive equity of assessments for street repairs without being bound to a thoroughgoing egalitarianism. One can question the responsiveness of government on a particular issue without endorsing all the implications of participatory democracy. Arguments from principle are a source of claims in everyday political argument. We select the criteria of judgment according to the characteristics of the particular controversy. Efficiency, equity, the recognition of rights and settled expectations are qualities of any social performance. In pointing to "neglected considerations" in any design for action, we do not commit ourselves to a rational ideology. We merely try to perfect a policy.

Argument from principle plays an important role in political discourse. Nonetheless, the ideal of acting on principle does not capture all that needs to be said about the method of practical political reason. Liberal rationalism produces a tension in political argument, but it does not resolve it. The significance of abstract norms becomes apparent only in particular situations. Perhaps universities should be organized to work systematically to the benefit of the "least well off," and perhaps they should not. Perhaps the extent of wilderness preservation should be determined by considerations of aggregate social utility or the preferences of individuals revealed in their "willingness to pay" for some measure of solitude, and perhaps it should not. Such theoretical imperatives are but bold conjectures that may or may not make sense in light of considerations of practice.

Those who would speak for principles take the measure of entrepreneurial initiative and the prudential claims of the trustees of prevailing practice. But the claims of each have standing as we seek to give direction to our collective life. Some further mode of analysis is required to resolve the quandaries that arise in political deliberation, when the voices of those who speak from these distinctive perspectives have been heard and appreciated.

PRAGMATIC ANALYSIS: STARTING FROM PROBLEMS

The pragmatist focuses neither on projects, practices, nor principles but on problems, which are precisely, in Dewey's definition, those occasions for judgment which arise out of conflicting valuations of existing patterns of activity. In theories of policymaking, the role of the pragmatic analyst is frequently taken to be that of the mediator, one who would negotiate meaning to the end of collective action. The orthodox, incrementalist prescription for doing this is to propose marginal adjustments in the going concern, adjustments that might make things "better" in the eyes of the protagonists, moving by successive approximations, reopening the argument on which aspects of practice are to be regarded as problematic with each successive iteration. The process is serial and remedial.[16] In theory the pragmatic analyst is the neutral adjudicator, the contriver of consent. Pragmatism is often associated with simple expediency and tough-minded realism. The goal of policymaking is to contrive a reform that will "work in practice."

However, when pragmatic analysis is understood as a function in political discourse, its implications appear in an entirely different light. When the issue is one of deciding on an indicated course of action when principled claims are brought against entrepreneurial projects or prevailing practice, the neutral stance of the analyst cannot be sustained. Now pragmatic analysis will have to take the form of an argument, a case either for reforming practice in the name of principle or for exempting practice from the force of some principled claim.

I think this formulation is closer to the spirit of philosophical pragmatism. For Dewey reform was always understood as change that worked in the direction of the perfection of the democratic polity, the "community of inquiry" persistently engaged in the critical examination of its own philosophy and purposes. However, pragmatists always held that the application of liberal principles was context-dependent. The evolutionary, part-Darwinian, part-Hegelian themes in Dewey gave great weight to experience, to those institutions and solidarities that had stood the test of time.

In the end, then, pragmatic judgment is the search for means for accommodating principle to practice, for advancing the liberal democratic project without destroying the integrity of existing institutions. The search is for a suggestive fit between theory and practice. The "reflective equilibrium" of pragmatic analysis is not a matter of ordering and bounding abstract norms in relation to one another but of assessing their pertinence to specific activities.

OF THE ORGANIC INTERDEPENDENCE
OF THE MODES OF ANALYSIS

The purpose of policy science, as that of political theory generally, is to teach a discipline of thought that can be generally recommended to those who assume responsibility for public choice. This, I shall also assume, is the classic meaning of practical reason, in the Aristotelian tradition.

In recent years policy theory has been very much preoccupied with the problem of uncertainty and the cognitive limitations of the individual. Hence one must somehow simplify complexity by disregarding nonessential elements in the situation of choice. This presupposes a cognitive focus, and it is variously recommended that we concentrate on the project at hand and the means to achieve it, our role and obligations in relation to an ongoing undertaking, some maxim of choice that could be endorsed consistently and universally, or the problematic situation as defined by conflicting valuations of an existing pattern of activity.

Political philosophy similarly counsels that public decisions must be grounded in some conception of public interest and the common good. We must be able to give good reasons for our decisions, reasons that are open to public scrutiny and that establish the propriety of our acts. Yet in the Western tradition it has been deemed appropriate to cite as justification for action the willingness of others to affiliate freely with it, a conception of "my station and its duties," the conformity of an action to some categorical rule, or the suggestiveness of a proposal as a way out of collective perplexity.

My view is that none of these approaches, taken in isolation, provides an adequate method of decision or a sufficient rationale for public choice. Rather, all are intertwined and interdependent in the process of political discourse as they are in the individual process of reflection on matters of public concern.

The merit of innovative projects is properly judged not by assent alone but in relation to the values of established practice, to norms of rightful authority prescriptive throughout the liberal order, and, in the end, the contrivance of a way of acting that reconciles these considerations and concerns. Trusteeship is tradition-bound and unreflective unless appraised through other disciplines of thought. The maxims of formal liberalism are sterile and formal unless applied to particular human activities and concerns. And pragmatism is merely expediency unless its object is to reconcile the claims of principle and practice.

Nor are these four positions mutually exclusive in practical reason. The considerations representative of each intertwine, either in our deliberations with ourselves or in discussion with others. Perhaps, inevitably, at the outset of inquiry one of these will represent a predominant cognitive focus for the individual. We will start from a conception of a project, a sense of obligation, from certain ideals or principles, or from a desire to resolve a controversy. But in the process of discourse, we may be led to broaden our consideration of the perspectives relevant to choice and in the end perhaps we may be led to change our minds. The trustee may "discover" that the institution that he or she felt committed to defend was inherently inequitable and becomes the champion of reform on principle. The pragmatic mediator may become the enthusiast of some novel undertaking. The social critic starts to search for proximate reforms of institutions. In a closed system of thought the solution to a problem is always inherent in the premises. In open systems it should always be possible to end up somewhere other than where one began. It is this capacity for exploration and discovery, the possibility of finding something new through the process of inquiry, that is a quality to be sought in models of both scientific understanding and collective, public choice.

What would be the role of policy science in such a conception of political deliberation and discourse? It is clear that I do not see policy science playing a differentiated role in the process of public debate. The methods of policy analysis do not provide the qualified practitioner with a specialized claim to knowledge. Rather, they reflect quite ordinary forms of political action and argument. In effect, the policy scientist may be entrepreneur, trustee, social critic, or pragmatic mediator.

However, the academic policy analyst may play a distinctive and peculiarly useful role in restoring balance in political argument. At any time, on any subject, the roles we have specified as essential to reasoned consideration of an issue tend toward a kind of natural disequilibrium. Momentum flows with the spirit of novelty, or defense of established ways, or the revelation of the flaws in the existing order, or hard-headed, immediate practicality. We seem always to be swept up in one of these enthusiasms. Such collective moods may mark the spirit of an age or may represent the momentary and transient "common sense" of a council or community seized with a specific problem.

Scholars on the whole have a propensity to think otherwise about matters, and their special function in political discourse may be to interpret matters in light of currently neglected perspectives. Thus in an atmosphere of criticism, inquiry would be ideally directed toward understanding the rationale of prevailing practice. When everything seems most settled, the speculative mind seeks novelty and innovation. When everything is chaotic and up in the air, it may be the moment for the detached academic to be merely practical.

As the partisan of neglected perspective, the scholar serves the interest of objectivity and of balance, of reasoned and deliberate judgment. Thus understood, the function of the policy scientist is to keep the argument open, not to resolve it. The ideal maxim for such a conception of policy science would seem to be Charles Sanders Pierce's dictum that one must "always keep the door open for further inquiry."

NOTES

1. This seems to be particularly apparent in Sir Geoffrey Vickers, *The Art of Judgment* (New York: Basic Books, 1965).

2. Morton White, *Social Thought in America: The Revolt Against Formalism* (Boston: Beacon Press, 1961). On the pragmatic foundations of political science see Bernard Crick, *The American Science of Politics* (Berkeley: University of California Press, 1959); Arthur Somit and Joseph Tannenhaus, *The Development of Political Science* (Boston: Allyn & Bacon, 1967).

3. Herbert A. Simon, *Administrative Behavior* (New York: Free Press, 1976) and David Braybrooke and Charles E. Lindblom, *A Strategy of Decision* (New York: Free Press, 1963).

4. Robert Goodin, *Political Theory and Public Policy* (Chicago: University of Chicago Press, 1982), 20.

5. Douglas T. Yates, Jr., "Hard Choices: Justifying Bureaucratic Decisions," in Joel L. Fleishman, Lance Liebman, and Mark H. Moore, eds., *Public Duties: The Moral Obligations of Government Officials* (Cambridge: Harvard University Press, 1981), 32-51.

6. Braybrooke and Lindblom, *A Strategy of Decision,* pp. 6-12.

7. Marcus G. Singer, *Generalization in Ethics* (New York: Alfred A. Knopf, 1961).

8 . John Rawls, *A Theory of Justice* (Cambridge: Harvard University Press, 1971), 48-51.

9. For an explicit statement of Rawls's reflective equilibrium as a method of policy analysis, see Peter G. Brown, "Assessing Officials," in Fleishman, Liebman, and Moore, *Public Duties,* pp. 289-305.

10. David C. Paris and James F. Reynolds, *The Logic of Policy Inquiry* (New York: Longman, 1983), 255-270.

11. Frank Fischer, *Politics, Values, and Public Policy: The Problem of Methodology* (Boulder: Westview Press, 1980).

12. Duncan MacRae, Jr., *The Social Function of Social Science* (New Haven: Yale University Press, 1976), 77-106.

13. Bertrand de Jouvenal, *Sovereignty* (Chicago: University of Chicago Press, 1959), 17.

14. Simon, *Administrative Behavior.*

15. Vickers, *The Art of Judgment,* pp. 25-35.

16. Braybrooke and Lindblom, *A Strategy of Decision.*

2

CAN POLICY ANALYSIS BE ETHICAL?

DOUGLAS J. AMY

Mt. Holyoke College

During the last decade, an increasing number of scholars and practitioners of policy analysis argued that policy analysis should become more ethical. By "ethics" they were not referring to the codes of behavior many professions have for dealing with such things as conflicts of interest. Rather, they were talking about ethics in the larger sense—the analysis of basic moral and value issues. They were calling on analysts to address more explicitly and systematically the normative dimensions of the policy choices they studied. For these advocates the need for a more ethical policy analysis was a pressing one. Many saw analysts as becoming increasingly involved in policy areas full of serious and complex moral questions—ranging from the Vietnam war to abortion policy—but at the same time being ill-equipped to address those kinds of questions. And it was argued that if analysts were to do their job and help policymakers and the public to understand fully the implications of these difficult policy decisions, a clearer exposition of the moral dimensions of those choices was needed.

Advocates of a more ethics-oriented policy analysis had other arguments as well, many of which I will consider shortly. But for the moment what is important is that for several years the movement to integrate ethical analysis into policy analysis was a growing intellectual force in the field. However, that movement now seems to be losing momentum. In particular, few practicing policy analysts have made a serious attempt to practice a more ethically oriented policy analysis. The question is, why? Why has the professional practice of policy analysis been reluctant to incorporate ethical concerns into its analytic methodologies? That question is the topic of this essay. To answer it, I will first consider the brief history of the movement to integrate ethical analysis into policy studies. Once the political and intellectual reasons behind this movement are clear, I will then explore the various reasons why this movement has not taken hold in the profession, and in the process uncover a set of obstacles that discourage analysts from engaging in ethical analysis. Finally, some consideration will be given to how these obstacles might be overcome.

THE MOVEMENT TOWARD
A MORE ETHICAL POLICY ANALYSIS

DISCONTENT WITH CONVENTIONAL POLICY ANALYSIS

The movement to integrate ethical analysis into policy analysis emerged in the 1970s, fueled by a number of intellectual developments. One was the growing discontent with conventional public policy analysis. By the early 1970s, critics had begun to point out an increasing number of serious deficiencies in the standard approaches to policy analysis. Much of this dissatisfaction focused on the way in which analysts approached the normative dimensions of policy decisions. Critics focused especially on cost-benefit analysis, which was, and still is, the primary method by which analysts deal with the normative issues that lie at the center of policy choices. Cost-benefit analysis was popular because it seemed to be a way to arrive at normative conclusions, to say which policy is best in an objective and scientific manner. It allowed analysts to venture into the murky realm of values, give precise answers, and at the same time maintain their social scientific credentials. However, critics argued that cost-benefit analysis had a number of glaring deficiencies as a tool of normative analysis. Their complaints were many, too many to discuss here,[1] but one of the foremost was that cost-benefit analysis only incorporates so-called hard or economic values—values that can be quantified in economic terms—and ignores the numerous soft-values or intangibles, such as community, beauty, and environmental balance, that cannot be so easily included in cost-benefit calculations. Ignoring these soft values not only leads to faulty normative recommendations, it was argued, but also renders the analyses less relevant to decisions makers, who are normally quite interested in these dimensions of policy questions. Thus as one leading environmental analyst lamented, standard policy analyses "are not about what people care about."

In the early 1970s these kinds of concerns about cost-benefit analysis and policy analysis as a whole led the American Academy of Arts and Sciences to sponsor an interdisciplinary study group to explore why policy analysis tended to be not very useful to policymakers and the public, especially in the area of environmental policy, and to make recommendations for reform. The result was an important book, *When Values Conflict,* which proved to be one of the first steps in the movement toward integrating ethical concerns into policy analysis.[2] In the course of their first meetings, the study group, which included Laurence Tribe, Robert Socolow, and Robert Dorfman, soon came to the conclusion that the core problem they were dealing with was not merely the inability of cost-benefit analysis to incorporate soft values, but the inability of policy analysis as a whole to approach issues where conflicting values were at work. Significantly, they noted that conventional techniques such as cost-benefit analysis assumed general agreement on societal priorities and values in America, an assumption that no longer seemed legitimate after the turbulent politics of the 1960s. As they explained,

> Inherited from an era when certain basic values and ideals seemed to be more clearly (if tacitly) understood and widely (if not universally) shared, the intellectual and institutional techniques available . . . to *any* policy-oriented research institute seem distinctly ill adapted to the task of helping to reach important decisions in a more fragmented society, a society which, for a variety of reasons, is no longer confident about the priorities among its values, and which is becoming increasingly aware of the inherent difficulty of choosing among values in conflict, coupled with the increasingly unavoidable need to do so.[3]

The study group concluded that an approach to policy analysis was needed that better addressed these difficult value issues. But like many first explorations of this area, they gave only the vaguest suggestions as to what such an approach might actually look like.

About the same time that the AAAS study group was formed, Martin Rein was becoming concerned that conventional policy studies were largely irrelevant to the deliberations of policymakers. A leading policy analyst, Rein concluded that much of this lack of utilization was due to the inability of policy analysis to comes to grips with the moral and values choices that lie at the heart of most important policy decisions. "Above all," he argued, "social policy is concerned with choices among competing values."[4] And any analysis that could not address these core issues was bound to be of only minimal usefulness to those concerned with those issues. He traced analysts' inability to deal with these normative dimensions of policy choices to the positivist methodology that most used. For Rein the main culprit was the fact-value dichotomy that characterized the positivist approach. Analysts automatically assume that normative issues are purely subjective and irrational, and that as good policy scientists they can legitimately investigate only the empirical dimensions of policy questions. This means that they can deal with normative question in only two ways, both of which Rein saw as undesirable. First, and most common, was what he called the "value-neutral" approach in which analysts simply ignore normative policy questions, considering them not amenable to rational analysis. But to adopt value neutrality is to be mute concerning the most important dimensions of policy decisions and to invite dismissal by policymakers and the public. The other alternative within the positivist framework is what Rein called the "value-committed" approach to analysis, in which one uses policy analysis to promote one's own personal subjective values, an approach he associated with Marxist analysis. He rejected this approach as well, arguing that it would produce obviously biased analyses that would be utilized only by those who already shared one's values.

The problem with both of these approaches, Rein argued, is that they adhere to the positivist assumption that values are entirely subjective. He called for a third approach, a "value-critical" approach to analysis that would neither ignore values nor take them for granted but instead would make them the center of analysis, submitting them to careful and systematic study. This kind of analysis, he argued, would be much more relevant to the concerns of policymakers and the public.[5] Thus like the AAAS study group, Rein was calling for some kind of ethical analysis to become a central part of policy analysis; but also like the AAAS group, he was at that time disappointingly vague about what this might look like in practice.

ANALYSIS AS IDEOLOGY

By the mid-1970s there was another development in policy analysis that began to force analysts to confront the necessity of ethical analysis. It was the increasing realization that conventional policy analysis techniques were not objective and value neutral but contained fundamental normative biases. Much of the path-breaking work in this area was done by Laurence Tribe in his famous essay in *Philosophy and Public Affairs,* "Policy Sciences: Analysis or Ideology?"[6] Much of Tribe's argument was epistemological in nature, concerning how policy analysis structures our knowledge of the world. He argued that all analytic methods look at the world in certain limited ways, including some parts and excluding others, and thus they are biased. These analytic biases can have important normative and political repercussions. Or to put the problem another way, all policy analysis methodologies contain certain assumptions about what issues are worth analyzing, what facts are important to look at, what the public good consists of, and so on—and all of these assumptions result in giving a normative slant to the final policy recommendations. To be clear, the argument here is not that analysts are personally biased but that the analytic methodologies themselves are.

This view of policy analysis as ideology was also later put forward by others, such as Fred Kramer, Brian Fay, and Paul Diesing.[7] Kramer, for example, argued the systems analysis used by Robert MacNamara and the Department of Defense during the Vietnam war served ideological purposes, that it tended to give a distorted and overly optimistic view of how the war was going, and obscured the fundamental underlying problems of that policy. He also concluded that it was fruitless to try to expunge all methodological biases from analytic techniques. Instead he recommended that analysts become more aware of the political and normative biases that are inevitably present in their analytic tools and be more willing to discuss and debate them. In this way these critics of "objective" policy analysis highlighted the need for analysts to become more sensitive to normative and ethical issues in analysis, and thus made more obvious the necessary overlap between the fields of ethics and policy analysis.

PUBLIC ADMINISTRATORS DISCOVER ETHICS

Also stimulating more interest in ethics and public policy were the upheavals in public administration that were taking place in the 1970s.

A set of political and intellectual developments converged in a way that prompted scholars and practitioners of public administration to become more interested in ethical questions. In the political world the scandals involving Watergate, the CIA, and the FBI produced much soul-searching about how administrative personnel could so easily engage in unethical and illegal activities. Some believed that part of the fault was in the training of administrators, which was primarily technocratic in nature and did little to sensitize them to the human and ethical results of their decisions. In hopes of combating this problem, graduate programs in public administration began to offer classes in ethics.[8]

At about the same time there emerged an intellectual movement called the "new public administration," which began to attack the traditional dichotomy between administration and politics and focused more attention on the normative side of administrative decisions.[9] It was argued that administrators routinely make important political and value choices and are not simply neutral implementors of policy, and thus they should be more thoughtful and sensitive to this normative dimension of their work. Hart and Scott, for example, criticized administrators for relying too much on technocratic rationality and ignoring the more important "metaphysical" dimensions of their decisions.[10] These authors called for administrators to be trained in moral and political philosophy so that they would be better equipped to address the deeper human and philosophical implications of their decisions.

Hart and Scott attributed much of the poor quality of public administration decisions to this neglect of basic ethical and philosophical questions. Irving Janis made a similar point, although he arrived at it from a very different direction. Janis wrote extensively in the 1970s about why administrators were capable of making disastrous policy decisions. In *Groupthink* he sought to identify those institutional and psychological factors that led policymakers to make the enormous mistakes involved in such fiascos as the Bay of Pigs, the Vietnam war, and Watergate.[11] Among a number of factors he cited the tendency of administrators to neglect to raise or systematically explore the moral implications of their decisions but simply to assume that they are on the side of right. He argued that better policy decisions have come about when these moral questions are confronted directly and honestly. For Janis, investigating ethical questions was not simply a philosophical exercise but a practical way of improving the quality and workability of policy decisions.

The point was reiterated by Anthony Lake, a former foreign policy analyst in several administrations and currently a professor of international relations. He argued that ignoring ethical analysis not only runs the risk of encouraging decisions that are immoral but can also produce impractical decisions.[12] He suggested that policymakers who are interested in effective and pragmatic decision making must be interested in all the consequences of their actions, including the moral consequences. Pragmatic decision making is based on reality—and the human consequences of policy decisions are an important part of reality that must be considered. Being concerned about the ethical implications of public policies serves to make one more sensitive to what is actually happening to real people in the world, and this is important information for those concerned with making effective policy. Conversely, ignoring ethical consequences is to ground one's decisions less in reality—to make them less realistic—and this, Lake argued, is one of the reasons we sometimes pursue the kind of impractical and self-defeating policies that characterized our involvement in the Vietnam war.

ETHICISTS STRIVE TO BE RELEVANT

The 1970s also saw ethicists working to make their work more relevant to public policy questions. Like social scientists during that time, many ethicists were possessed with the idea of making their work more relevant to solving the country's pressing social and political problems. Unlike policy scientists, many ethical philosophers had long abandoned positivism and the notion that ethical decisions were totally subjective and not amenable to analysis or debate. Many believed, as Paul Taylor had argued in the 1960s, that some rationality could be introduced into the discussion of ethical questions—that a systematic analysis of these issues was possible.[13] One of the earliest products of efforts to turn these new analytic skills to public policy issues was the creation of the journal *Philosophy and Public Affairs* in 1971. It was a conscious effort to show that philosophical analysis, including ethical analysis, could be relevant and useful in deliberations over difficult policy issues ranging from abortion to war to affirmative action.

Among other things, ethicists and philosophers have been interested in demonstrating that there are other legitimate forms of ethical analysis besides the utilitarianism of cost-benefit analysis, and that these alternative approaches could and should be applied to policy decisions.

For example, some ethicists developed a notion of "rights' as an alternative to cost-benefit analysis, arguing that some policies, such as a minimum level of health care for the poor, are justified as a basic right, even though they are inefficient from a cost-benefit point of view.[14] Gradually, some policy analysts, such as Steven Kelman of the Kennedy School at Harvard, began to appreciate how this notion of rights could shed important light on many contemporary political debates, such as that over environmental policy.[15]

Eventually ethicists concerned with public policy questions began to find a home in a number of institutes that were dedicated to illuminating the connections between these two fields. Foremost among these is The Hastings Center, which has made important contributions to a number of policy debates, especially in the biomedical area. For example, a Hastings research project developed the notion of "brain death" that now serves as the legal definition of death in over twenty states. This kind of work by ethicists helped to make the policy analysis community aware that fruitful cross-fertilizations between these two fields could take place.

TOWARD A SYSTEMATIC APPROACH
TO ETHICAL POLICY ANALYSIS

By the mid-1970s, the most pressing question in the movement toward a more ethical policy analysis was not whether ethical analysis was needed but what it would look like in practice. Up to that point few had done more than speculate about how ethics could be integrated into policy analysis. However, in the mid-1970s some analysts began to develop a more systematic approach. C. W. Churchman, one of the founding fathers of systems analysis, suggested what is now called a "forensic approach" to ethical issues, which basically consists of an organized debate among various analysts and policymakers with differing normative perspectives on a policy issue.[16] Such debates could air ethical issues and clarify hidden assumptions.[17] Also in this period Duncan MacRae developed a more systematic approach, offering a number of logical rules that could be used to structure the debate over ethical issues in policy.[18]

It was not until the late 1970s that some more methodologically sophisticated approaches were developed. Several scholars of policy analysis, agreeing with earlier critics who faulted the positivist assumptions underlying analysis, began to explore newly developed techniques in postpositivist social science for approaches that could incorporate an ethical dimension into the study of policy questions. Bruce Jennings, Martin Rein, and Frank Fischer offered visions of what a postpositivist, ethically aware policy analysis methodology might look like.[19] To date, the most important of these efforts has been Fischer's *Politics, Values, and Public Policy: The Problem of Methodology.*[20] Weaving together approaches developed by ordinary language theorists, moral philosophers, phenomenologists, and political theorists, Fischer constructed a complex and intellectually rigorous approach to policy questions that integrates the empirical, theoretical, and normative dimensions of these issues. Through this kind of work, the ethics and policy analysis movement began to come of age methodologically.

THE NEGLECT OF ETHICS BY PRACTITIONERS

Despite all this attention to ethics and policy analysis in the 1970s, concern has seemed to wane in the 1980s. Although there is still lively interest in the area among some scholars of policy analysis and some of the more philosophical analysts, the effort to integrate ethics and policy analysis has made very little impact on the world of professional policy analysis. Few practicing analysts have tried to incorporate ethical concerns and methodologies into their work. Moreover, interest in this topic has lessened even in academia. Current graduate students seem less concerned with the larger issues, including ethical ones, and one teacher of an ethics and policy analysis course reports that his course is now rated one of the least useful by students in his program. The question, of course, is why this lack of interest by practitioners? Neglect of ethical analysis is certainly not due to lack of good reasons to use it. As we have seen, a number of persuasive reasons can be given for the relevance of ethics to policy analysis and policy decisions. But although the philosophical battle over the relevance of ethics to policy analysis has been won, the larger war over whether it will actually be used by analysts seems largely to have been lost. The rest of this essay will attempt to explain why. To do so, we must explore the unforeseen but fundamental contradictions that exist between ethics and policy analysis. We will find that the reasons why ethics has not been integrated into policy analysis are not intellectual but rather professional, political, and psychological in nature.

OBSTACLES TO
AN ETHICAL POLICY ANALYSIS

ETHICS AND THE POWER RELATIONS OF ANALYSIS

One of the main reasons ethics has largely been ignored by policy analysts has to do with the power relationships that characterize the profession.[21] As a rule, policy analysts work for someone. They have clients for whom they are doing analysis. Typically, most practicing analysts work in government, so their clients are either administrators or legislators. But the identity of these clients matters less than the fact that such clients exist and that analysts have a strong professional interest in maintaining a good relationship with these superiors. Analysts interested in maintaining good analyst-client relationships are well advised to steer clear of serious ethical analysis in their work. Most clients have strong commitments to policy goals and values and would not be pleased to receive a study that calls these basic commitments into question. Yet once an analyst begins to engage in ethical analysis, it is just those kinds of basic normative commitments that will end up being examined.

The effect of client-analyst power relationships on dampening any desire to engage in ethical analysis is perhaps strongest in government bureaucracies, where much of professional policy analysis takes place. Bureaucracies are characterized by strongly hierarchical power relationships, where subordinates are expected to follow orders and to promote agency goals and values. Bureaucracies are not egalitarian debating societies, and they are not designed to encourage frank discussion and dissent. Indeed, as one prominent political scholar, Arnold Meltsner, has pointed out, questioning basic agency goals can be decidedly bad for the analyst's career: "The bureaucratic situation encourages analytical work within the consensus of ongoing programs and approved policies. Therefore the policy analyst who departs from the bureaucratic consensus is bound to run the risk of being attacked, discredited, ignored, or even fired."[22] In other words, ethical analysis and those who use it are often seen as threats to the organization and its values. Because ethical analysis necessarily involves the examination of clashing normative perspectives, it almost inevitably raises arguments critical of reigning policy and the smooth pursuit of the dominant values of the organization, whatever they may be. Thus a serious investigation of organizational values and priorities would not have been welcome either in the proenvironmental Interior Department under Carter or in the prodevelopment department under Reagan. Facing this kind of hostile reaction, it is not surprising that most analysts have little interest in exploring basic ethical questions and are content simply to accept their client's normative perspective.

GROUPTHINK AND THE NEGLECT OF ETHICS

The power relationship between clients and analysts is only one of the factors that encourage analysts to ignore ethical analysis. Indeed, there is reason to believe that even when those hierarchical relationships are absent, ethical questions still tend to be downplayed. There are a number of reasons for this. One problem involves the group dynamics that take place in policymaking groups, a phenomenon that has been studied extensively by Janis. Janis acknowledges that administrative hierarchies are one major stumbling block to the full analysis of policy implications, including their moral implications. In addition, when such power relationships are minimized, such as when the administrative leader leaves the room and the staff discusses policy alternatives among themselves, there is a better chance for frank ethical debate and dissent to take place.[23] However, he also points out that even in these relatively egalitarian situations powerful group pressures are at work that tend to discourage individuals from seriously investigating differing ethical positions. According to Janis, subtle and overt pressures toward conformity often tend to create the condition he calls "groupthink"— the situation of false group consensus that suppresses a thorough analysis of policy implications. Importantly, one of the main results of groupthink is "an unquestioned belief in the group's inherent morality, inclining the members to ignore the ethical or moral consequences of their decisions."[24] Among the factors helping to maintain this unquestioning approach to moral questions are (1) "the self-censorship of deviations from apparent group consensus, reflecting each member's inclination to minimize to himself the importance of his doubts and counter-arguments," and (2) "direct pressure on any member who expresses strong arguments against any of the groups' stereotypes, illusions, or commitments, making clear that this type of dissent is contrary to what is expected of all loyal members."[25]

It seems, then, that we must add group pressure to hierarchical power relations as a factor that inhibits ethical policy analysis. Both are characteristics of bureaucratic life and are bound to be felt strongly by analysts working in that environment.

THE TECHNOCRATIC ETHOS

Yet another factor that inhibits the use of ethical analysis is the technocratic ethos that has come to infuse the profession of policy analysis. All professions cultivate a certain image—a mystique—that serves to promote and legitimize the work of its practitioners. In the case of policy analysis, this professional image is of the analyst as technician. Analysts prefer to portray themselves as purely technical advisors whose analysis is value-free and apolitical. This image is deeply rooted in the history of the profession. When policy analysts were making their first large inroads into the federal government in the early 1960s, it was fashionable to believe that policy questions no longer revolved around "passionate" ideological questions but were primarily technical in nature. Moreover, social scientists' unquestioned faith in the positivist approach seemed to suggest that a value-free, technocratic approach to policy issues was possible. Analysts assumed that they could easily draw a sharp distinction between normative questions and factual questions. In practice this meant that analysts would focus on questions of means, while leaving questions of ends to policymakers. It was thought that politicians would set societal goals, and analysts would give them technical advice on how these goals could best be achieved.[26]

This technocratic image continues to serve a number of important professional functions for analysts. Primarily it serves to legitimize the role of the analyst in the political system. Analysts are unelected, and as such they have no persuasive political justification for participating in the policymaking system. But their claim to be technocrats serves as their ticket into the halls of power. Their involvement is politically acceptable because their work is portrayed as value-free and they supposedly address only questions of means. So in much the same way that eunuchs were thought safe to be allowed to work in harems, policy analysts who are technocrats and thus "neutered" politically are considered safe to be included in the policymaking process.

Given that positivism and its notion of value-free analysis serves these important professional interests for policy analysts, it should not be surprising that they have not rushed to embrace ethics. To engage in ethical analysis would require abandoning many of the central tenets of positivism; and this in turn would undermine the carefully tended technocratic image of the analyst and the comfortable role that the profession has carved out for itself in the policymaking system. There is an intimate connection between the intellectual distinctions made in positivism (the fact-value dichotomy, the means-ends dichotomy) and the important distinctions made between the professional roles of analysts and policymakers. As ethics begins to blur the intellectual distinctions, it also begins to blur the professional distinctions. This can only make everyone uncomfortable. For this reason analysts continue to cling to such questionable positivist notions as value relativism and value-free analysis, outdated as they are. The positivist approach to values may be intellectually weak, but it still has a number of professional advantages for the analyst. It seems likely, then, that one of the major reasons that ethics is ignored by analysts is its tendency to threaten both the intellectual and political legitimacy of the profession.

ETHICS AND BUREAUCRATIC POLITICS

The fact that ethics is antitechnocratic not only helps to explain the reluctance of analysts to supply ethical analysis but also points to why administrators in particular fail to demand it. Administrators are reluctant to encourage ethical investigations because they too have a professional interest in maintaining a technocratic image. Being policymakers, administrators constantly face political risks and criticisms for their decisions. Being unelected policymakers, bureaucrats are particularly vulnerable to the accusation that they are using their discretion to go beyond their legislative mandates and engage in actual policymaking. In order to protect themselves and minimize these risks, they often take refuge in a technocratic defense of their decisions, asserting that they are not making policy but merely implementing it, and that they are not making value decisions but merely deciding how most efficiently to design a program. Of course, the notion that bureaucratic decision-making is nonpolitical is nothing more than an illusion, but it is an illusion that is useful to the political and professional survival of administrators.

The problem with ethical analysis is that it tends to weaken this valuable political shield. If, as some scholars have suggested, administrators were to engage in ethical analysis and make public the ethical deliberations that went into their decisions, this would be admitting that they in fact are engaged in normative policymaking.[27] When confronted with a group of inquisitive reporters, irate citizens, or hostile congresspersons, it would make little political sense for bureaucrats to begin discussing the various ethical issues involved in their decisions. It is much safer to fall back on more standard technocratic justifications.

This is not to say that administrators are not aware of or never consider the ethical implications of their decisions. These implications often may be the subject of informal discussions. Rather, the point is that such ethical deliberations are ad hoc, and they are unlikely to be made public or to be the subject of careful and systematic investigation in formal agency studies and reports. Instead, the dominant style of public justification for administrative decisions remains technocratic, because it increases the appearance of political legitimacy and presents the fewest political risks. To acknowledge and investigate publicly the ethical difficulties surrounding agency policies would only invite unwelcome public scrutiny. It would amount to painting a target on one's chest.

Anthony Lake, who has been both an administrator and a scholar, also makes the point that the nature of bureaucratic politics often encourages analysts and administrators to censor any private ethical concerns they might harbor. He found this tendency particularly evident during the Vietnam war:

> The men involved in making decisions on Vietnam in the early 1960s were aware of, and must have been privately concerned with, the human dimensions of their decisions. But such concern as they felt was not allowed to be included in their formal, written recommendations and analyses. It simply is not *done*.[28]

It is not done, Lake points out, because of the bureaucratic rules of behavior in the White House and the State Department. In these institutions a kind of bureaucratic machismo reigns, and this attitude interprets any deep concern for ethical issues as a sign of political and intellectual weakness—an unwillingness to make the "tough" policy decisions that foreign policy requires. As Lake explains, "Policy—good steady policy—is made by the 'tough-minded.' To talk of suffering is to lose 'effectiveness,' almost to lose one's grip. It is seen as a sign that one's 'rational' arguments are weak."[29] This, then, is yet another way in which the bureaucratic environment encourages technocratic over ethical forms of discourse and policy analysis. This pressing need for administrative decision making to appear purely pragmatic and tough-minded limits the terms of policy debate and works to preclude the open and probing evaluation of the human consequences of these decisions.

THE PSYCHOLOGICAL RISKS OF ETHICAL ANALYSIS

There are, then, a number of factors that inhibit the use of ethics in policy analysis, including the nature of administrative institutions and technocratic ethos that dominates the profession. It should be pointed out, however, that some analysts may be less vulnerable to these pressures than others. Specifically, it is likely that independent analysts, such as those who work in academia, may be in a better position to use ethical analysis in their work. Being freer from client and peer pressure and less dependent on a technocratic approach to legitimize their work, these practitioners face less professional risk from ethical analysis. It is revealing, for example, that in the area of energy policy the analyses that have most explicitly addressed the basic moral and ethical issues involved in the choices between alternative energy systems have been done by analysts such as Amory Lovins who have worked outside of government.[30]

But this is not to say that independent policy analysts are immune from all the pressures that inhibit the use of ethical analysis. Indeed, there is one more obstacle to employing ethical analysis over which even politically independent policy analysis tend to stumble: the psychological and emotional risks involved in this kind of analysis.

It is psychologically difficult to engage in ethical analysis. Ethical analysis involves asking questions that can be disturbing to the analyst. In thoroughly analyzing ethical questions, analysts inevitably have to question deeply held moral commitments, often including their own. For example, during an investigation of such morally difficult issues as abortion, pornography, or war, analysts might easily find that the justifications they have always held for their own positions are not nearly as flawless as they first thought, or that there is much previously unnoticed merit in the arguments of the opposition. Moreover, ethical analysis has an annoying tendency to raise more questions than it answers. In addition, the answers that do come from ethical analysis are not always exact and reassuring. The results may be ambiguous, and few people are comfortable living with ambiguity at such a basic philosophical level. In this sense, then, the fact that analysts are human and that most humans shy away from questioning their own basic ethical commitments can be a powerful force discouraging the use of ethical analysis. To make matters worse, some observers have suggested that policy analysts may be particularly sensitive to the psychological difficulties of ethical analysis. Daniel Callahan, director of the Hastings

Center, a leading institute for the study of ethics and public policy, has observed that certain personality types tend to be drawn to certain fields and that those who are drawn to policy analysis have a propensity to be very uncomfortable with the kinds of analysis involved in ethical investigations:

> I think the people drawn to policy analysis tend, on the whole to be people of a rather practical, activist orientation, and rather resistant to specula- tive, and inherently murky, issues. And ethical issues are certainly that. Moreover, I think that those trained in economics are particularly resistant to working on philosophical issues, or taking on ethical problems. Since most policy analysts are trained in economics, I think part of the problem lies there.[31]

In a sense, then, we return to a problem involving the technocratic nature of the policy analysis profession. The technocratic approach that most analysts are trained in may be not only politically convenient for the analyst but psychologically and emotionally convenient as well.

Janis has observed that the emotional risks involved in ethical questioning are a major factor in encouraging the emergence of groupthink. Serious ethical deliberations bring much stress, and policymakers and analysts already facing stressful situations may not want to add to their psychological burdens. Indeed, Janis found that the more stressful the policy decision, the less likely decision makers are to examine their moral assumptions.[32] This is particularly true in situations of crisis, in which decision makers are very concerned with bolstering their self-confidence and their sense of moral righteousness. Ironically, this tendency is even more pronounced if policy decisions involve the use of violence or other obviously morally questionable impacts—impacts that would easily raise feelings of guilt in the decision maker. Thus it is exactly when ethical analysis is most needed that, for psychological reasons, it is most unlikely to take place.

Janis found that the effort to avoid emotionally threatening ethical questions not only leads people to preempt their own investigation of the moral dimensions of the issues but also prompts them to discourage others from raising these questions. "When most members [of the policymaking group] fall back upon the familiar forms of social pressure directed against a member who questions the group's wisdom or morality, they are in effect protecting psychological defenses that help them to keep anxiety, shame, and guilt to a minimum."[33] It is significant that in most of the policy decision fiascos Janis studied, he found that the group deliberations that produced the worst decisions where often characterized by much self-confidence and a generally tranquil emotional atmosphere. Janis contrasts this with the stormy meetings that took place in situations in which analysts and decision makers successfully dealt with a pressing political problem. In the Cuban missile crisis, for instance, the deliberations of the president's advisory group generated much painful emotion. Bobby Kennedy in particular expressed his gnawing doubts about the morality of several proposed military options and forced many difficult but ultimately beneficial discussions about those ethical issues.[34] Janis concludes that the quality of the final policy decision is highly dependent on how frank and challenging the policy deliberations are.

In short, arriving at the ethically best policy decision is often an emotionally and psychologically painful process, one that few analysts and policymakers willingly embrace. Although this tendency may be most pronounced in the context of administrative decision making, these factors are also inevitably at work on the independent analyst as well. Indeed, the analyst who is working largely alone may have little awareness of the self-censorship that is taking place regarding the ethical dimensions of his or her investigation. Without someone else to provide a different moral perspective to challenge the analyst's own deeply held ethical assumptions, they may go largely unnoticed and unquestioned. Thus working alone may in some ways be just as hazardous to an analyst's ability to do serious ethical analysis as working in bureaucracies.

TOWARD A MORE ETHICAL
POLICY ANALYSIS

Writing in 1978, John Rohr warned that "unless the current interest in ethics is *institutionalized,* there is real danger that the profession as a whole may grow weary of well-doing as new issues and events present themselves."[35] Unfortunately, his prophecy has come true. The interest in ethics has waned not simply because it has gone out of fashion, but, as we have seen, because of powerful political, professional, and psychological forces that have actively discouraged the incorporation of ethics into policy analysis. Thus it is no accident that the concern for ethics has not been institutionalized. In many ways the institutional nature of policy analysis is quite hostile to ethical analysis, and it seems unlikely that ethics will easily be incorporated in a widespread or systematic way into the profession.

Of course, this is not to say that the *idea* of an ethical policy analysis is not a viable one. There are many reasons to believe that an ethical policy analysis is a worthwhile and intellectually workable idea. But whether or not a good idea is put into practice is a political matter, which is to say that it depends on the particular interests that benefit or suffer from its implementation. Unfortunately, ethical analysis threatens in many ways the interests of professional policy analysts and their clients. Many more professional and psychological benefits flow from the narrow technocratic approaches that currently characterize the profession. And so these approaches continue to dominate, despite their many intellectual and moral deficiencies. In short, there is a real politics to policy analysis methodologies, and this politics works against efforts to integrate ethics into the profession.

Although the prospects for an ethical policy analysis are somewhat bleak, they are far from hopeless. Indeed, it is important not to be too pessimistic about the prospects of ethical policy analysis, for this would only lessen further the chance of it being used. My analysis of the prospects for an ethical analysis is intended to be realistic, not pessimistic—to simply make it clear that it is naive to expect ethics to easily become an institutionalized part of policy analysis. But to say that an ethical policy analysis is difficult and unlikely is not to say that it is impossible. Thus the key question becomes, How can we encourage the increased use of ethical analysis? There would seem to be two answers: We can try to increase the supply of ethical analysis or increase the demand for it.

Increasing the supply of ethical analysis involves encouraging analysts to use this type of approach more often in their work. This encouragement can and has taken several different forms. For instance, one could familiarize analysts with ethical analysis during their training and argue its relevancy. There are now professional graduate programs that include courses concerning policy analysis and ethics. One can also exhort analysts to use the tools of ethical analysis in their work, pointing out the reasons why it would improve policy analysis. This has been a common approach among those who promote a more ethical policy analysis. All such efforts to increase the supply of ethical analysis are laudable and should be continued. However, if the analysis in this essay is correct, these efforts alone are akin to spitting into the wind. The institutional and political realities of policy analysis mean that such well-intentioned efforts will produce only minimal results. For this reason it seems impractical to rely on practitioners or the profession of policy analysis to be the driving force behind any movement toward a more ethical policy analysis.

It seems much more promising to try to increase the demand for ethical policy analysis. Primarily this would involve getting the clients of policy analysis to demand more serious analysis of the ethical dimensions of policy issues. Clearly ethical policy analysis could prosper if administrators and other clients of analysis could be won over, for they could make it more politically and institutionally acceptable for analysts to engage in this kind of analysis. This, of course, is easier said than done. The obvious sticking point is how to motivate administrators to demand this kind of analysis.

There are three possible approaches to this problem. First, one can appeal to the moral sense of policymakers, arguing that ethical issues and ethical analysis should be at the center of policy deliberations. However, such appeals have been made in the past with little obvious success; and so one might wait in vain for the emergence of a set of ethically enlightened administrators. Much more likely to work is a second approach: showing administrators that ethical analysis is in their interest, that it will help to produce better policy decisions. Recall that both Lake and Janis have argued that ethical analysis can be of practical use in helping to craft more realistic policies and in avoiding serious policy mistakes. Stressing this attribute of ethical analysis to policymakers could be much more effective than mere moral exhortation as a way of prompting them to take ethical issues seriously. For example, Lake suggested that if one wants foreign policymakers to take into account ethical considerations such as human rights, one not only makes a moral appeal but must also attempt to show how these concerns can help to produce realistic policies that serve the interests of the United States.[36] And if one can be successful in getting administrators to realize the practical and political advantages of ethical analysis, then this naturally would encourage them to demand more of it from their staff.

Of course, it is unlikely that the practical benefits of ethical analysis will always be evident to administrators and other policymakers, so a third form of encouragement will probably be necessary: the use of political pressure, particularly from the public. The strategy here is straightfoward: If considerable public pressure is put on administrators to confront the ethical dimensions of a particular policy issue, then they would feel more of an obligation to justify their decisions on these grounds. This in turn would make ethical analysis more politically relevant for administrators and make them more likely to demand it from their staff. In effect, public pressure is another way to make it in the self-interest of administrators to confront ethical issues directly.

Can such public pressure work? There is evidence that it already has in some areas. Consider, for example, the rise of hospital ethics committees. During the last few years, an number of hospitals have set up ethics committees to make recommendations about the difficult ethical decisions that arise in patient care.[37] Of particular concern have been decisions to terminate treatment, such as in so-called Baby Doe cases involving infants with severe birth defects, and in "right to die" cases involving hopelessly ill patients. Until recently such decisions were made on an informal and ad hoc basis by the doctor and the patient's relatives. These new ethics boards are designed in part to help make these difficult decisions more systematically and rationally. For our purposes it is important to note that these committees have come about in large part because of public pressure on doctors and hospital administrators to confront these ethical problems more directly. Specifically, groups and individuals in the right-to-die and right-to-life movements have focused increased attention on these decisions, requiring doctors and administrators to justify their decisions publicly. Some of these cases have ended up in court, which also has put considerable legal pressure on doctors and hospital administrators. In short, because of all of these pressures, conducting a systematic ethical analysis of these decisions is now in the legal and political self-interest of these decision makers.

The rise of hospital ethics committees provides an encouraging example of how decision makers can be motivated to take ethical issues more seriously—and how that kind of analysis can be institutionalized. Of course, these committees are relatively new, and it remains to be seen what their eventual impact will be. Moreover, it is not clear whether these kinds of committees would be feasible or even desirable in public sector bureaucracies that typically deal with very different kinds of decisions. Nonetheless, this example illustrates how public pressure can encourage decision makers to look more deeply into ethical issues, and this is a lesson that can be usefully applied to the political sphere. Indeed, one can find instances in which public pressure did force political decision makers to examine more closely the ethical implications of their decisions.

Consider the issue of human rights in American foreign policy. During the late 1970s, this concern became an important consideration in our foreign affairs. In part this new emphasis was a response to public pressure to reevaluate the morality of past foreign policy efforts, particularly in light of the ethical questions raised by Vietnam. In more recent times the federal government has been made to examine the ethical issues surrounding our support of the white minority government of South Africa, and in this case the pressure to do so has come mainly from the bottom up.

Such reliance on public pressure, however, is not without its problems. The moral concerns of the public are often fleeting. Moreover, there are often sharp disagreements between various segments of the public as to how relevant ethical concerns are in various policy areas. Indeed, often there are intense political struggles over whether a particular policy choice should be seen primarily in ethical terms. Consider a current issue such as divestment in South Africa. Advocates of divestment have put much effort into emphasizing divestment as a moral issue, whereas those opposed to divestment have tried persistently to shift the discussion to other terrain—arguing, for example, that moral and political considerations should not guide investment decisions. Clearly, then, not all groups have an interest in emphasizing the moral dimensions of these decisions. It was seen earlier that one of the main obstacles to the ethical analysis of policy issues in government bureaucracies is the self-interests of various actors and groups. This is also the case in the larger political system.

Unfortunately, there is not adequate space here to examine all the implications of these strategies to promote more ethical policy analysis. I believe, however, that these suggestions point in some hopeful directions. The basic point underlying these suggestions is this: Policy analysis exists in a larger political context and responds to the political pressures put upon it. Thus we can expect more ethical policy analysis only if policymakers or the public demand it. In this sense, the ultimate fate of ethical policy analysis does not lie in the hands of policy analysis professionals but will be determined by the struggles taking place in the larger political system. If the battles to define and approach public policy decisions more ethically can be won in the halls of power and in the streets of the nation, then the practitioners of policy analysis will follow suit.

NOTES

1. For a recent summary of the ongoing complaints about cost-benefit analysis, see Daniel Schwartzman, Richard A. Liroff, and Kevin G. Croke, eds., *Cost-Benefit Analysis and Environmental Regulations* (Washington, DC: The Conservation Foundation, 1982), especially chapter 4.

2. Laurence Tribe, Corinne S. Schelling, and John Voss, eds., *When Values Conflict* (Cambridge, MA: Ballinger, 1976).

3. Tribe, Schelling, and Voss, *When Values Conflict*, p. xii.

4. Martin Rein, *Social Science and Public Policy* (New York: Penguin, 1976), 140.

5. Rein, *Social Science and Public Policy,* pp.78-79.

6. Laurence Tribe, "Policy Science: Analysis or Ideology," *Philosophy and Public Affairs* (Fall 1972): 66-110.

7. Fred Kramer, "Policy Analysis as Ideology," *Public Administration Review 36* (Sept.-Oct. 1975): 509-517; Paul Diesing, *Science and Ideology in the Policy Sciences* (New York: Aldine, 1982); Brian Fay, *Social Theory and Political Practice* (London: George Allen & Unwin, 1975).

8. For a description of some of these programs, see Joel L. Fleishman and Bruce Payne, *Ethical Dilemmas and the Education of Policymakers* (Hastings-On-Hudson, NY: The Hastings Center, 1980).

9. See Frank Marini, *Toward a New Public Administration* (Scranton, PA: Chandler, 1971).

10. D. Hart and W. Scott, "Administrative Crisis: The Neglect of Metaphysical Speculation," *Public Administration Review* 33 (January-February): 415-422.

11. Irving Janis, *Groupthink,* 2nd ed. (Boston: Houghton Mifflin, 1982).

12. These points came from personal discussions with Anthony Lake and from his article (with Roger Morris) "The Human Reality of Realpolitik," *Foreign Policy* 4 (Fall 1971): 157-162.

13. Paul Taylor, *Normative Discourse* (Englewood Cliffs, NJ: Prentice-Hall, 1961).

14. One of the first to argue the case for rights over cost-benefit analysis was Tribe in his article "Policy Science: Analysis or Ideology." The thinking of Ronald Dworkin has also been important to this movement to analyze policy issues in terms of rights. See his *Taking Rights Seriously* (Cambridge, MA: Harvard University Press, 1977).

15. Steven Kelman, *What Price Incentives* (Boston: Auburn House, 1981).

16. C. W. Churchman, *The Design of Inquiring Systems* (New York: Basic Books, 1971).

17. Irving Janis has also suggested a version of this forensic approach. See *Groupthink*, chapter 11.

18. Duncan MacRae, *The Social Function of Social Science* (New Haven: Yale University Press, 1976).

19. See the articles by Jennings and Rein in Daniel Callahan and Bruce Jennings, *Ethics, the Social Sciences, and Policy Analysis* (New York: Plenum, 1983).

20. Frank Fischer, *Politics, Values, and Public Policy: The Problem of Methodology* (Boulder: Westview Press, 1980).

21. For an earlier version of some of the arguments in this section, see Douglas J. Amy, "Why Policy Analysis and Ethics are Incompatible," *Journal of Policy Analysis and Management* 3, 4 (1984): 580-587.

22. Arnold Meltsner, *Policy Analysts in the Bureaucracy* (Berkeley: University of California Press, 1979), 292.

23. Janis, *Groupthink,* p. 142.

24. Ibid., p. 174.

25. Ibid., p. 175.

26. See Callahan and Jennings, *Ethics*, p. xvii.

27. See Douglas Yates, "Hard Choices: Justifying Bureaucratic Decisions," in Joel Fleishman et al., eds., *Public Duties: The Moral Obligations of Government Officials* (Cambridge, MA: Harvard University Press, 1981).

28. Lake and Morris, "Human Reality of Reapolitik," p. 159.

29. Ibid., p. 160.

30. Amory Lovins, *Soft Energy Paths* (Cambridge, MA: Ballinger, 1977).

31. Daniel Callahan, personal correspondence.

32. Janis, *Groupthink,* p. 258.

33. Ibid., p. 257.

34. Ibid., pp. 147-148, 151.

35. John Rohr, *Ethics for Bureaucrats* (New York: Marcel Dekker, 1978), 51.

36. This example came from a number of personal conversations with Anthony Lake at Mount Holyoke College, fall 1985. His comments and suggestions were very helpful in developing many of the arguments in this concluding section of the essay.

37. My thanks to the editors of this volume for bringing these committees to my attention, and to Bruce Jennings for giving me much helpful information about their workings. For those interested in more information about these committees, see Ronald E. Cranford and A. Edward Doudera, *Institutional Ethics Committees and Health Care Decisionmaking* (New York: Health Administration Press, 1984).

PART II

Policy Expertise and the State:
The Technocratic Bias

3

POLICY SCIENCE AND THE ADMINISTRATIVE STATE: THE POLITICAL ECONOMY OF COST-BENEFIT ANALYSIS

JOHN BYRNE
University of Delaware

The idea of governing under the constraint of a benefit-cost test of contemplated public actions is not new. Inspired by Jeremy Bentham's argument that, morally speaking, society's problem is the provision of the greatest happiness for the greatest number, it has been urged in one form or another in certain philosophic and economic circles for nearly two centuries. Until recently, however, government by felicific calculus had gone largely untried.

The central advantage claimed for cost-benefit government is that it would discipline public choice so that scarce public and private resources are rationally allocated to their highest valued uses. In this way, it is argued, contemporary social well-being is optimized and future happiness enhanced through reosurce conservation. To accomplish these ends, however, will require fundamental changes in the governmental decision-making process. The current domination of this process by political interest and power has resulted, according to cost-benefit advocates, in a systematic distortion of the value of resources and their public uses. What is required to remedy this situation is the recognition that the paramount problems of governance are not those having to do with power and conflict but with the efficient administration of state actions. Supporters of cost-benefit tests of government policy do not deny the existence of conflict; indeed, many assert its unavoidability. But it is argued that this recognition impels attention to the problem of how conflict should be managed by the state. In this context, cost-benefit analysis is offered as a viable alternative to politics. With it otherwise amorphous issues of governance purportedly can be resolved in an orderly manner and the rationally superior public action for many, if not all, social problems discovered.

The tenability of this proposal rests upon displacing politics with administrative forms in deciding issues of governance. Indeed, the advocacy of cost-benefit government represents an implicit, if not explicit, endorsement of the administrative state. Curiously, however, the desirability of such a displacement is seldom addressed. It appears that cost-benefit government, suitably debugged and with possible allowance for certain "inalienable" rights, is presumed inherently good and preferred. Concern is focused almost exclusively on whether and to what extent such a mode of governance can be implemented. Despite a divergence of opinion on feasibility, there remains a common presumption that installment of cost-benefit tests for public actions would be desirable.

The desirability of cost-benefit analysis, and the technocratic system of governance that it requires, cannot be resolved by presumption. If the tenability of cost-benefit analysis hinges upon the emergence of the administrative state, then ultimately the use of this technique to decide public policy specifically, and the nature and role of state power generally, hinges upon the preferability of such a system of governance. My argument against cost-benefit rule is focused on the normative and ideological implications of the use of this technique to decide questions of power and policy and the displacement of politics that is essential to its effective use.

THE RULE OF REASON

Cost-benefit analysis is now an established, if still controversial, tool of public policy making and evaluation. The national government especially is a frequent user, employing the technique for such purposes as determining acceptable levels of various pollutants, setting industry standards of worker health and safety, assessing the feasibility of safety improvements in automobiles, and evaluating the impact of alternative technologies on social and economic welfare. But although the uses of this mode of analysis are growing, they nonetheless continue to be confined to decisions made in executive branch agencies. Legislative and judicial decisions are seldom if ever based on such logic. Even in the executive branch, cost-benefit calculations usually play only a minor role in policy decisions. The limited integration of this tool into the policy apparatus has raised the problem that only parts of a policy may be subjected to the rigor of analysis, whereas others continue to be formulated on grounds that either contradict or neutralize those applied in analysis.

Thus advocates have directed their attention increasingly to the problem of expanding the use of cost-benefit analysis. Not surprising, much of the criticism as well as advocacy of cost-benefit analysis have been preoccupied with the appropriateness of this technique to certain classes of problems and to the value implications of its use in identifying solutions. Normative dilemmas, if they are recognized, are seen to derive from the nature of the problem to which the technique is applied rather than from the implication for governance of its use. For advocates and many critics, the key questions have become, "To what range of problems is cost-benefit analysis applicable?" and "Under what conditions would its contribution be optimized?" Responses to these questions can be separated into two groups: those which recognize social order as necessarily imperfect and treat cost-benefit analysis as an organizing rather than calculative framework for addressing social concerns, and those which see the use of this technique as part of an effort to establish formal rational criteria in government decision making. The first is characterized by a pragmatic understanding of social problems and deemphasizes the formal features of cost-benefit procedures in favor of the heuristic value of its general logic and perspective. The work of Alice Rivlin and Tom Beauchamp[1] is representative of this approach. The other, more formal approach stresses the precision and ethical superiority of cost-benefit decision making and calls for a decisive role to be played by such analysis. The arguments of E. J. Mishan and David Braybrooke and Peter Schotch[2] are indicative of this latter understanding.

For "informalists" such as Beauchamp and Rivlin, the practical conditions of *realpolitik* urge the use of cost-benefit analysis. The contemporary problem of governance is seen to be one of establishing rules of reason by which to decide issues of public concern in an otherwise untidy world of power and politics. Although cost-benefit analysis cannot deliver the ultimate rules of governance, nevertheless this technique is seen as important and valuable for the opportunity it provides for arriving at a rational accommodation of the moral conflicts of an irrational world. In this respect cost-benefit analysis represents an attractive solution to problems cf modern governance offering the prospect of escape from total reliance on power and politics. Thus, for example, Beauchamp claims that cost-benefit analysis is a pragmatic necessity in "real" moral life where rights frequently conflict. It provides a "morally adequate"[3] means of decision making that evaluates political decisions against the standard of aggregate welfare, a standard that "at least on some occasions is mandatory from a moral point of view."[4] Some critics charge that such a standard would lead to the denial of basic rights if the costs of doing so were less than the collective benefits. Beauchamp argues, however, that consistent with the familiar rule-utilitarian position, cost-benefit analysis should not be immunized from the restraining control of moral rules.[5] The force of moral rights will not be contravened if a "loose sense" of the cost-benefit technique is adopted in which the objective is to determine whether a particular action is "acceptable," "reasonable" *within* the boundaries of morality.[6]

Rivlin expresses a similar attitude toward the problems of society, based on her considerable experience in the federal bureaucracy:

> The choices are genuinely hard and the problems are extraordinarily complex and difficult. It is hard to design an income maintenance system that will both assure adequate incomes to the needy and encourage people to work, or a health financing system that will both assure proper care to the sick and encourage efficient use of health insurance. . . . If any analyst thought it was going to be easy to make social action programs work better or to make more rational choices among programs, he is by now a sadder and a wiser man.[7]

In this complex world values will not be easily quantified and often will be in conflict. What can be achieved is not the definitive solution but the reasonable one, founded on an informed understanding of the general levels of costs and benefits and their distributions: "who would benefit from a policy and who would pay its costs."[8] Echoing the point, Boulding suggests that

> even though economic measurement may be abused, its effect on the formulation of moral judgments is great, and on the whole I believe

beneficial. The whole idea of cost-benefit analysis . . . is of enormous importance in the evaluation of social choices and even social institutions. We can grant, of course, that the "real" dollar . . . is a dangerously imperfect measure of the quality of human life and human values. Nevertheless, it is a useful first approximation, and in these matters of difficult choices, it is extremely useful to have a first approximation that we can later modify.[9]

The value of cost-benefit analysis is thus in the discipline it brings to the policy process and the ability it provides for addressing social problems in a systematic manner. As Rivlin asserts, "The crucial questions now are . . . organizational."[10]

While recognizing that the value of cost-benefit analysis relates to its capacity to yield rational solutions of social problems, "formalists" such as Mishan and Braybrooke and Schotch see no means of using this technique within the contemporary world of politics. For these advocates, no minor modification of the world as it is will suffice. The problems are, as Mishan observes, constitutional and concern the ethical premises that serve as "a common context of aspirations."[11] At issue are the inescapable conflicts not only among alternative social policies or objectives but between these and questions of rights and needs. Seen in this light, cost-benefit analysis cannot be divorced from the most general value implications of social organization and action.

Equally clear, Mishan argues, is that use of cost-benefit analysis cannot be restricted to the role of consultative input into policy decisions. Requests to " 'organize' the new data" and provide a framework for comparing alternative policies that would extend extraordinary power to the consultant-analyst that, practically speaking, cannot be limited.[12] What must be demanded instead is that the framework and organization employed are based upon nonarbitrary economic principles of allocation. Cost-benefit analysis draws its justification, as Mishan demonstrates, from allocative "propositions at the centre of welfare economics" which are represented in the "virtual constitution"[13] of society. Specifically, the technique is guided by the principle of Pareto optimality:

> If, in any situation it is found to be impossible to make *any* change without making some individual in the group worse off, the situation is defined as Pareto-optimal or Pareto-efficient. . . . A change is defined to be Pareto-optimal, if in the transition from one situation to another: (1)

every individual in the group is made better off; or (2) at least one individual in the group is made better off and no one is made worse off.[14]

The elevation of cost-benefit analysis to constitutional status rests, as Liebhafsky[15] has pointed out, on the presupposition that Pareto optimality is a *Grundnorm* upon which the validity of all other norms depends. As such, the *Grundnorm* of Pareto optimality cannot and should not be constrained by the requirements of political consensus; as with all constitutional rules, it antecedes consent. For Mishan, then, the impetus is to moor cost-benefit analysis to the "guiding rules" that "can truthfully claim to rest on a widely accepted ethical base."[16] Once achieved, the cost-benefit calculus "on any ethical ranking, would . . . transcend economic decisions reached by political processes, democratic or otherwise. . . . For decisions reached by the political process will almost always rest on a narrow basis of consent."[17]

Braybrooke and Schotch propose a similar system of governance intended to deliver the formalist vision of a transcendental social order beyond social and ethical conflicts brought about through the exercise of "right" reason. Their proposal represents perhaps the most explicit conception of governance as a process of rational problem solving. Governing begins with the scrutiny of issues of collective concern to determine whether they involve, respectively, questions of rights, needs, and preferences. Rights and needs are to be addressed by means of threshold analyses. In the case of rights, "whether a policy conforms to a peremptory consideration is to be treated as a matter of fact that can be ascertained by comparing the features of the policy with the requirements set forth in the consideration."[18] Response to potential rights violations is to take one of two forms: Either the policy is not to be enacted until and unless the cause of violation is removed; or the policy is to be enacted on the condition that fair compensation of victims, again to be regarded as a matter of fact, can be assured by a compensation scheme that presumably would have to satisfy the criterion of cost-effectiveness as well. Observance of minimum needs thresholds is also to be required of any proposed policy. Such thresholds are to be established from objective analysis of "minimum standards of provision."[19] Any remaining public policy problems are considered in this scheme to stem from conflicts of preferences. Within an institutional framework that provides for prior checks for violations of basic rights and needs, cost-benefit analysis has the role of resolving subjective "interest" conflicts according to the criterion of maximization of objective social benefit. In this type of framework, cost-benefit analysis represents a particular stage of analysis within a general framework of objective analysis of moral problems.

Despite important differences in the way advocates conceptualize the possibilities and limits of cost-benefit analysis, governance via a cost-benefit norm is promised to elevate policymaking above the inefficiency and irrationality of politics. Moreover, advocates project a common set of conditions for the optimal use of this technique. The social world is generally approached as one in which problems occur or may be treated as occurring relatively independently of one another and are bounded in scope. In some versions, such as the Braybrooke-Schotch scheme, this independence condition is extended to the moral dimensions of social problems as well, with an expectation that rights, needs, and preferences can be addressed separately without distorting the nature of the "problem." To this independence condition about the nature of social problems advocates add important conditions regarding the nature of their solution. The set of alternative solutions to a particular problem is treated, where such a set exists, as an analytically finite and commensurable one. This means that if solutions exist, there is always a superior one. Where no solutions exist, no rational engagement of the problem is available and no public action can be justified. A third set of conditions concerns the issue of valuation. The costliness of a particular problem and the implementation of its solution, as well as the worth of any advantages that might result (beyond the elimination of the particular social problem itself), are regarded by advocates as objectively knowable. Of special importance, these values are thought to be available to the analyst without recourse to individuals or communities who might be affected by the contemplated public action.

If these conditions can be met—and much of the debate surrounding cost-benefit analysis is absorbed by this question—a distinct political opportunity emerges. Insofar as social problems can be treated as independent and bounded in scope, their solution regarded as a question of optimizing net benefit, and the availability of objective measures by which to evaluate competing solutions confidently assumed, government by right reason would seem to be within our grasp. Historic social conflicts such as those concerning the distribution of wealth and the public provision of basic rights and needs, as well as more recent ones such as the protection of the environment, worker and product safety, and balanced economic growth, would all appear to reduce to discovering and implementing the best alternative and therewith to be resolvable through procedures of rational calculation. This is because in a world made safe for cost-benefit analysis, conflict is the result not of irreconcilable substantive differences, as much of political theory has traditionally argued, but of the use of faulty "decisional premises."[20] Correcting those premises that distort our understanding of the true costs of public services, or that encourage suboptimal supply (either over- or undersupply) of such services, should lead, in a world fashioned from the postulates of cost-benefit analysis, to the virtual elimination of social conflict. Indeed this is precisely what is envisioned by advocates of the widespread use of cost-benefit analysis.

Engaging the problems of society from the vantage point of cost-benefit analysis is an exciting proposition for its advocates. It heralds the possibility of the triumph of reason over power and the displacement of politics with analysis. To some this triumph and displacement are instrumental but not complete, as they cannot be. To others a fundamental reordering of society and government is necessary. In both cases, however, the basic aspirations are the same—only the expectations about the level of accomplishment differ. Perhaps because of the attractiveness of such a triumph, and because only the level of accomplishment is in dispute, advocates tend to be unpersuaded of the tenuousness of the conditions necessary for cost-benefit analysis to be fully effective. But regardless of whether the feasibility of these conditions is conceded, the basic objections to a world made amenable to cost-benefit analysis remain.

WHAT'S WRONG WITH
BEING REASONABLE?

The worlds projected in formalist and informalist visions of cost-benefit government would require a profound transformation in the basis of governance. Fundamentally, these worlds call for the abandonment of rule by consent in favor of the rule of reason. The replacement of consent with reason as the foundation of governance is intended to dispense with the inefficiency and irrationality of politics, but in fact it dispenses with democracy in favor of the administrative state. The issues that normally give rise to questions of democratic participation and consent are simply without salience in the transformed world of cost-benefit analysis. Indeed, the ideals of democracy could not be tolerated in the new world, and only its veneer would survive the transformation.

CONSUMER SOVEREIGNTY AND
THE DECLINE OF THE CITIZEN

Government by cost-benefit analysis has no need of a participative citizenry. The processes of public decision making depend in such a model upon the identification of objective values. It is only with their identification that rational solutions can be found. To involve the citizenry in the process of identifying values could only result in contamination of the process, for citizens can offer merely subjective assessments of their idiosyncratic circumstances. To operate effectively, the world of cost-benefit analysis must be insulated from, and preemptive of, the participation of its citizens.

The arguments in a recent U.S. Supreme Court case covering the 1980 cotton dust standard set by the Occupational Safety and Health Administration (OSHA)[21] illustrate the tension between cost-benefit rule and democratic participation. At issue in the case was whether the OSHA standard could be challenged on the ground that it failed to pass a cost-benefit test. The 1970 enabling legislation mandated the promulgation of a standard that "most adequately assures, *to the extent feasible,* on the basis of the best available evidence, that no employee will suffer material impairment of health" from contact with cotton dust.[22] The American Textile Manufacturers Institute and the National Cotton Council of America, representing industry, argued that the "to the extent feasible" requirement should be interpreted to include the demonstration of net benefit. Not to do so, it was claimed, would extend to the Secretary of Labor and OSHA extraordinary discretion to interpret the requirement as mandating a workplace "utopia" free of risks and hazards based upon the unrealistic and irresponsible ideal of absolute safety.[23] Justice Rehnquist, in a minority opinion supporting the industry position, was even more blunt: The cotton dust standard, he asserted, represents a choice of the balance to be observed between the statistical possibility of death or serious illness and the economic costs of avoiding death or illness; but Congress, by exacting the law without conducting a cost-benefit analysis or defining some other objective standard to determine this balance, abdicated its elected responsibility.[24]

A majority of five justices with one abstaining concluded that a cost-benefit test of the cotton dust standard was not required because Congress, in establishing the need for the standard, had chosen "to place preeminent value on assuring employees a safe and healthful working environment limited only by the feasibility of achieving such an

environment."[25] Any further analysis of the standard's costs and
benefits beyond that implicitly performed by Congress when it passed
the 1970 Act would be, in the minds of the Court majority, an obstruc-
tion of legislative will.[26]

What this case illustrates is the constitutional upheaval implied by the
installment of cost-benefit rule. If accepted, the industry argument and
Rehnquist dissent would have required the substitution of purported
objective values[27] for democratic participation as the basis of legitimacy
for government policy. Under their vision of governance, a constraint
on policy choice based on apparent objective circumstances (in this
specific case, the medical, engineering, and economic facts surrounding
textile manufacture) is dictated in order to ensure responsible policy
selection. Without such a constraint, values could be introduced that
obscure a rational understanding of the facts of the situation (such as the
placing of preeminent value on a safe and healthful work environment)
and that may lead to unjustifiable intrusions of political activity into
society's affairs. Participative government in this view should confine
itself to discovering the objective conditions of the issue at hand and
affirming them in public policy. This is to be contrasted with the Court
majority position, which denied the necessity of a cost-benefit constraint
on policy choice and thereby preserved the opportunity for political
participation in setting the boundaries of such choice, rather than
merely the opportunity to select among preselected alternatives. Under
cost-benefit rule such an opportunity would be denied.

But if participation is precluded, what is left of the idea of citizen?
Little more than a glorified notion of consumer. In a world of cost-
benefit analysis, governance is a consumption good. Citizens decide
whether and to what degree they are satisfied with the products of
governance, but they have no responsibility for the production of
governance or even overseeing its production. Indeed, the expectation is
that citizens have no substantial interest in such matters beyond the
desire for objective government. The problem of political sovereignty,
so hotly debated in Western political theory, is discovered to have little
more meaning, rationally speaking, than economic utility won or lost, as
measured by triangles of benefit under demand curves.

FREEDOM = OBJECTIVITY; JUSTICE = EFFICIENCY

Without an active citizenry, and with an objectively grounded
intolerance of democratic participation, can such a world be demo-

cratic? The notion of democratic cost-benefit rule would require, to say the least, a novel use of the term. Consider, for example, the classic association of democracy and freedom. "Free" in the new world refers neither to the absence of constraints on choice or action nor positively to the pursuit of collective goals such as the elevation of the intellectual and moral character of society, the promotion of social equality, and the like. Such definitions presuppose the cost-effectiveness (at least) of freedom, a judgment that must necessarily be questioned. Instead, freedom under cost-benefit rule refers to the appreciation of objective existence. It is the knowledge that decisions about one's future are based upon and limited to "the facts" that make one free in this world. This is not to say that the worlds projected by the advocates of cost-benefit government would not be populated by those sensitive to democratic ideals of freedom. Rather, it is to argue that a world fashioned from the postulates of cost-benefit analysis is indifferent to concerns with democratic freedom.

If cost-benefit rule is unconcerned with democratic freedoms, it likewise shows little regard for the need to ground governance in principles of justice.[28] As with ideals of freedom, those of justice do not find a central place in the administrative state, not because of an aversion within the mechanics of cost-benefit analysis to matters of justice but, rather, as the result of an indifferent regard to them. What is fair, moral, respectful can be incidental only to what is of maximum net benefit. Cannot such qualities either be monetized and included in rational calculations or, as Braybrooke and Schotch suggest, treated as peremptory considerations? In one sense they can be, and many writers have attempted to explain such a possibility.[29] But their suggestions appear to be negatively rather than positively motivated as a response to the charge by critics that such matters cannot be adequately incorporated. Little attention seems to have been given to the question of the desirability of doing so.[30] Most important, the issue only begins with the question of whether these dimensions can be incorporated in the cost-benefit calculus. It must also be ascertained: with what confidence can they be included, especially in comparison with what are considered the nonnormative dimensions of policy issues; and at what cost to our understanding of the role and importance of these considerations would this be done?

Again, consideration of a recent U.S. Supreme Court decision[31] is useful. In a 1981 case concerning the constitutionality of warrantless inspection of mines, the Court with one dissent held that

a warrant may not be constitutionally required when Congress has
reasonably determined that warrantless searches are necessary to further
a regulatory scheme, and the federal regulatory presence is sufficiently
comprehensive and defined that the owner of commercial property
cannot help but be aware that his property will be subject to periodic
inspections undertaken for specific purposes.[32]

The legal arguments underlying the decision are complex and
concern differences historically made by the courts between privacy
rights pertaining to the home and those pertaining to commercial
property under the Fourth Amendment. But suppose that such
differences were not decisive in the case. Would it be appropriate to
substitute a cost-benefit test as the condition for authorizing a
warrantless search? That is, could the surprise inspection be justified if
the expected benefits in terms of deterred harmful activity outweighed
the costs to mining owners' privacy and other expenses? Clearly the
Supreme Court's concern with privacy rights would be of incidental
importance under a cost-benefit test. Indeed, the act of violation itself
would be secondary to the extent of harm. If the mine violations that
might be found were expected to be petty and the deterrent effect slight,
a cost-benefit rule would not only fail to support the inspection, but
would furnish grounds as to why a search would be *unjustifiable*. That
is, used as a rationale of law, the cost-benefit test could sanction a
finding that enforcement of the law would be unjust. This result is not
peculiar, of course, if the legitimacy and purpose of law are located in an
equation of justice with the optimization of net benefit. However, it does
raise the interesting paradox of law violation as just, due to questions
not of conscience but of prudence. In this regard Ronald H. Coase's
essay on social cost[33] takes cost-benefit reasoning to its logical
conclusion by conceiving social harm as "necessarily reciprocal." Under
this framework harm is not exclusively a condition of victims because,
insofar as laws are enforced to protect or compensate victims, an
additional harm is created in the form of the reduced utility/wealth of
prosecuted violators. A truly novel idea of justice!
    If in the administrative state the achievements of governance are not
judged by the extent to which the governed are free and public actions
just, then what is to be the measure? The success of government, if we are
being reasonable, is to be measured by whether it works efficiently. In a
society governed by right reason, government is held accountable for the
delivery of policies of maximum yield relative to the amount of

resources used—that is, policies that satisfy the optimality *Grundnorm*. Government has little to do with the goal of ensuring that public actions are moral, normatively preferred, or fair. Although such qualities may perhaps be deemed desirable, their "intuitive"[34]—or, more exactly, normative—foundations preclude them from being central commitments in the constitution of Pareto-optimal society.

HYPOTHETICAL DEMOCRACY

If such a foundation of governance is to be called democratic, it is democracy without the attributes that have traditionally been thought to be fundamental to the idea. Cost-benefit rule imputes little value to democratic processes of decision making, preferring calculation to consent as the basis of public choice. It ascribes no special importance to the ideals of democratic freedom and justice, reserving ideal status instead for the purportedly objective and efficient decision. Ultimately it is right reason, not democratic participation or values, that is cherished and nourished under cost-benefit government.

But might it not be argued in defense of cost-benefit tests of government policy that democratic attributes can be grafted onto the decision-making process; that the above criticisms prove only the non-essentialness of democracy for cost-benefit rule, not its incompatibility; and that the real issue avoided by such criticisms is the prosperity of citizens under such rule? That is, are we not overlooking the fundamental importance of the *results* of government—whether the greatest happiness is provided for the greatest number? That, at the end of the day, is what cost-benefit rule supposedly delivers, and what democracy may not.

First, caution should be observed in conceding the compatibility of the democratic graft. As Mishan has pointed out, accommodating democracy may be more costly than avoiding it:

> Decision-making through the political process, especially in a liberal democracy, is time-consuming. Even if the democratic process, alone and unaided, were somehow able to offer to each person the same opportunities and the same combination of goods that he already receives through the market, economists would have no difficulty in convincing people that the substitution of voting mechanisms for the pricing mechanism would take up an unconscionable amount of time and effort.[35]

Furthermore, where political decisions are unavoidable, a strong case based on the yardstick of results can be made for using the market rather than the vote as the model for decision making:

> And yet, prodigal though it would be in the use of time and effort, it is hardly conceivable that the political process will bring about an allocation of goods and resources as satisfactory as that brought about through the market. Whatever the outcome of the political process, it is highly unlikely . . . that such an outcome could not be materially improved by introducing pricing mechanisms. And, if some improvements can be effected by the introduction of such pricing mechanisms, they can also be effected by simple allocation rules (such as net or proportionate benefit rule) which "stimulate" the workings of the price mechanisms.[36]

Thus democratic compromises may be too expensive and inferior in deliverable results compared to those achievable by "econocracy,"[37] as one writer has termed cost-benefit government. Cost-benefit advocates do not want to get too carried away with democratic ideas.

Democracy's advocates should be equally uneager to accept its compatibility with cost-benefit rule. Even if the value of certain democratic mechanisms could somehow be warranted as positive and sizable, their function in this form of government would likely not be very encouraging. For example, representational voting might remain in the world of cost-benefit analysis, but the rationale for its retention would be quite different from that of traditional democratic theory. As noted earlier, cost-benefit analysis is predicated on the assumption that if normative dilemmas exist, they exist as attributes of the problems engaged and not as attributes of social analysis itself. This being the case, how are the problems for analysis to be selected without bias under cost-benefit rule? Clearly any selection must be normative, for it necessarily will favor consideration of one normative dilemma over another. To have some technical apparatus of analysis determine which problems are investigated and which are not would obviously undermine the very basis of authority on which rational society operates. But "democratic" voting removes at least the appearance of such a problem by transferring blame to the citizenry and its subjective proclivities. The insidious result is that a democratic mechanism is used to relieve the administrative state of democratic responsibility.

The fundamental problem with cost-benefit reasoning on this score, however, is that it misrepresents the issue. By challenging democracy to yield utilitarian results, advocates presume the normative legitimacy of the criterion of net benefit while completely devaluing democratic results. It is as though the choice of democracy were inherently utilitarian. The possibility that decisions arrived at through democratic participation and consent could be valued in themselves independently of their economic implications is simply not recognizable from a cost-benefit perspective; such a notion makes no sense because it ignores the constitutional status accorded to efficiency. There is a fallacy, of course, in this line of reasoning which Weinrib has dubbed the "fallacy of results" and which he illustrates with the following analogy:

> Assume that Jones loves playing golf and plays eighteen holes every Sunday morning. One particular Sunday Jones realizes that he cannot spare the time to play his usual game. Instead he goes out into his back yard, digs a hole, and drops the ball into it eighteen times. When questioned about his peculiar behavior, he explains, 'Well, since it was impossible to play golf, I decided to mimic what happens when I actually play golf. Golf, as you know, is a game which results in a ball being repeatedly deposited into a hole in the ground. Of course, this is not the whole game, which includes the process by which this result is to be attained. But surely the result is the most significant part of the game, so that is the element which I reproduced. After all, what I was playing was not actual golf (that was impossible in the circumstances), but only hypothetical golf.' It is unlikely that this explanation will persuade many golfers to try hypothetical golf when circumstances prevent the playing of actual golf. . . . [And] a claim by Jones that his commitment to actual golf led him to try hypothetical golf would be regarded as incoherent, since the challenge which is integral to the former is completely lacking in the latter.[38]

To reap the promised benefits of cost-benefit rule, it will be necessary to forego democracy of the actual kind for a hypothetical variety, a bargain not without its costs.

The intolerance of the administrative state to participation and debate on questions of values is traceable directly to the distinctive attribute of this system of governance—its lodging of authority in technocratic reason rather than political consent. There is no place in the workings of this system for majority votes and minority objections to interfere in, much less withhold legitimacy from, public actions dictated by rational analysis. Cost-benefit analysis and the technocratic system of governance it implies depend upon right reason to convince us of the sensibleness of policies selected by its use. In this respect the achievement of a world in which the contributions of cost-benefit analysis to policy are optimized is the achievement of irresistibility for the decisions and actions of government. It is a world in which we must abandon political choice, participation, and dissent to gain efficient and unassailable social order.

CLASS AND COST-BENEFIT ANALYSIS

Perhaps the most embarrassing problem with being reasonable in the cost-benefit sense is that it can provide no escape from the world of power and politics. The conditions necessary for the effective use of cost-benefit analysis in matters of public policy are normative and ideological. They favor certain conclusions about the social order over others and certain actions in that world over others. These conditions are neither morally modest nor trivial. They cannot be represented as mere analytic devices to focus attention on certain relevant attributes of social problems because they introduce systematic bias that can be removed only by violating the requisite conditions for the use of this technique. Indeed, the technique is imbued with values that strongly favor the status quo.

Three analytic conditions, as noted in an earlier section, are assumed in cost-benefit analysis: that social problems are independent and bounded in scope; that alternative solutions for problems are commensurable and finite; and that objective values exist for measuring the cost of problems and benefits of solutions. The independence condition provides closure to the calculation of costs and benefits and is therefore an essential requirement for the performance of cost-benefit analysis. If social problems are largely interdependent, then the costs and benefits of certain actions to resolve these problems cannot be assumed to aggregate mainly in the first few orders of effect. It also means that what might at first appear, in terms of direct costs and benefits, to be the superior solution may not be so superior after indirect effects are accounted for.

The obvious license taken in characterizing social problems as independent and bounded in scope should be fully recognized. But its unreality is not the primary problem. Rather, it is the implication that effective government requires that social problems be engaged in "manageable" units; that a policy perspective that divides social problems into their component parts is not only adequate but preferable on rational grounds. Such an understanding presumes that basic change is always less desirable than a series of marginal ones and that no change is less costly than significant change, if for no other reason than that the "sunk costs" of the status quo are always sizable. It encourages the view that social problems need not be engaged from the vantage point of the collectivity, that issues of governance do not concern the whole of society but only the individuals and communities affected under a piecemeal definition of the problem. Policy, constrained in this manner, poses no threat to the existing order and thereby implicitly, if not explicitly, confers approval upon its persistence.

The condition imposed by the cost-benefit framework on the nature of solutions to social problems is equally necessary from the standpoint of the validity of cost-benefit analysis, yet highly normative in the context of public policy. The condition that alternative solutions, when such exist, be finite in number and commensurable is essential if any calculation is to take place. Indeed, a singular advantage of cost-benefit analysis—the precise comparison of rival solutions—hinges on the commensurability and finiteness of alternatives. There can be no assurance of a superior alternative without this condition.

Commensurability and finiteness among alternatives presume, however, that any conflict that may exist among them is reconcilable. Such an assumption might be reasonable in purely economic contexts where individuals select among alternatives all of which are desirable to them and for which interactive effects upon others (externalities in the language of economics) do not exist to any significant degree. But implanted in the world of political choice and conflict, this condition is far from innocuous. It promotes the view that the exercise of state power is indeed largely an administrative issue, having to do with organizing public action in such a way that it efficiently services nominally contending interests. But on what grounds is one to suppose that political conflict is not real? Certainly such a question is not empirical but normative. The reasons for accepting this understanding of collective conflict must derive from certain desired attributes of decisions based upon it. What might these be?

If conflicting political solutions are ultimately commensurable, then there is no need to depend upon subjective individuals to discover the right solution, with all the inefficiency that would involve in terms of both time and resources. Indeed, relying on contending parties to develop solutions to their problems is a clearly inferior course to follow when a commensurable calculus is available to ferret out the inevitable exaggerations of each side. Thus one stands to gain efficiency and precision by the commensurability condition. Such gains, however, can be looked at just as easily as enormous costs. To say the least, this view of political solution is extraordinarily antagonistic toward the possibility that radical changes are needed to solve social problems. Ruled out by the commensurability condition are solutions in which the status quo suffers losses that cannot be "netted out" by gains elsewhere because the conflicts involved are irreconcilable (e.g., expropriation and divestment policies). Additionally, commensurability implies that where proposed solutions cannot be compared, public action cannot be defended. This suggests that from the perspective of cost-benefit analysis, the focus of governance is not and should not be the intractable problems of civilization. If such a view is intended to act as a proscriptive limit on public action, what an extraordinary limit it is. To employ this method effectively, the most consequential problems must be forsaken for the most manageable. If instead it is intended only as a restriction on the use of cost-benefit analysis, the silence of this technique on the fundamental questions of governance belies claims of its significant value in grappling with social problems. Under either interpretation, the dilemma with accepting this condition is that it puts a substantial premium on public inaction, on doing nothing or at least little, and discourages significant concern for the most difficult social problems. How else is such a posture to be understood if not as a massive endorsement of the status quo?

The most significant and controversial claim is that objective values exist to measure problems and alternative solutions. It is on the basis of this claim, more so than any other, that the image of cost-benefit analysis as nonnormative is based; it is what gives cost-benefit analysis the aura of "hard" social science.[39] The most prevalent measure of value employed in cost-benefit calculations is market price. Whether it is the cost of equipment and salaries of personnel necessitated by a new environmental rule imposed on an industry, or the budget savings of government programs eliminated by a change in the rule, cost-benefit calculations rely heavily on market prices to measure alternative possibilities. But are prices objective measures of collective value? Certainly only in the rare circumstance of perfect competition would conventional price theory suggest that this would be the case. And even there assumptions regarding income distribution equity, economic mobility, information cost and availability, and the like would be required to assure at least approximate equality of starting positions.

Such assumptions cannot be made in this world without serious distortion. Moreover, as has been pointed out, "perfect competition is . . . a logical category; it does not describe any real world situation nor one that is attainable and hence cannot serve as a norm or standard to be achieved in the world in which we live."[40] When the assumptions undergirding perfect competition are dropped, the meaning of prices as measures of value is greatly complicated. In a world where all are not equal, those more equal than others have a greater opportunity to influence prices.

Such differential influence can have profound consequences. For example, if one considers the problem of condemnation to clear land for a new highway, can existing housing prices be used as objective measures of the costs of such condemnation? The all too predictable consequence of their use, of course, is that slums become the optimal places for building highways. Similarly, in monopolistic and oligopolistic markets in which firms can pass on increased costs to them in the form of higher prices, should such prices be used to determine costs and benefits? Many examples could be cited with the same implication: Prices in an unequal world cannot readily be taken to represent nonnormative and nonideological measures of collective value.

In addition, the use of prices raises the problem of the individual versus the collective as the unit of measure. The presumption even in the ideal circumstance of perfect competition is that the sum of individual valuations constitutes a collective determination of value at a specified level of production. Yet much of this century's contribution to economic theory suggests that this equality is often tenuous. The theories cf public goods and externalities point to vast areas of "social" production in which aggregate and collective value need not be synonymous.[41] Indeed to represent them as such may, according to these arguments, yield socially inefficient as well as inequitable results. The areas in which aggregate-collective equality cannot be preserved, of course, coincide almost completely with the domain of governance. If, therefore, cost-benefit analysis is to be employed in resolving such issues, either its use must be curtailed to the exception where aggregate expressions of value can be taken to stand for collective value, or this theoretical dilemma must be ignored. If the former, cost-benefit analysis once again retreats to an excuse for public inaction; if the latter, the purported objectivity of its measure of social value is reduced to dogma.

The other principal measures employed in cost-benefit calculations are taken from social and actuarial distributions. These include

demographic distributions of age, race, sex, occupation; epidemio-
logical distributions of disease, symptoms, and the like; economic
distribution of goods and services production, use, and cost; and so on.
They are used by the cost-benefit analyst to develop projective
information on likelihoods of certain outcomes. One of the central
problems with their use, however, is that they incorporate patterns of
social inequality into the cost-benefit calculation. For example, if the
problem were to which of two medical research programs should public
funds be allocated to yield maximum net benefit, and one program was
concerned with a disease found prominently among whites and the other
among blacks, likelihoods would suggest that, *ceteris paribus*, the first
program would prove of higher net benefit because whites tend to live
longer than blacks in this country. Yet such a determination would
amount to an endorsement of an economic and social system that was an
essential factor in determining this differential. Again, numerous
examples could be offered identifying normative issues associated with
the use of supposedly objective social and actuarial distributions. In
sum, the "objective" values employed in cost-benefit analyses cannot be
represented in the context of public policy formulation as neutral and
nonnormative.

Cost-benefit analysis as a tool for evaluating issues of governance
injects considerable and significant normative content. This content
largely favors incremental change and often no change at all. Significant
social problems of inequality and injustice are undervalued or not
valued at all by this procedure. And this mode of analysis projects values
arrived at mainly by individuals without regard to their collective
consequences as social values or fails to provide any assessment
whatsoever. Certain of these attributes can be, and have been, used with
ingenuity to obstruct policies defending the existing order. But taken
together, they make clear that the most likely beneficiaries of cost-
benefit analyses in the long run are those most interested in preserving
the social and economic system largely as it is.[42]

CONCLUSION

In sum, the advocacy of cost-benefit analysis as a mode of governance
is based on two flawed premises: first, that the basic dilemma of modern
governance is how to arrive at rational definitions and ultimately
solutions of complex social problems; and, second, that cost-benefit
analysis provides one important method for achieving rationalization of

our problems and that it can furnish nonnormative solutions to our normative social problems. Cost-benefit analysis is not neutral, does not offer nonnormative solutions, and cannot rationalize social problems without considerable violence to our understanding of these problems. The problems of modern governance, moreover, are not mainly administrative and in need of technical definition. They are political, as they have always been, and require the exercise of political will and choice. Athough such solutions will necessarily be inefficient, temporary, and confused by some measures, this is a small price to pay compared with what has so far been offered as so-called nonpolitical alternatives. The rational utopia projected by advocates of cost-benefit analysis ultimately depends upon surrender to the irresistibility of right reason. In this respect, the use of cost-benefit analysis to decide matters of governance is by no means a modest proposal that we "enjoy the advantages of the latest intellectual techniques."[43]

If we are serious about the evaluation of state power and its use, a far more rigorous approach is needed than what is delivered by cost-benefit tests. The truths found by this mode of analysis consist mainly of "a discovery of the meaning of the assumption originally made";[44] in this instance, the meaning of the optimality *Grundnorm*. Self-sealing analysis of this kind can only confirm the validity of "the efficient outcome." There is *no* other conclusion available: "Once a policy has been adopted or a decision has been made which leads to . . . an 'optimal' result, further inquiry into the problem is precluded. The problem has been solved when the analysis reaches the *Grundnorm*."[45] To achieve an understanding of the costs and benefits of existing and alternative social arrangements that is not self-sealing, we will have to go beyond Pareto optimality (of either the pragmatic or pure variety). Instead, a theory is needed that integrates economic, political, and ideological factors in the analysis of systems of social valuation; a theory, in particular, that accounts for the institutional nature of social value rather than a method that simply manipulates the artifacts of social value. As Liebhafsky notes, "a cost-benefit study is a quantitative statement of the qualitative judgements of the economist making the study," and "ought to be recognized for what it is . . . a piece of evidence presented by one side or the other."[46] Such evidence is not a substitute for an understanding of political economy or its operation.

NOTES

1. Alice Rivlin, *Systematic Thinking for Social Action* (Washington, DC: Brookings Institution, 1971); Tom L. Beauchamp, "The Moral Adequacy of Cost-Benefit Analysis as the Basis for Government Regulation of Research," in Norman E. Bowie, ed., *Ethical Issues in Government*, Philosophical Monographs, Third Annual Series (Philadelphia: Temple University Press, 1981), 163-175.

2. E. J. Mishan, *Cost-Benefit Analysis* (New York: Praeger, 1976); David Braybrooke and Peter K. Schotch, "Cost-Benefit Analysis Under the Constraint of Meeting Needs," in Bowie, *Ethical Issues in Government*, 176-197.

3. Beauchamp, "The Moral Adequacy of Cost-Benefit Analysis," p. 163. Beauchamp also characterizes the technique as a "means to moral ends."

4. Ibid., p. 164.

5. Ibid., pp. 172-173.

6. Ibid., see pp. 166-167 for a definition of a "loose sense" of cost-benefit analysis; and pp. 169 and 172, respectively, for an identification of "acceptable" and "reasonable" as primary criteria.

7. Rivlin, *Systematic Thinking*, p. 5.

8. Ibid., p. 16.

9. Kenneth E. Boulding, "Economics as a Moral Science," *American Economic Review* 59 (1969): 7.

10. Rivlin, *Systematic Thinking*, p. 15.

11. Mishan, *Cost-Benefit Analysis*, p. 385

12. Ibid., pp. 382-383.

13. Ibid., p. 382, 385.

14. James M. Buchanan and Gordon Tullock, *The Calculus of Consent: Logical Foundations of Constitutional Democracy* (Ann Arbor: University of Michigan Press, 1962), p. 172.

15. H. H. Liebhafsky, " 'The Problem of Social Cost'—An Alternative Approach," *Natural Resources Journal* 13 (1973): 616-619.

16. Mishan, *Cost-Benefit Analysis*, p. 385.

17. Ibid.

18. Braybrooke and Schotch, "Cost-Benefit Analysis," p. 187.

19. *Ibid.* See pp. 179-181 for an analytic definition of such standards.

20. This term is used by James G. March and Herbert A. Simon to describe the basis of organizational behavior and is the core idea for their definition of organizational-administrative, as distinct from political, authority. See their *Organizations* (New York: John Wiley, 1958); also Herbert A. Simon, *Administrative Behavior: A Study of Decision-Making Processes in Administrative Organizations*, 3rd ed. (New York: Free Press, 1967). The relationship between cost-benefit analysis and organization theory has received little attention despite the fact that they share virtually identical conceptions of decision and decision making.

21. American Textile Manufacturers Institute, Inc. et al. v. Raymond J. Donovan, Secretary of Labor, U.S. Department of Labor et al., *U.S. Law Week* 49(June 16, 1981): 4720-4736.

22. Ibid., p. 4720.

23. In congressional debate of the bill this was the principal objection of opponents. See Ibid., pp. 4727-4728.

24. Ibid., p. 4735: "Congress simply abdicated its responsibility for the making of a fundamental and most difficult policy choice—whether and to what extent 'the statistical possibility of future deaths should . . . be disregarded in light of the economic costs of preventing those deaths.' . . . That is a 'quintessential legislative' choice and must be made by the elected representatives of the people."

25. Ibid., p. 4733.

26. An earlier U.S. Court of Appeals ruling concluded precisely this and its view was specifically affirmed in the Supreme Court majority opinion.

27. In the third section of this chapter, the claim of objectivity is challenged.

28. Indeed, one proponent cf cost-benefit-type reasoning has argued that rights and justice should be administered so as to maximize their market value, thus substituting economic performance for justice as the primary aim of law. See Richard A. Posner, *Economic Analysis of Law* (Boston: Little, Brown, 1972), and also his "Utilitarianism, Economics and Legal Theory," *Journal of Legal Studies* 8 (1979): 103-140.

29. Buchanan and Tullock, *The Calculus of Consent;* Anthony Downs, *An Economic Theory of Democracy* (New York: Harper & Row, 1957); and Posner, *Economic Analysis of Law.*

30. A prominent exception is the utopian writings of Milton Friedman. See his *Capitalism and Freedom* (Chicago: University of Chicago Press, 1962); and *Free to Choose: A Personal Statement,* with Rose Friedman (New York: Harcourt Brace Jovanovich, 1979).

31. Raymond J. Donovan, Secretary of Labor v. Douglas Dervey et al., *U.S. Law Week* 49 (June 17, 1981): 4748-4753.

32. Ibid., p. 4748.

33. Ronald H. Coase, "The Problem of Social Cost," *Journal of Law and Economics* 3 (1960): 1-44. For a critique of neoclassical economic views of the law, see H. H. Liebhafsky, "Price Theory as Jurisprudence: Law and Economics, Chicago Style," *Journal of Economic Issues* 10 (1976): 27; and John Byrne and Steven M. Hoffman, "Efficient Corporate Harm: A Chicago Metaphysic," in Brent Fisse and Peter A. French, eds., *Corrigible Corporations and Unruly Law* (San Antonio, TX: Trinity University Press, 1985), 101-136.

34. See Braybrooke and Schotch, "Cost-Benefit Analysis," p. 189, where it is argued that ideals such as justice and equality depend upon nonrational justification.

35. Mishan, *Cost-Benefit Analysis,* p. 384.

36. Ibid.

37. See Peter Self, *Econocrats and the Policy Process: The Politics and Philosophy of Cost-Benefit Analysis* (London: Macmillan, 1975). Econocracy is defined at p. 5.

38. Ernest J. Weinrib, "Utilitarianism, Economics and Legal Theory," *University of Toronto Law Journal* 30 (1980): 321-322.

39. Liebhafsky, " 'The Problem of Social Cost,' " p. 620.

40. Ibid., note 22.

41. The dilemma in using market values as proxies of social value and market-based reasoning to devise government policy is examined in detail in J. M. Buchanan and G. F. Thirlby, eds., *L.S.E. Essays on Cost* (London: Weidenfeld and Nicoloson for the London School of Economics and Political Science, 1973). See also Buchanan's *Cost and Choice:*

An Inquiry into Economic Theory (Chicago: Markham, 1969). These statements of theoretical reservations are of special interest because they are by neoclassicists. Nonneoclassical objections to the equation of price with social value are, of course, numerous.

42. For additional discussion of the class bias of cost-benefit analysis, see Mark Green and Norman Waitzman, "Cost, Benefit and Class," *Working Papers for a New Society* 7 (May-June 1980).

43. Braybrooke and Schotch, "Cost-Benefit Analysis," p. 196.

44. Liebhafsky, "Price Theory as Jurisprudence," p. 27.

45. Liebhafsky, " 'The Problem of Social Cost,' " p. 625.

46. Ibid., pp. 622, 623.

4

POLICY EXPERTISE AND THE "NEW CLASS": A CRITIQUE OF THE NEOCONSERVATIVE THESIS

FRANK FISCHER

Rutgers University

> Despite centuries of concern with policy, we have little solid understanding of the relation of experts and intellectuals to the men of power.
>
> —Harold Wilensky
> *Organizational Intelligence* (1967)

Over the past twenty years policy experts have emerged as increasingly significant players in the game of politics. Most of the policy-oriented literature, however, has failed to grapple with the broad sociopolitical issues raised by this important development. One of the best examples is provided by the policy analysis literature. Largely a response to the need for policy expertise, public policy analysis has been one of the fastest-growing specializations in the social sciences. But most of the literature of "policy science" has assumed a rather narrow technical orientation. Much of it, in fact, has been devoted to methodological issues. Opting for an emphasis on procedure and technique, policy

Author's Note: *I am grateful to Alan Mandell, Kenneth Fox, and Steven Maynard-Moody for their helpful comments on earlier drafts of this essay. In addition, I would like to thank Melvyn Nathanson, Dean of the Rutgers-Newark Graduate School of Arts and Sciences, for a small grant that helped to support the writing of this chapter.*

analysts have largely shunned the political questions that accompany their new presence.

In view of this new role, it is fair to say that the policy science movement and its literature naively cling to a number of outdated assumptions. One is the overly simplistic assumption that better policy knowledge will lead to improved policy decisions. Another is the idea that good policy science is "value neutral." There is little in the contemporary experience that demonstrates the reliability of either assumption, although both remain firmly grounded in the discipline. Taken together, they perpetuate one of the discipline's most powerful myths: namely, that the concerns of policy science, if not all policy experts, transcend the play of politics.

One important exception to this trend in recent years has been the policy-oriented writings of the neoconservative movement.[1] Neoconservative social scientists, in large part writing in reaction to the uses of social science in the Great Society era, have singled out policy expertise as a political phenomenon that now threatens the future of representative government. The rise of these policy experts, increasingly taking the form of a "new class" striving for political power, portends the appearance of a technocratic system of government. The role these experts now play in the formulation of public policy is, according to the neoconservatives, the measure of their new power.

The neoconservative thesis is important for several reasons. It is put forward by a group of intellectuals, many of them so-called policy intellectuals, who have helped to shape the contemporary conservative assault on big government, the primary consumer of policy expertise. It also provides us with a usefully provocative literature that helps to cast light on the neglected political issues that now surround the policy expert's role. This chapter, as an effort to probe these issues, outlines the neoconservative position and attempts to assess its new class thesis as it pertains to both the expert role and the policy science movement. It proceeds in five parts. First, it examines the traditional patterns of policy expertise, and second, turns to a discussion of postindustrialism and the new class thesis. Against this background, the third and fourth sections trace the thesis through the Great Society experience and the conservative political response to it. Based on the themes developed in these sections, the closing discussion offers an alternative perspective on the politics of policy expertise and draws out its implications for the policy analysis profession.

POLICY EXPERTISE:
BASIC POLITICAL PATTERNS

The relation of knowledge to power has long been a central theme in social and political theory. Moreover, variants of the new class thesis are as old as the social sciences themselves. In the American experience, these issues have been most prominent in the Progressive era and the New Deal.[2] In these periods, as well as the more recent Great Society in the 1960s, both conservatives and radical theorists have typically portrayed top-level policy experts as members of a new class seeking to install themselves as the political and moral arbiters of public policy.

In some cases there is truth in this view. Men as disparate as Harold Croly and Rexford Tugwell, for example, can be found in these earlier periods calling for the ascendency of the expert. But the experience in all of these periods has been one of dashed hopes. Such movements have invariably encountered powerful political opposition. Indeed, the degree of hostility with which such expertise has generally been greeted has at various times posed serious threats to the future of the larger policy science movement. In view of the precarious nature of such political activity, the rank and file of the professional discipline have traditionally opted for a politically cautious orientation.

In general outline, this historical experience has given rise to a narrow professional perspective purportedly grounded in the scientific principle of "ethical neutrality."[3] Eschewing ethical and political analysis, the policy science profession has been shaped around a methodological orientation that emphasizes technical advice concerning policy effectiveness and program efficiency. In this role, the policy scientist functions as a social engineer whose task focuses mainly on the calculation of costs and benefits of alternative means (for achieving goals hammered out by legitimate legislative processes). Some experts, swept into the enthusiasm of this orientation, have paradoxically gone so far as to view the value-laden political dimensions of the policy processes as irrational interruptions that impede the methodological requirements of efficient decision making.

Thus, as members of a professional movement, these applied social scientists have pursued the development of a functional relationship to those in power. This has generally taken the form of a close cooperative relationship with the "men of action" (those who, by virtue of their important political and economic responsibilities, are seen to possess superior practical knowledge). In this arrangement social scientists supply technical knowledge about the efficient achievement of goals deemed necessary by these practical men of affairs. Only these men are viewed to be in the position to judge which of the social scientists' recommendations can be used, when, and how.[4]

Under this functional or service model of policy advice, then, social scientists do not expect all of their advice to be accepted and used. But this is not to suggest that they exercise no policy influence or initiative in the processes. Within the context of this relationship, these "service intellectuals" have often promoted themselves and their ideas as the representatives of reason—largely defined as technical reason—in policy processes. In this respect the policy science movement, in the name of efficiency and cost-effectiveness, can be likened to an interest group vying for influence among competing interests in a pluralistic decision-making process.

Some have argued that this service model of expertise and its ideology nicely fit the pluralist theory of democracy and provides policy-oriented social scientists with a legitimate stance from which to ply their trade. Whether or not this is true, the practice of policy expertise has generally reflected something more than the impartiality that this theoretical justification would imply. Historian Barry Karl, for example, has shown that in practice this service model often takes the form of a political strategy, or what he calls a "methodology of social reform."

According to Karl, this reform methodology involves a number of basic steps. The first step concerns the assembly of a group of social science experts, usually by a reform-minded president. This group devotes its time to defining a social problem and spelling out the need for specific political reforms. A larger group of journalists, philanthropists, and business leaders is then gathered to discuss the problem. The objective in this phase is to develop a consensus and to broaden the reform coalition. Following this gathering a study is produced "containing all of the information and interpretation on which reasonable men, presumably in government, would base programs for reform."[5]

Such a reform methodology is clearly compatible with the service orientation but need not be limited by it. From the historical evidence it is far from clear that policy experts are necessarily constrained by an agenda preestablished by those they serve. Indeed, given the dynamics of this methodology, they can be deeply involved in determining the agenda. To be sure, such a role only confers an indirect form of power— namely, a power based on the ability to persuade political leaders that certain courses of action should be taken. But it is nonetheless very real power that can be used at propitious moments to shape the course of events.

Although both liberal and conservative politicians have used this methodology, it has been the liberal reform administrations that have provided most of the propitious moments. Because the liberal administrations of the Democratic Party have typically shaped their political agendas around the call for social reform, it is not surprising that this methodology has largely served as a *liberal* reform strategy. The histories of the great liberal expansions—particularly in the Progressive Era, the New Deal, and the Great Society—reveal a fairly regular and predictable pattern of political conflict generated by the use of this reform strategy. Given the fact that liberal reform agendas have generally borne the mark of liberal policy experts, the conservative attack on these agendas has typically included an attempt to discredit liberal social scientists and their ideas. Portraying them as impractical, power-seeking, and elitist, conservatives have generally sought their speedy return to the quiet life of academe.

Attacked in this manner, the social scientists have usually retreated under the banner of the service model. In short, they concede only to having served the programs of their elected political leaders (which, of course, is true but represents something less than the full picture). The fact that these leaders were generally of the Democratic Party is thus portrayed as an issue for the political system, not the policy science profession.

POLICY EXPERTISE AND
THE NEW CLASS

Having examined the basic patterns that formed the policy expert's traditional relationship to power, the discussion now turns to the neoconservative thesis: the argument that an elite group of policy experts has begun to play a leading political role in the formulation of public policy. Portraying these experts as members of a "new class," neoconservatives maintain that they have established a new and much more politically significant relationship to power.

The neoconservative thesis is grounded in an important reality that is not to be slighted. The preceding discussion has made clear the fact that the policy expert's role is not a new concern, but never has the issue been more salient than today. Not only has policy expertise become a pervasive phenomenon in contemporary society, many theorists now contend that its continuing evolution presages the rise of a new configuration of power. Indeed, some theorists write of a phase of societal development based on the production and administration of knowledge. Often called the "postindustrial society," this new social configuration is one in which capitalist values associated with property, wealth, and production are steadily giving way to values based on knowledge, education, and intellect.[6] Such a transformation is said to portend the coming of a new society in which a technical elite will take its place alongside traditional economic and political elites in the governance of society generally.

The emergence of expertise is thus not in doubt. Since the latter part of the 1800s a large degree of control over the day-to-day workings of complicated economic, political, and social processes has indeed been delegated to professional experts. Professional associations and policy experts generally now constitute the "hidden hierarchies" of all major policy arenas, prompting some to speak of the "Professional State."[7] One can debate the specific dimensions of this phenomenon, but it is abundantly clear from the available evidence that expertise has become deeply embedded in the bureaucratic structures of modern government.[8]

In recent years this concern has been reflected in the growing literature on the "new class." Disillusioned by the corporate-welfare state, in the 1970s theorists of both the political left and the right began to link many of the political problems of modern society to the rise of a new class. The challenge tended to come first from the radical critics. For example, Alvin Gouldner wrote of the "liberal technologues of the welfare-warfare state"; Noam Chomsky spoke of the "New Mandarins"; and Robert Goodman criticized the "planning mandarins" of the military-industrial complex.[9] Later in the decade, as well as into the 1980s, the same refrains could be heard, this time from the "neoconservatives," a group consisting of disheartened liberals from the Great Society period. Here we find theorists such as Irving Kristol, Edward Banfield, Jeanne Kirkpatrick, Nathan Glazer, and Samuel Beer, among others.[10] Although both radical and conservative writers have long been interested in the new class issue as an intellectual problem, in recent years neoconservatives have brought the topic into the mainstream of contemporary political discussion. Indeed, the neoconservative attack on the new class has figured prominently in the political assault on the welfare state, particularly the Reagan administration's emphasis on deregulation.

At base, the neoconservative's polemic against the new class is an attack on professional expertise and the modern role of the universities. The authority and legitimacy of this new elite are traced to their knowledge and professional credentials, the key commodities of the emerging postindustrial society. From this perspective the universities, as the purveyors of these commodities, constitute the institutional power bases of this new elite. Some argue that elite universities are increasingly being turned into policy "command posts." The "ivory tower" is described as becoming a sort of forward position from where the new elite can direct the government's weapons to policy targets, usually visible only to itself.[11]

Many concede that the grand outline of this "technocratic takeover" has in reality yet to fully materialize.[12] But as Banfield cautions, this must not overshadow the fact that the new class is emerging. Already it represents a significant challenge to our traditional democratic institutions, particularly the legislative system and political party structures. Banfield describes the unfolding threat in these terms:

> Policy science . . . appears as one in a long series of efforts by the Progressive Movement and its heirs to change the character of the American political system—to transfer power from the corrupt, the ignorant, and the self-serving to the virtuous, the educated and the public spirited. . . . These were the motives that inspired proposals to replace politicians with experts in the legislatures and to do away with political parties.[13]

Experts may not have replaced legislators yet, but neoconservatives are quick to point out that they are found everywhere *in* legislatures. Portrayed as part of the intellectual cadre of the liberal establishment, these policy experts are not only presented as ambitious, arrogant, and elitist; they are seen as the products of an adversary culture that is hostile to traditional American values, particularly the institutional practices of corporate capitalism. Defending democracy against these "unelected representatives" has become the defining agenda of the neoconservative movement.

How do we assess this neoconservative argument? Clearly these writers have identified an important political phenomenon, but coming to agreement on an interpretation of this development is another matter. Such an assessment is complicated by a number of factors. One long-standing problem has been the subtle and usually anonymous nature of the expert's power. Being neither publicly elected nor reviewed, the expert and his or her influence is generally difficult to measure. Indeed, for this reason the power of the expert has developed rather opaquely. To the degree that the phenomenon is upon us, it seems to have happened before we noticed it.

Another problem in assessing the new class thesis can be attributed to the fact that a good deal of the writing (on both the political left and the right) has been advanced to serve an ideological function. Often the intent has been to scapegoat the new class as an impediment to either market capitalism or democratic socialism. For this reason the new class literature tells us very little about the role of expertise in policymaking or about the struggles that have shaped its role.

To assess this thesis it is thus necessary to turn to other sources of data. Although such data have generally been hard to come by, over the past ten or fifteen years sufficient fragments have appeared to make such an assessment feasible. Much of the data pertain to the Great Society era and its aftermath, the touchstone of the neoconservative argument. Although this work has largely failed to capture the larger political dynamics of this phenomenon, it does provide an empirically oriented literature upon which to base an assessment.

POLICY EXPERTISE AND THE GREAT SOCIETY

The first step in the assessment is to set the neoconservative thesis in a substantive context. For this purpose the discussion turns here to the Great Society and the neoconservative interpretation of the liberal policy intellectual's role in the development of the war on poverty.

A number of important political and intellectual events helped to set the stage for the Great Society. In particular it is essential to note that the period preceding this era was marked by a belief in the "end of ideology." Put forward by writers who could later be counted among the neoconservatives, the thesis asserted the fundamental triumph of liberal capitalism over bureaucratic socialism. According to this view, further debate about these ideologies would only impede progress toward the American ideal. The remaining task was seen to be largely technical in nature. It was time for the ideologue to step aside for the social engineer. Through technical expertise, such as that to be provided by the newly developing policy sciences, the task ahead was mainly a matter of fine-tuning the engines of liberal capitalism.[14]

Such ideas began to give rise to a new technocratic creed. Basic to this outlook was the idea that the guidance of complex economic and social processes could be based on the empirical propositions of the social and policy sciences. Drawing primarily on economics and systems analysis, the challenge was to technically employ "objective" scientific information to regulate smoothly the processes of social and political change.[15] These ideas reached their pinnacle in the Great Society of Lyndon Johnson. As a protege of Roosevelt in the 1930s, Johnson was no stranger to the use of expertise in the formulation of goverment policy. Indeed, he was deeply committed to the kinds of liberal social reform developed by the policy advisors of the New Deal period. In his own words, in fact, the Great Society was to be the fulfillment of the New Deal legacy.

In much the same way that policy-oriented social scientists served the New Deal, they flourished in nearly every domain of the Johnson administration. Social scientists not only played a major role in two wars—the Vietnam war and the war on poverty—they also devised and implemented throughout the federal government a comprehensive technocratic system of social planning and budgetary decision making, the Planning, Programming, Budgeting System (PPBS). In his statement introducing this new planning technique, Johnson hailed it as a revolution in policy decision making that would help to plan and coordinate his effort to end poverty in America. It was a high moment in the technocratic movement. To use Moynihan's phrase, it was clear evidence of the "professionalization of reform."[16]

Theodore White went so far as to describe this period as the "Golden Age of the action intellectual." For White it was nothing less than the appearance of a new system of power in American politics. These new intellectuals, acting in concert with political leaders in both the White House and Congress, were the "driving-wheels" of the Great Society. As a new generation of intellectuals with special problem-solving skills, they sought "to shape our defenses, guide our foreign policy, redesign our cities, eliminate poverty, reorganize our schools," and more. These policy professionals represented a "bridge across the gulf between government and the primary producers of really good ideas." The White House served as "a transmission belt, packaging and processing scholars' ideas to be sold to Congress as programs."[17]

Such enthusiasm was also reflected in the influential report issued by the National Academy of Sciences, *Government's Need for Knowledge and Information*. As a paradigm of the liberal methodology of reform in action the report was prepared by a blue-ribbon commission of social scientists and policy experts, and its message was widely disseminated to leading journalists, politicians, and philanthropic institutions. Reflecting on the fact that "the federal government confronts increasingly complex problems in foreign affairs, defense strategy and management, urban reconstruction, civil rights, economic growth and stability, public health, social welfare, and education and training," the report's message was this:

> The decision and actions taken by the President, the Congress, and the executive departments and agencies must be based on valid social and economic information and involve a high degree of judgment about human behavior. The knowledge and methods of the behavioral sciences, devoted as they are to an understanding of human behavior and social institutions, should be applied as effectively as possible to the programs and policy processes of the federal government.[18]

In short, the social sciences had much to offer policymakers. Indeed, by implication the report can be read to argue that social scientists are better equipped for policymaking than the legislators and citizens who inform the traditional political processes. For this reason the report concluded that the social sciences needed increased financial support from the government to continue developing the theory and methods that were to contribute to better policy design.

The government did in fact contribute vast sums for applied social research. During this period it became customary to speak of policy expertise as a "growth industry." Spurred by the Great Society programs, the expenditures for applied or policy-related social research jumped dramatically. For example, federal agency spending climbed from about $235 million in 1965 to almost $1 billion in the ensuing decade.[19] Such funds brought into existence a number of major research institutions, both public and private, and greatly increased the amount of university-based policy-oriented social research. Accompanying this process was a sizable increase in the number of social scientists. During the decade of the 1960s this group increased by 163%, an increase larger than that registered by any other major occupational group.

No government programs were more closely associated with this policy research than the Great Society's antipoverty programs. It is not easy to generalize about complex governmental programs, but one thing that clearly stands out in the analyses of the antipoverty program is the central role of the "policy intellectual." Throughout the design and implementation of these programs the influence of such experts frequently played an important role in determining the course of events.

To be sure, the precise nature of the policy professional's role has been a sensitive and controversial issue in many circles, especially liberal circles. In part this can be attributed to the neoconservatives' polemical attack on the liberalism of the period. For neoconservatives, the antipoverty effort represented one of the most blatant exercises of new class power. The recognition and analysis of these events remain a basic touchstone upon which their movement was built.

To the neoconservative the critical question is this: Where did the antipoverty programs come from? Prior to the Great Society there was very little interest in poverty in America. As Glazer pointed out, there was nothing behind the war on poverty "like the powerful political pressure and long-standing support that produced the great welfare measures of the New Deal—Social Security, Unemployement Insurance, Public Welfare, Public Housing."[20] The massive political and ideological support that produced these reforms of the 1930s simply did not exist in the early 1960s. Antecedent to initiation of the antipoverty programs, for example, there were no poverty protest movements per se. To be sure, poor black people were marching in the streets, but *formally* their demands were directed at achieving civil rights, not the elimination of poverty. Comparatively speaking, their numbers were usually small and their cause was far from popular in the nation as a whole. Moreover, there was little political discussion about poverty in the leading intellectual journals; and organized labor, to the degree that it was concerned, had little success in interesting its members in the plight of the poor.

About these facts the neoconservatives are largely correct. There was little political pressure on policymakers to focus on poverty. Indeed, one does not have to take the evidence here from the neoconservatives alone; radical social scientists such as Piven and Cloward make the same point.[21] What does remain controversial, however, is where such political initiatives did come from.

The answer is that they came from inside the White House. Essentially, the main pressure for this massive governmental assault on poverty was initiated *inside* the Kennedy and Johnson administrations. And it is here that the neoconservatives pick up their new class polemic. For them the poverty agenda was the work of a well-staffed cadre of intellectuals—in large part academics—assigned to the job of thinking about social reform. Some were old New Dealers, but many were drawn from the growing ranks of post World War II social scientists. Together they constituted what one neoconservative called the "Great Society braintrusters."

The braintrust was indeed a significant political reality; about that there is no question. Enjoying easy access to President Johnson, these policy professionals discovered a chief executive who knew not only something about poverty but even a great deal more about politics. In a short period of time—perhaps six months from the time Johnson assumed the presidency in 1964—the array of programs and bills drafted by these policy experts was shaped into a major legislative program and delivered to Congress under the banner of the war on poverty. The chief lobby for the program was the White House, which sent a parade of officials to speak in favor of the legislation. As Bibby and Davidson put it, "Congress was asked not to draft the war on poverty, but rather to ratify a fully prepared administration program, and invited though hardly encouraged, to propose marginal changes."[22]

Once a poverty bill was enacted, the White House and its policy advisors retained the initiative. For one thing, legislation for the Office of Economic Opportunity was written to assure that it could be managed from the top. This was accomplished by deliberately granting broad political discretion to professional administrators appointed by the White House. For another, the news media were inundated with facts and rhetoric emanating from the White House on the plight of the impoverished one-fifth of the nation, a group until then largely ignored. In conjunction with this effort, the president enlisted a host of private organizations—foundations, professional associations, and corporations—to proselytize the public to support the administration's war.[23] As Piven and Cloward put it, "very rapidly, poverty became a major newsbeat."[24] In a manner patterned on the techniques of the reform methodology, the Johnson administration and its policy elites had reinstated poverty as a major issue for the first time since the New Deal.

Beyond the issue of who initiated the poverty program, much has also been made of the specific influence of professional thinking on the content of poverty programs. Neoconservatives in particular are prone to underscore the Economic Opportunity Act requirement that community action programs be carried out with "maximum feasible participation" of the poor themselves. Many observers have argued that this was one of the most politically important aspects of the entire antipoverty program. Typical of the legislation in general, this provision was inserted into the law in the absence of any significant political demand from the poor. It was introduced, according to neoconservatives, largely because intellectuals of the social welfare profession believed the measure to be indispensable to effective social action. The literature of the field, as they point out, used such terms as the involvement of "indigenous nonprofessionals" to describe the community participation process.[25] Its effect, if not always its purpose, was to bring these nonprofessionals into a working coalition with poverty experts at the expense of elected local and state officials. Neoconservatives are not wrong when they argue that no other single program had less political consensus than this measure. Certainly none generated more political heat.

CONSERVATIVE POLICY ANALYSIS: POLITICIZING THE POLITICAL

The war on poverty ran into many obstacles. For one thing, by the time the antipoverty programs were fully operational, the Vietnam conflict had unexpectedly claimed much of the fiscal dividend that was to be used for poverty programs. Whether or not it is fair to say that the war on poverty was a failure remains a debated point. (In large part the answer depends on what criteria one uses to evaluate it.) On one point, however, there is little dispute: The program was a disappointment.

The public, in the face of disappointment, began to lose its fascination not only with a war on poverty but with the "action intellectuals" as well. This first began to surface over the conduct of the Vietnam war. As foreign policy experts became more deeply mired in a losing war, major divisions broke out among themselves. It wasn't long, given internal dissension, before the wisdom of the policy elites was being questioned by the larger public. And this concern soon spread to the poverty planners as well.

In the case of the antipoverty programs, the neoconservative movement played a primary role in articulating this dissatisfaction. In the years that followed, neoconservatives succeeded in elevating their critique of the "technocratic takeover" to a central issue in leading journals of political opinion. Indeed, thanks to these writers, it emerged as a major feature of the political dialogue of the 1970s reaching its acme in the election of Ronald Reagan. In this section I shall first examine the nature of their complaint, and then turn to a discussion of its influence on conservative politics and policy analysis.

It is not easy to ferret out the precise nature of the neoconservative complaint against technocracy and its policy science techniques.

Invariably it is said that policy scientists, trained in the art of abstract model building, lack experience in practical politics. For another thing, it is frequently said that they are unable (or unwilling) to speak the language of either the policymaker or the ordinary citizen. Still another criticism stresses their failure to produce "usable knowledge." As one writer put it, "study after study fails to turn up a direct link between data and decisions."[26]

If the analytical payoff of the policy sciences has been so divorced from the decision-making processes, why, then, all the concern about a new elite? Is it not just a matter of time before such a group withers away from ineptitude? The trouble seems to lie elsewhere. For writers such as Kristol and Banfield, it is in reality more a matter of the questions that are being raised than the solutions being proposed.[27] In their view policy scientists exhibit a special talent for finding fault with the American political system. One reason is rooted in the nature of their scientific methodologies; another is traced to the nature of politics in the emerging postindustrial society.

Committed to the ideals of scientific rationality, particularly the principles of technical efficiency, policy scientists are said to suffer from a distorted view of political realities. Against the ideals of technical rationality, nothing in the political world seems to work. Policy problems appear to abound in every area in a system that is described as slow and inefficient. But these are not *real* problems, according to neoconservatives. Political problems are not defined by scientific criteria external to the situation; they are determined by the political actors themselves. In the political world a problem exists only if political groups say that it exists. Perversely, then, the policy sciences busy themselves finding fault where none exists. For Banfield this constitutes a form of "metaphysical madness."[28]

Were it not for the cumulative effect of this phenomenon, the neoconservatives might be content to relegate such complaints to the intellectual realm of methodology. But in the emerging postindustrial society, where knowledge itself becomes a primary political commodity, these practices create pressure for policy change. By bringing to consciousness "problems" that would otherwise remain invisible to both politicians and the public, policy experts become an independent force for social change. The fact that experts tell people that a problem exists sets up a social disequilibrium that can be translated into a political demand for compensatory action.[29] Indeed, according to the neoconservatives, this dynamic has been a key component of the liberal strategy for social reform. The ability to translate such pressures into a political reform agenda has played a key part in the successes of liberal democratic reformers. The Great Society agenda is a primary example.

During eras in which policy intellectuals have managed to elevate themselves to significant positions of influence, conservative politicians and publicists have typically hounded them with harsh criticisms. One of the most common conservative strategies has been to portray them as the agents—witting or unwitting—of creeping socialism in America. Given the experts' precarious position in the political system, this tactic has almost always been sufficient to put them on the defensive, usually followed by a propitious retreat to the safe haven of the "ivory tower."

In the 1970s things started to change. The neoconservatives began to advocate a new strategy to sever the connection between liberal reform and policy expertise. In the face of the newly emerging "knowledge society," they counseled the more traditional conservatives to drop their typically one-sided animosity toward intellectuals in general and urged them to reach out to their own often forgotten conservative bretheren in the academic realm. For neoconservatives the time had come to counter expertise on its own terms. A modern conservative movement, they argued, must itself get into the policy expertise business. Because of the inevitable coming of the "new class" phenomenon in a complex technological society, conservatives were exhorted no longer to view the phenomenon as an aberration in the patterns of American politics. According to the neoconservatives, expertise was now here to stay, and it was time for conservatives to train and hire their own experts, what William Simon called the creation of a "conservative counter-intelligentsia."[30]

No one was more important in launching this movement than Irving Kristol. For Kristol, the new class had become the "permanent brain trust" of American politics. Having long sought their place in the sun, these new class members were now "in the process of seizing and consolidating" their political position. In view of their critical role in modern government and industry, conservatives must now launch a struggle to win their political allegiances. Kristol put it this way: "If one cannot count on these people to provide political, social, and moral stability—if they do not have a good opinion of our society—how long . . . can that stability and good opinion survive?"[31]

Traditional rhetoric aside, the new men, as Kristol cautioned his fellow conservatives, are not yet "doctrinaire socialists." Although it might prove impossible to convert them to the businessman's free market ideology, in Kristol's view they can nonetheless be educated in the realities of business and economics, particularly the need to maintain a sizable private sector. This requires the development of a new ideology to guide the politics of this emerging class. Steinfels, Berube, and Gittell, in fact, argue that the formation of this ideology has been the primary mission of Kristol and the neoconservative intellectuals generally.[32]

Such ideological work had to be buttressed by an active involvement on the part of the corporate leaders, a role heretofore largely shunned. Specifically, steps had to be taken to establish a working political relationship between business leaders and the conservative members of the new class. Most important, top executives were asked to invest in both conservative-oriented research and educational projects. And this they did. Throughout the 1970s corporate elites financed the development of a multimillion-dollar network of conservative think tanks, research centers, and educational programs.

One of the prime movers behind this effort was William Simon. In his conservative manifesto, *A Time for Truth*, he explained the agenda in these words: "Funds generated by business (by which I mean profits, funds in business foundations and contributions for individual businessmen) must rush by multimillions to the aid of . . . scholars, social scientists, writers and journalists who understand the relationship between political and economic liberty." In addition to supplying money "for books, books, and more books," he urged his fellow businessmen to "cease the mindless subsidizing of colleges and universities whose departments of economics, government, politics, and history are hostile to capitalism" and to redirect these grants to those with a more "pro-business" orientation.[33]

Much of this money has been channeled through a number of powerful conservative think tanks that have come to play a central role in shaping the conservative policy agenda. Most important are the American Enterprise Institute for Public Policy Research, the Hoover Institution, the Heritage Foundation, the Institute for Contemporary Studies, Freedom House, and the Institute of Educational Affairs, each of which produces a steady flow of books, pamphlets, and reports for the media, the public and the universities.[34] Where for decades the prestigious Brookings Institution served Democratic administrations with both advisors and advice, these newer conservative institutes have become its counterparts for Republican administrations. It is, of course, difficult to measure the influence of these research institutes, but it is clear that they have been very influential in shaping the "Reagan Revolution." For example, it is estimated that more than two-thirds of the Heritage Foundation's policy recommendations were adopted by the Reagan administration in its first term.[35] In short, policy intellectuals were again shaping a presidential agenda. The difference was political: this time they were strictly conservative.

The result of these developments has been a significant politicization of policy expertise. Although policy analysis has always harbored political biases, in the past they have usually been fairly covert (thus providing the traditional claim of value neutrality with the appearance of plausibility). Today, however, many policy professionals openly operate in an adversarial style that makes their political biases quite explicit. Indeed, some policy analysts now readily concede their role as "hired guns." As recently as ten years ago, it would have been difficult to find a project director of a major research institution who would easily acknowledge the ideological character of his or her work. Today that has changed. Take, for instance, the remarks of Stuart Butler of the Heritage Foundation:

> It is naive, in the public policy area, to assume that people don't have an ideological predisposition toward things. Every economist subscribes to a school of economics.... Unlike other institutions that pretend ideological neutrality, we're conservative, no bones about it. We don't pretend to be anything different from what we are. [36]

Whereas the basic impetus for this adversarial style was the changing political climate, within the policy sciences themselves there were a number of technical considerations that helped to facilitate a conservative opposition to the traditionally dominant liberal bias. Particularly important was growing recognition of the complexity of the kinds of social problems that the Great Society had set out to resolve, as well as the limitations of the research techniques employed to measure their amelioration. To liberal policy analysts in the mid-1960s solving social problems often seemed to be merely a matter of commitment and resources, but by the 1970s a more cautious breed of politicians and social scientists saw only complexity and unanticipated consequences. For instance, in the case of poverty research, Henry Aaron put it this way:

Such puzzles as why earnings are distributed as they are and how policies of various kinds would affect the distribution, or what makes prices and wages increase and how to alter that rate of increase, are at least as complex as any addressed in the physical or biological sciences. Underlying these puzzles are all the variations in human personality and the mystery of its development . . . , the operations of labor markets involving the decisions of millions of businessmen and tens of millions of workers, and the myriad laws that guide and shape behavior, often indirectly and in surprising ways.[37]

In the face of this complexity "any particular set of facts will be consistent with a variety of theories and that it may be impossible or excessively costly to acquire the data that would permit analysts to reject false theories."[38] What starts in theory as an objective science of policy analysis thus turns out in practice to be a highly subjective and interpretive mode of inquiry. Given this reality, the political mood of the times, along with the persuasiveness or prestige of the policy advocate, will usually be the primary determinants of the acceptability of a particular policy proposal. In short, as the conservatives have demonstrated, the practice of policy analysis can become very political.

FROM POLICY INNOVATION TO EVALUATION

The beginnings of this conservative approach to policy research first appeared during the Nixon administration. In his bid for the presidency, Nixon took advantage of the apparent policy failures associated with both the Vietnam war and the war on poverty. Throughout his campaign he attacked both of these wars and the efforts of those who helped President Johnson direct them. After the election, the profile of policy intellectuals faded rapidly from center stage. Although Moynihan was recruited to bridge the political gulf between Nixon and the academic community, the political tone of the new administration was set by lawyers and businesspeople.

This is not to suggest that social science disappeared from the political scene. Indeed, retooled to address the conservative agenda, social science played an important role in the Nixon administration. One of the first steps in the ideological transition was a shift of federal spending toward conservative think tanks, particularly the American Enterprise Institute and the Hoover Institution. In fact, the Hoover Institution, traditionally involved in international studies, added a domestic policy analysis program to its activities in order to undertake the assignment.[39]

Under the aegis of this Republican administration and its conservative think tanks, this new orientation applied principally to the analysis of domestic social policy. Essentially the traditional reformist orientation of policy analysis—emphasizing social problem solving and the creative design of public programs—quickly vanished from the scene. In its place emerged an emphasis on a relatively new technique: evaluation research. Where policy analysis focuses largely on the implications of *prospective* public goals, evaluation research is *retrospectively* aimed at the measurement of program outcomes. Moynihan set the tone for this transition by arguing that the role of social science had been misunderstood. "The role of social science," as he put it, "lies not in the formulation of social policy, but in the measurement of its results."[40]

The role of evaluation research had already begun to emerge in the latter part of the Johnson years. It was largely a response to early signs of disenchantment with a number of social programs. Increasingly prominent in these circles was the idea that many of the programs were founded upon questionable social science assumptions and findings. Antipoverty programs, it was pointed out, had been designed under the constraints of both time and politics. For this reason much of the policy advice behind their construction was based on the best *available* information. As Wilson put it, a good deal of what passed for "expert advice" was necessarily based on educated guesses, personal opinion, or ideological assumptions.[41] Evaluation research was in part an attempt to develop a more scientific basis for policy intervention. Emphasis in the academy rapidly shifted from analysis to evaluation. Indeed, both on and off the campus, evaluation research emerged as a growing industry.

Although politicians were seldom interested in the scientific foundations of policy research, they were nonetheless interested in finding out "what works." Thus as early as 1967, Congress amended some of the basic poverty legislation to include evaluation requirements. After 1969, the Nixon administration significantly extended the practice by adding newer and more stringent mandates for measurement of program outcomes. The primary reason given for the new practice was the sheer increase in social spending, especially for human resources. Politicians and the public were increasingly interested in what they were getting for their money. Social scientists, as evaluation researchers, were to provide answers.

For the Nixon administration, then, evaluation research was much more than just another bureaucratic requirement. Essentially it was seen as a core component of the administration's larger effort to bring management reform to the federal bureaucracy. Toward this end Nixon took steps to upgrade evaluation and to institutionalize it as a managerial function. The most important step in this direction was the establishment of the Office of Management and Budget (in place of the Bureau of the Budget). The reorganization was explicitly intended to strengthen the evaluation function by harnessing it to OMB's budgetary power.[42] In the future programs would have to show results or lose their funding.

Through this institutionalization of evaluation in the budgetary process, OMB took a strong role in monitoring the progress of these evaluations. Ostensibly the agency's interest in these evaluations was largely financial in nature; it sought to terminate those programs that did not conform to the administration's conception of cost-effective results. However, although the growth of social programs was reason enough to justify a financial interest in program outcomes, the evidence suggests political motives as well. In short, low-cost social experiments combined with rigid evaluation requirements were often used to subvert or eliminate expensive social programs beneficial to Democratic constituencies.[43]

A number of practices illustrate the administration's political use of evaluation research. One of the most important was the contrast between the evaluation criteria required for war on poverty programs and those required for other programs aimed at assisting such interests as agribusiness, urban renewal, railroads, and the merchant marine. In the case of the former, every effort was made to demand rigorous results justifying continuation of the program, whereas none of the latter—described as "older, well-established and 'safe' domestic programs"—had such evaluation requirements attached to them. Particularly under scrutiny were those programs aimed at altering the established power structures, such as the community action program with its participation requirements. As Morehouse put it, "program evaluation requirements were an important by-product of a general policy to bring controversial programs under control."[44]

The administration had chosen just the right methodology for this purpose. A close look at these techniques reveals an underlying bias that conveniently serves a conservative political orientation. The policy analyst (often in the role of planner or advocate) is generally biased toward social change; the evaluation researcher is biased in the opposite direction. Designed to review existing programs, evaluation research tends to be cloaked in skepticism. In part this skepticism is grounded in the nature of the sociopolitical role assigned to evaluators. Because they are asked to supply evidence to justify the continuation of public programs, evaluators are typically cast into a "show me" attitude that puts the burden of proof on those who wish to continue a particular program.[45] It is essentially the attitude of the budget office. In short, the methodology nicely complements the role.

For the political decision maker, then, an emphasis on evaluation builds a conservative bias into the policy decision processes. But for the evaluation researcher the bias is usually less a function of his or her political orientation than the nature of the methodology itself. As an experimental mode of research, evaluation research—like science in general—is based on tough-minded doubt. Doubt and skepticism are inherent in the very theory upon which experimental science is based, particularly the principle of falsification (operationalized through the concept of a "null hypothesis"). Based on falsification (or disproof) rather than proof per se, the experimentally oriented techniques of evaluation research require cautious skepticism. In a world of imperfect knowledge there is always one more variable that must be taken into account; there are experimental conditions that introduce uncontrolled variances; data that are invariably scarce; and so on. Given the fact that rigorous scientific verification remains the official standard for rendering valid policy judgments, the complexity of most policy problems can be marshaled to render an empirical assessment inconclusive, if not wrong.[46] Indeed, in these terms policy evaluations are beyond proof. As illustrated by the much-debated Head Start evaluations, they remain at best exercises in interpretation.[47]

Evaluation findings thus tend to be negative. In a situation in which it is difficult to prove anything, a mixed assessment is about the best one can hope for from evaluation research. Translated from the world of science to political decision making, a mixed assessment is usually enough for the conservative budget analyst to justify putting a program on the fiscal chopping block.

Nowhere was this process more clear than in the evaluation of poverty programs. Far from documenting the successes of these programs, the primary long-term effect of the massive accumulation of poverty-related findings generated by evaluation techniques was corrosion of the ideological faiths upon which these political programs were built.[48] In the mind of the general public, these findings left the impression that there was not a great deal to show for the money that had been spent on poverty programs. Evaluation research could not have provided better ammunition for the conservative opposition. In their eyes the war on poverty had failed and they had the research to demonstrate their case.

The influence of this conservative orientation was soon to show up in the policy analysis profession more generally. By the mid-1970s the language of the discipline began to reflect this new emphasis. In place of the earlier bias toward liberal advocacy, much of the policy language began to emphasize the needs of public management. One sign of this was the focus of a prestigious new professional association, the Association of Public Policy and Management. The association's publication, *The Journal of Policy Analysis and Management*, is dedicated to bringing together the interests of policy analysts and public managers. In fact, this general concern gave rise to a new and expanding field of study called "knowledge utilization," largely designed to develop linkages between the creation of policy knowledge and its administrative uses.[49]

COST-BENEFIT ANALYSIS AND DEREGULATION

Although the development of the conservative approach to policy research first appeared in the Nixon years, not until the Reagan era did it formally emerge as part of the new class challenge. Under Reagan this has been most vividly played out in the administration's efforts to dismantle the federal regulatory system.

Few presidents have been as anti-intellectual as Ronald Reagan. But even Reagan has felt obliged to legitimate his policy agenda with an academic theory (in many ways an important political confirmation of the emerging "knowledge society"). Indeed, "Reagonomics" was put forward as the product of a new development in economic theory, "supply-side economics." Essentially, Reagonomics is a turn away from the evaluation of public programs to a more direct assault on their very existence. Beyond a determination of which programs work, the new emphasis is on limiting government programs altogether. The president enunciated his new policy emphasis in these words: "Government is not the solution to our problem . . . government is the problem."[50]

To effectuate this new political thrust, policy science was again called upon to play a special role. Following earlier but limited initiatives by the Carter administration, Reagan sought to employ cost-benefit analysis (CBA) as the major test for determining the future of public programs. Toward this end, cost-benefit analysis was institutionalized in the policy process through the Office of Management and Budget. Its job was to oversee and ensure that all programs pass this analytical test.

Cost-benefit analysis has, of course, long been a standard technique in the policy scientists' tool kit. Unlike evaluation research (designed to measure existing programs), cost-benefit analysis is generally a pre-decision technique used to compare alternative policy choices. In contrast to other prospective approaches in policy analysis, cost-benefit analysis stresses economy and efficiency over creativity and innovation. Thus, as in the case of evaluation research, conservative politicians have found cost-benefit analysis to be conveniently compatible with their own biases.

Largely a technique developed by economists, the basic logic of cost-benefit analysis is quite simple: It involves totaling up all of the costs and benefits of a policy or program to determine its net value. In practice, however, it is far from a simple operation. Although it has often been helpful in technical decision making (such as Defense Department decisions dealing with military procurement), its uses in the social and political realm have been the subject of a great deal of disagreement, both theoretical and practical. In social policy it has proven quite difficult to quantify policy inputs and outputs. Many have complained that the technique systematically underplays social objectives that cannot easily be measured in quantitative terms.[51]

In spite of these long-standing disputes, the Reagan Administration has elevated cost-benefit analysis to serve as the *primary* test for making policy decisions. With no shortage of support from conservative think tanks, administration officials have persistently argued that such a test is the essence of rational decision making itself. And the message has had an impact. In more and more quarters of the policy analysis profession cost-benefit analysis has emerged as the primary analytical technique. For some, cost-benefit analysis is largely the definition of good policy analysis.[52]

In particular, cost-benefit analysis has been directed at government regulation. Regulation was identified by the Reagan administration as one of the most malevolent aspects of the liberal welfare state. At the heart of the problem was the new class. The regulatory system, in this view, has been captured by new class reformers hostile to traditional capitalist values. As Weaver put it,

> The New Regulation... is the social policy of the new class—that rapidly
> growing and increasingly influential part of the upper-middle class that
> feels itself to be in a more or less adversary posture vis-à-vis American
> society and that tends to make its vocation in the public and not-for-profit
> sectors. Over the past decade it has come to be represented by a broad
> constellation of institutions—the "public interest" movement, the national
> press,various professions . . . , government bureaucracies, research
> institutes on and off campus, the "liberal" wing of the Democratic party,
> and the like. By means of its regulatory policy, the new class is . . .
> transferring power from the managerial class to [itself], and from
> [corporations] to more fully public ones—i.e., to the government.[53]

Essentially the effort to dismantle regulation was designed to
undercut the political influence of these new class reformers. The first
step, aimed at their purported hostility to capitalist values, was to
subvert their use of noneconomic—social and political—criteria in the
regulatory decision-making process. This was to be accomplished
through the introduction of cost-benefit analysis. By mandating cost-
benefit requirements for all regulatory and administrative agencies (a
process called the "regulatory impact assessment," or RIA), the administration sought to impose an "economic grid" on all policy decision
making.[54] Because of CBA's basic market bias, its use would impose on
the regulatory system a business-oriented decision-making-framework
that systematically deemphasizes social benefits. In the language of the
RIA's architects—namely, conservative economists closely associated
with the American Enterprise Institute and the Heritage Foundation—
CBA would build the canons of economic rationality into the bureaucracy's incentive system. James Miller candidly described the nature of
the system this way:

> The CBA executive order says to them: even if you get a nonconforming
> proposal past your agency heads, even if you've captured them or just
> plain fooled them, that proposal is likely to be caught at OMB—and
> there's not a chance in Hades of your capturing those people. So if you
> want to get ahead, you're going to have to write new rules and review
> existing rules in conformance with principles set forth by the President in
> the executive order. I believe that as internal agency procedures and the
> mechanisms for centralized review settle into place, agency personnel will
> voluntarily comply.[55]

Basically what these internal agency procedures are designed to do is
impose a business language on policy discourse. Through a requirement

that all decisions be explained and justified in terms of costs and benefits, a business bias is implicitly imbedded in the deliberation process. Other modes of argumentation, particularly those grounded in the language of the "public interest," are rendered inadmissible—unless, of course, they should happen to pass the cost-benefit test.

Examination of those programs that do manage to demonstrate their cost-effectiveness sheds a revealing light on the politics underlying the administration's use of cost-benefit analysis. For programs or regulatory rules that pass the cost-benefit test, OMB has employed a number of back-up tactics. One has been to tie up an undesireable regulatory rule in methodological analysis. As Zinke has argued, the purpose can be either to generate an alternative study with negative findings or merely to stall the implementation of an unacceptable regulation.[56] Because the determination of costs and benefits is frequently tied to a wide range of uncertain assumptions, it is almost always possible to challenge a particular analysis on methodological grounds. This point was underscored by Dr. Morton Corn, director of the Occupational Safety and Health Administration (OSHA) in 1976:

> After arriving at OSHA, I engaged in an indepth consideration of cost-benefit analysis, applying the methodology to the coke oven standard. . . . With the dose response data at our disposal, various assumptions were used to ring in changes on different methodologies for estimating benefits. The range in values was so wide as to be virtually useless. The conclusion I reached after this exercise was that the methodology of cost-benefit analysis for disease and death effects is very preliminary, and one can almost derive any desired answer.[57]

The point that CBA can be used to justify almost any conclusion is perhaps best illustrated by Russell Settle.[58] Independent of OSHA, Settle studied the agency's 1972 asbestos standard. His conclusion shows that CBA results are in large part determined by policymakers' assumptions, particularly those pertaining to the identification, monetarization, and discounting of future benefits. Employing a wide range of reasonable alternative assumptions, Settle calculated as many as 72 different estimates of the net benefits of OSHA's asbestos standard, from high to low.

In numerous cases OMB is reported to have attempted to assist an agency's ability to generate desirable analytical results by funding efforts to improve available data. For example, in the case of Federal

Trade Commission regulations, OMB has poured a substantial amount of money into research that assists staff analysts in identifying the *costs* of trade regulations while, at the same time, helping the Environmental Protection Agency to eliminate research that makes it easier to quantify *benefits.*[59]

In other cases where there is fairly clear evidence from the outset that CBA calculations are unlikely to support the administration's preferences, OMB has resorted to more direct political tactics. Ample evidence has been assembled to show that OMB, where deemed necessary, has tabled its own request for a CBA review. Zinke, for example, points to cases in which the central budget staff squelched various analyses of housing industry subsidies at the Department of Housing and Urban Development (HUD). He quotes one official as saying that in some cases if HUD wanted to carry out a cost-benefit analysis of a particular housing rule, the agency would literally have to fight for the permission to do it.[60]

Cost-benefit analysis, then, has emerged as a major *political* methodology of the Reagan administration. This is not to say that information on the costs and benefits of a public program are not an important—and at times an essential—ingredient for policy decision making. Rather, it is to point out that the cost-benefit technique, like evaluation research or any other methodology, can be only one component of an adequate policy science. Given the full array of normative and empirical data that potentially bear on a policy judgment, to misrepresent one type of data as sufficient is to build bias and distortion into the decision-making process. Perhaps in one sense data can be neutral (and thus speak for themselves), but as soon as they are introduced into a political process, all such claims must be abandoned. Thus, in order to judge a policy methodology and its data, it is essential to know something about the political purposes of those who employ it.

AN ALTERNATIVE PERSPECTIVE

At this point the question of new class power—at least as it pertains to the policy scientists—readily yields to a more sophisticated explanation than the sort typically rendered by neoconservatives. It is clear that neoconservatives have identified an important political phenomenon: Modern-day policy professionals play an increasingly important role in the policymaking process. Indeed, in some cases they may be prime movers behind a policy agenda, as the war on poverty experience illustrated. Although policy professionals fell far short of becoming a "new priesthood," it was not wrong to speak of the professionalization of reform.

At the same time, however, it is inaccurate to characterize this phenomenon as a "technocratic takeover." It is clear from the foregoing discussion that technocrats have not become a dominant elite per se. This is not to deny that they have striven for political influence; rather, it is to argue that the neoconservatives' emphasis on the political machinations of an ambitious group of policy professionals is simplistic and insufficient. The evidence presented here illustrates the need for a more systematic explanation. In this view it seems to be less a matter of a new and unrepresentative elite conniving for power than a matter of the ideological and technical realities of postindustrial politics ushering this new group to the fore.

Policy experts, as noted at the outset, have traditionally been quick to specify their role as functionaries to the power elite. Little, if anything, in the foregoing account would suggest a transformation in the *basic* patterns of this political relationship. The principal actors here are still the economic and political leaders of the two ruling parties. With the exception that the conservatives themselves have now strategically entered the technocratic game, the emergent pattern must be seen as a contemporary variant of the earlier patterns of policy expertise.

In cases such as the Great Society, in which policy professionals would appear to have stepped beyond their role as functionaries, such expert behavior must be interpreted at something less than political autonomy. What neoconservatives fail to acknowledge is that such behavior occurs only at the discretion of political elites. Policy experts were busy pushing forward antipoverty legislation because Democratic Party leaders, particularly President Johnson, sanctioned their role. Without this sanction, these activities would not have taken place.

This is not to deny that the process has conferred a new status on policy experts. Rather, it is to argue that this new role does not represent a *basic* change in the underlying political structure of society. What has begun to change, however, is the *terrain* of politics. In the "knowledge society" expertise has become a key commodity essential for political control.

What does it mean to say that knowledge is becoming the terrain of politics? It is clear, regardless of one's assessment of the postindustrial thesis, that knowledge and expertise now play important roles in mediating policy decisions. Experts may not make the final decisions about policy, but they increasingly serve as intermediaries between elite decision makers and the groups toward which specific policies are aimed. This confers an indirect but significant form of power upon experts. It usually means that in the name of expert knowledge, policy advisors gain significant influence in shaping the discussion of policy alternatives, if not the specific outcomes. It also means that in some instances experts *broker* political options between elite decision makers and particular interest groups. In those cases in which the experts innovate an option acceptable to elite leaders, they will sometimes even appear to have initiated the policy itself. The antipoverty program is an important example of one such illusion.

The importance of this new terrain is underscored by the neoconservatives' efforts to cultivate their own policy experts. What is more, such efforts tell us a good deal about their understanding of the expert's relation to power. The neoconservatives' strategy, contary to their rhetoric, is clearly compatible with the conviction that those who have expertise are not necessarily those who control it. Indeed, this chapter has shown that neoconservatives have turned the expert's commodity into an object of political struggle for control of the liberal capitalist state.

The terms of this struggle also reveal a significant ideological flaw in the neoconservative position. Neoconservatives regularly argue that knowledge elites are a threat to democracy. But if this is their primary concern, their solution is scarcely designed to remedy the problem. Indeed, by challenging the Democratic Party's use of policy expertise with a counterintelligentsia, they implicitly accept—and approve of—the evolving technocratic terrain. Developing a conservative cadre of policy analysts cannot be interpreted as a measure designed to return power to the people.

Neoconservatives doubtless maintain that *their* policy advisors speak for different political values: Rather than the welfare state and bureaucratic paternalism, conservative experts advocate democracy and free market individualism. Such an argument, however, fails to address the critical issue. As a system of decision making geared toward expert knowledge, technocracy—liberal or conservative—necessarily blocks meaningful participation for the average citizen. Ultimately only those who can interpret the complex technical languages that increasingly frame economic and social issues have access to the play of power. Democratic rhetoric aside, those who nurture a conservative intelligentsia in reality only help to extend an elite system of policy-making.

Moreover, the idea that the neoconservative thesis itself ultimately supports the ascendancy of technocracy converges with the argument put forth by Steinfels, Berube, and Gittell. For them neoconservativism is essentially an elitist ideology for the new class. In the realm of policy expertise this appears to mean the development of an ideology for a new group of conservative policy professionals. The neoconservative involvement in the rise of right-wing think tanks, which in turn have emphasized policy techniques compatible with basic conservative biases, is clearly evidence that helps to support such an argument.

Finally, what are the implications of this analysis for the policy analysis profession and its principal standard of conduct, value neutrality? Policy experts are not entirely naive when it comes to the subject of political influence. The policy literature is filled with references concerning the influence of partisan politics on analysis. The implications of the discussion here, however, suggest that the standard professional perspective on the problem is basically one-sided.

Typically, the professional literature focuses on the politician's misuse or abuse of the policy expert's data. The analyst, by and large, is portrayed as a relatively impartial evaluator struggling against the pressures of partisan politics. Underplayed, if not altogether missing, is a sense of the degree to which the policy expert can (and often does) complicitly join the political fray. Rarely does the literature concede the kind of involvement portrayed in the analysis of the Great Society experience and its aftermath. Not only do we see the ways in which policy professionals—both liberal and conservative—commit themselves to particular politicians and ideologies, we also become aware of the ways in which both the techniques and methodological assumptions of the discipline periodically shift to accommodate changing political winds. Although the profession continues to sell policy analysis as an applied science dedicated to an impartial pursuit of practical knowledge, in reality it is clear that the discipline's public image and methodological approaches are significantly shaped by external political influences. Indeed, we have seen here that the practice of policy analysis, if not the discipline, is increasingly adopting an adversarial orientation.[61] In this light it is not surprising to learn that some writers have begun to identify a new type of expert role on the political landscape: the "policy entrepreneur." The policy entrepreneur, as Polsby explains, is an expert who not only develops a policy idea but also actively works with interest groups and politicians to promote its adoption.[62] With the rapid growth of competing think tanks, such policy entrepreneurship is becoming increasingly prominent.[63]

Clearly, this advocacy role requires more attention than it is getting in the professional literature. Not only does it have profoundly significant implications for our understanding of the policy expert's role, it also raises very important questions about the nature of policy analysis training. Until these issues are addressed in the context of actual policy analysis practices, the discipline's self-proclaimed impartiality can only serve as a professional ideology that obscures the expanding power of the policy expert.

Coming to grips with these issues requires that we recognize the policy science movement to be, like any other scientific or professional movement, an organizational enterprise with interests beyond the production and dissemination of knowledge. Like other professional organizations, it is subject to the political pressures of its times, including the view of itself it both creates and propounds. If we are to learn anything from the experiences reported here, it is this: An adequate understanding of the policy professions must not be limited to the methodological discussions that too often serve to define the subject. Only when these methodological issues are couched in the larger political context that surrounds them can we begin to grasp the role of policy expertise.

NOTES

1. Peter Steinfels, *The Neoconservatives* (New York: Simon & Schuster 1979); and Lewis A. Coser and Irving Howe, eds., *The New Conservatives* (New York: Quadrangle, 1973).

2. Mary O. Furner, *Advocacy and Objectivity: A Crisis in the Professionalization of American Social Science: 1865-1905* (Lexington: University of Kentucky Press, 1975); and Richard Kirkendall, *Social Scientists and Farm Politics in the Age of Roosevelt* (Columbia: University of Missouri Press, 1966).

3. Frank Fischer, *Politics, Values, and Public Policy: The Problem of Methodology* (Boulder: Westview Press, 1980).

4. One of the early, influential statements of this position was advanced by John R. Commons. See Kirkendall, *Social Scientists and Farm Politics,* pp.3-5.

5. Barry Karl, "Presidential Planning and Social Science Research: Mr. Hoover's Experts," in *Perspectives in American History*, Vol. 111 (Cambridge, MA: Charles Warren Center for Studies in American History), 347-409.

6. See, for example, Daniel Bell, *The Coming of Post-Industrial Society* (New York: Basic Books, 1973).

7. Corrine L. Gilb, *Hidden Hierarchies* (New York: Harper & Row, 1966); and on the "professional state" see Frederick C. Mosher, *Democracy and the Public Service* (New York: Oxford University Press, 1968).

8. Gene M. Lyons, *The Uneasy Partnership* (New York: Russell Sage Foundation, 1969).

9. Alvin W. Gouldner, *The Coming Crisis of Western Sociology* (New York: Avon, 1970); Noam Chomsky, *American Power and the New Mandarins* (New York: Vintage, 1969); and Robert Goodman, *After the Planners* (New York: Simon & Schuster, 1971).

10. See Steinfels, *Neoconservatives*.

11. Ibid., especially chapter 10.

12. The term "technocratic takeover" is used by Samuel H. Beer, "In Search of a New Public Philosophy," in Anthony King, ed., *The New American Political System* (Washington, DC: American Enterprise Institute for Public Policy Research, 1978), 44-55.

13. Edward C. Banfield, "Policy Science as Metaphysical Madness," in Robert A. Goldwin, ed., *Bureaucrats, Policy Analysts, Statemen: Who Leads?* (Washington, DC: American Enterprise Institute for Public Policy Research, 1980), 5.

14. See Chaim I. Waxman, ed., *The End of Ideology Debate* (New York: Funk and Wagnalls, 1968).

15. Jürgen Habermas, *Legitimation Crisis* (Boston: Beacon 1975).

16. Daniel P. Moynihan, "The Professionalization of Reform," *The Public Interest* (Fall 1965): 6-16.

17. Theodore H. White, "The Action Intellectuals," *Life* (June 9, June 16, June 23, 1967).

18. National Academy of Sciences, *Government's Need for Knowledge and Information* (Washington, DC: Government Printing Office, 1968).

19. See Clark C. Abt, *Toward the Benefit/Cost Evaluation of U.S. Government Social Research* (Cambridge, MA: Abt Associates, 1976).

20. Cited by Moynihan, "Professionalization of Reform," p. 7.

21. Frances Fox Piven and Richard A. Cloward, *Regulating the Poor* (New York: Pantheon, 1971).

22. John Bibby and Roger Davidson, *On Capitol Hill* (New York: Holt, Rinehart & Winston, 1967), 236.

23. Elinor Graham, "Poverty and the Legislative Process," in *Poverty as a Public Issue*, Ben B. Seligman, ed. (New York: Free Press, 1965), 243-244.

24. Piven and Cloward, *Regulating the Poor*, p. 258; and Sar Levitan, *The Great Society's Poor Law* (Baltimore: Johns Hopkins University Press, 1969), 94.

25. Daniel P. Moynihan, *Maximum Feasible Misunderstanding: Community Action in the War on Poverty* (New York: Free Press, 1969); and Nelson W. Polsby, *Political Innovation in America* (New Haven: Yale University Press, 1984), 128-145.

26. Banfield, "Policy Science as Metaphysical Madness," pp. 6-7.

27. Ibid., p. 18; and Irving Kristol, "Where Have all the Answers Gone?" *National Forum* LXIX, 1 (1979): 12-14.

28. Banfield, "Policy Science as Metaphysical Madness," p. 1.

29. Robert E. Lane, "The Decline of Politics and Ideology in a Knowledgeable Society," *American Sociological Review* 31 (October 1966): 662.

30. William Simon, *A Time for Truth* (New York: Reader's Digest Books, 1979).

31. Irving Kristol, *Two Cheers for Capitalism* (New York: Basic Books, 1978), 141-145.

32. Maurice R. Berube and Marilyn Gittell, "In Whose Interest is the 'The Public Interest'?" *Social Policy* (May-June 1970) 5-6; and Steinfels, *Neoconservatives,* p. 279.

33. Simon, *A Time For Truth.*

34. John S. Saloma, *Ominous Politics: The New Conservative Labyrinth* (New York: Hill and Wang, 1984), especially chapter 2.

35. See "Bad Advice from Heritage," *Public Administration Times* (January 1, 1985), 2; and Charles L. Heatherly, ed., *Mandate for Leadership: Policy Management in a Conservative Administration* (Washington, DC: The Heritage Foundation, 1981).

36. Quoted in Martin Tolchin, "Working Profile: Stuart M. Butler," *New York Times* (July 22, 1985): 10.

37. Henry J. Aaron, *Politics and the Professors: The Great Society in Perspective* (Washington, DC: The Brookings Institution, 1978), 57.

38. Ibid.

39. James Everett Katz, *Presidential Politics and Science Policy* (New York: Praeger, 1978), 204.

40. Moynihan, *Maximum Feasible Misunderstanding*, p. 193.

41. James Q. Wilson, "Social Science and Public Policy: A Personal Note," in Lawrence E. Lynn, Jr., ed., *Knowledge and Policy: The Uncertain Connection* (Washington, DC: National Academy of Sciences, 1978), 82-92.

42. Larry Berman, *The Office of Management and Budget and the Presidency,* 1921-1979 (Princeton: Princeton University Press), 105-130.

43. Katz, *Presidential Politics,* 200-205.

44. Thomas A. Morehouse, "Program Evaluation: Social Research Versus Public Policy," *Public Administration Review* (November/December 1972): 873.

45. Allen Schick, "From Analysis to Evaluation," *American Academy of Political and Social Science Annals,* 394 (1971): 57-71.

46. Mark H. Moore, "Statesmanship in a World of Particular Substantive Choices," in Goldwin, *Bureaucrats, Policy Analysts, Statesmen,* p. 33.

47. Frank Fischer, "Critical Evaluation of Public Policy: A Methodological Case Study," in John Forester, ed., *Critical Theory and Public Life* (Cambridge: MIT Press, 1986), 231-257.

48. Aaron, *Politics and the Professors,* p. 159.

49. On "knowledge utilization" see the journal *Knowledge: Creation, Diffusion, Utilization,* published by Sage Publications.

50. John Schwarz, *America's Hidden Success* (New York: W.W.Norton, 1983), 22.

51. See, for example, Steven Kelman, *Cost-Benefit Analysis and Environmental Regulation: Politics, Ethics, and Methods* (New York: The Conservation Foundation, 1982).

52. For a spirited defense of this position see, John McAdams, "The Anti-Policy Analysts," *Policy Studies Journal,* 13, 1 (1984): 91-102.

53. Paul H. Weaver, "Regulation, Social Policy and Class Conflict," *The Public Interest* 50 (Winter 1978): 59.

54. Susan J. Tolchin, "Cost-Benefit Analysis and the Rush to Deregulate: The Use and Misuse of Theory to Effect Policy Change," *Policy Studies Review* 4,2 (November 1984): 213.

55. "Deregulation HQ: An Interview on the New Executive Order with Murray L. Weidenbaum and James C. Miller, III," *Regulation* (March/April 1981): 16.

56. Robert Clifford Zinke, "Cost-Benefit Analysis and Adminstrative Decision-Making: A Methodological Case-Study of the Relation of Social Science to Public Policy" (Unpublished doctoral dissertation, Department of Public Administration, New York University, 1984).

57. Cited in Office of Technology Assessment, *Preventing Illness and Injury in the Workplace* (Washington, DC: Government Printing Office, 1985), 283.

58. Russell Franklin Settle, "The Welfare Economics of Occupational Safety and Health Standards" (Unpublished doctoral disseration, Department of Economics, University of Wisconsin, 1974).

59. Nancy DiTomaso, "The Managed State: Governmental Reorganization in the First Years of the Reagan Administration," in Richard G. Braungart and Margaret M. Braungart, eds., *Research in Political Sociology* (Greenwich, CT: JAI Press, 1985), 141-166.

60. Zinke, "Cost-Benefit Analysis and Administrative Decision-Making," p. 257.

61. On some implications of this adversarial style see Jeanne Guillemin and Irving Louis Horowitz, "Social Research and Political Advocacy: New Stages and Old Problems in Integrating Science and Values," in Daniel Callahan and Bruce Jennings, eds., *Ethics, The Social Sciences, and Policy Analysis* (New York: Plenum, 1983), 187-211.

62. Polsby, *Political Innovation in America*, pp. 167-174.

63. On think tanks and policy entrepreneurship, see Philip Boffey,"Heritage Foundation: Success in Obscurity," *New York Times* (November 17, 1985): 62.

PART III

Normative Theory and Methodology

5

INTERPRETATION AND THE
PRACTICE OF POLICY ANALYSIS

BRUCE JENNINGS
The Hastings Center

The greatest trust between man and man is the trust of giving counsel. For in other confidences men commit the parts of life; their lands, their goods, their child, their credit, some particular affair; but to such as they make their counsellors, they commit the whole: by how much more they are obliged in all faith and integrity. . . . There be [those] that are in nature faithful and sincere, and plain, and direct; not crafty and involved; let princes, above all, draw to themselves such natures. Besides, counsellors are not commonly so united, but that one counsellor keepeth sentinel over another; so that if any do counsel out of faction or private ends, it commonly comes to the King's ear.

—Francis Bacon

In a democratic age we perhaps find it difficult to share Bacon's appreciation of the moral significance that resides in the activity of giving counsel on matters of state. One reason for this is that we no longer have kings who commit the whole of their public selves, their bodies politic, in trust to their advisors. We have instead "policy-makers"—a neutered, technocratic term suitably shorn of the symbolism, if not the substance, of rulership—who draw on the specialized expertise of policy analysts. The image of a political trust that is also a moral trust does not resonate clearly in a liberal democratic and bureaucratic world of impersonal rule, the sovereignty of processes rather than persons. Another reason for our distance from Bacon's concern is that we seem to lack any very rich understanding of what giving political or policy counsel is about—what modes of political and social knowledge, judgment, and prudence it entails; what ethical responsibilities it bears; what shapes its practice might take in a governance that cultivates democracy instead of curtailing it.

Over time a great many political theorists who, like Bacon, were concerned to bridge the gap between theory and action have developed a conception of the practice of giving political counsel that I regard as ethically richer and epistemologically more adequate than the standard account of applied social science that underlies policy analysis today. These older theorists viewed political counsel as the application of practical reason (*phronesis*) informed by enlightened common sense, what in our current idiom we would call interpretive social science.

The aim of counsel, so conceived, is threefold: (1) to grasp the meaning or significance of contemporary problems as they are experienced, adapted to, and struggled against by the reasonable, purposive agents who are members of the political community; (2) to clarify the meaning of those problems so that strategically located political agents (public officials or policymakers) will be able to devise a set of efficacious and just solutions to them; and (3) to guide the selection of one preferred policy from that set in light of a more general vision of good of the community as a whole as well as the more discrete interests of the policymakers themselves.

In sum, the counselor must construct an interpretation of present political and social reality that serves not only the intellectual goal of explaining or comprehending that reality but also, and more important, the practical goal of enabling constructive action that moves the community from a flawed present toward an improved future. Contrary to Marx, who held that interpreting the world and changing the world were two distinct, if not antithetical, enterprises, the traditional conception of counsel presses interpretation into the service of change. Not just any change but change that is itself directed by the human moral values and possibilities that the practice of interpretation uncovers.

In this essay I shall analyze some of the reasons why we seem to have lost this older conception of counsel, and explore how we can recover or rehabilitate that conception in a new understanding of the practice of policy analysis as it might be (and I believe sometimes is) constituted today. My focus will be on the epistemological and methodological foundations of policy analysis, broadly defined as policy advice, informed by perspectives drawn from the social sciences and the humanities, that pertains to the initial definition of policy problems, the identification of policy options, and the evaluation of policy choices. My analysis will be constructed around a comparison of three different models or second-order reconstructions of the practice of policy analysis—policy analysis as science, policy analysis as advocacy, and policy analysis as counsel. These models are grounded in different philosophical accounts of the social scientific knowledge base of policy analysis, which need to be explored. In addition to their philosophical foundations, I also want to examine the ethical and democratic implications of these models.

At first glance, my focus on models or theories of policy analysis may seem unduly abstract. But in this case abstractions matter. Models provide, so to speak, a reflexive self-understanding of the practice of policy analysis for its practitioners, its "clients," and observant citizens. I believe that the most widely, albeit tacitly, held models are neither adequate as descriptive representations nor acceptable as prescriptive, regulative ideals. Consequently, policy analysis today is a practice in search of both a self-identity and a profession. Its theorists—practitioners who step back from its practice and systematically attempt to make sense of what they are doing, or commentators who try to examine its role and effects in our political system—find it difficult both to give a public account of what policy analysis is and to articulate what values it should profess.

In fact, there have been remarkably few synthetic attempts to develop a theory of policy analysis, considering the way the field has grown in size and influence since the 1960s.[1] Most theories that do exist have tended to employ a model of policy analysis based on a positivistic conception of its social scientific knowledge base and an "engineering model" of applied social science supplemented by techniques such as decision theory or cost-benefit analysis. This model, policy analysis as science, may describe the implicit image of policy analysis embedded in the curricula of most professional schools of public affairs and many leading textbooks on policy analysis[2] (where most of the available secondary reconstructions of policy analysis are to be found), but it does not accurately represent—and cannot methodologically or ethically guide—the actual or potential practice of policy analysis. For this we should turn to a model I shall call policy analysis as counsel, which, inspired by the traditional conception of counsel mentioned earlier, views the practice of policy analysis as mode of policy-oriented social interpretation based on a hermeneutical, rather than a positivistic, conception of social science.

Thus far this interpretive turn has not been taken in the theory of policy analysis to any significant extent. Instead, there has been a shift in fashion of late from policy analysis as science to policy analysis as advocacy as a preferred model. This shift returns us in a curious way to something Bacon, who was no stranger to policy advocacy at court, feared: "crafty and involved" advisors who "counsel out of faction or private ends." And it returns us as well to a procedural solution that Bacon saw as a necessary expedient in the absence of an ethos of public trust: a system of countervailing roles and incentives, akin to the adversarial legal system, in which "one counsellor keepeth sentinel over another."

The conception of policy analysis as advocacy has been given a new lease on life by the fact that policy analysis as science has been subjected to a telling—and I think decisive—critique in recent years. What has emerged from this critique is a much chastened conception of policy analysis, a policy analysis shorn of its once prized value neutrality and scientific objectivity. As a result, many who can no longer subscribe to policy analysis as science have turned—prematurely and unnecessarily, in my estimation—to policy analysis as advocacy as the only philosophically viable and politically honest alternative.

My argument is that if we carefully think through the epistemological and normative implications of recent criticisms of scientific or positivistic policy analysis, we will come to two conclusions: First, these criticisms of positivism permit a different, but still fully serviceable and rational, conception of "objective" policy advice. Second, they do not entail advocacy as a substitute for science but rather suggest the alternative notion of policy analysis as counsel. This notion is more attractive than advocacy, both as an ethical profession for policy analysis and as a way of enabling the practice of policy analysis to strengthen rather than erode democratically legitimate governance.

THE PRACTICE OF POLICY ANALYSIS

Before taking up the three models of policy analysis I have distinguished, something more should be said about the notion of policy analysis as a practice. Then I will present a hypothetical case to focus the connection between the epistemological and the ethical issues, which is my theme.

Policy analysis today is a practice in search of a profession. It is a "practice" in at least two senses. First and most simply, it is an activity that is widely practiced not only by those in university settings who have made it their academic speciality but also by an increasingly large number of individuals directly employed by federal and state agencies, congressional committees, commissions, private sector institutes, consulting firms, lobbying groups, and the like. Nonetheless, amid this diversity of different species of policy analysts, the outlines of the genus, policy analysis, are beginning to take shape. We recognize the distinctive timbre of its voice in the chorus of different voices—of politics and ideology, of need and interest—that join together, not often harmoniously, in the song of policymaking. When we speak of "policy analysts" we now have a tolerably clear sense of the type of people being referred to, the roles they play, and the special contributions they make.

We are also beginning to have some prescriptive sense of what policy analysis should and should not be, and of what policy analysts should and should not do. This is due, in part, to the fact that policy analysis is a practice in a second, more technical sense: It is a distinctive, rule-governed form of activity that has its own internal protocols, methods, and conventions of discourse.[3] This development gives one the starting point for a normative conception of policy analysis. As a practice in this sense, policy analysis is something that can be done well or badly, competently or incompetently, and its own internal norms establish criteria for evaluating the competency of a specific performance within the practice.

Moreover, if policy analysis has become a recognizably distinct mode of inquiry with its own conventions, idioms, and functions, it has also started to become a "profession" in recent years. Professions are special kinds of practices; they differ from other occupations in several ways. They have their own theoretical and technical knowledge base, they have their own certifying or gatekeeping educational institutions, they are self-regulating and set their own criteria for admission and acceptable practice standards, and so on. Although policy analysis will probably always lack certain attributes characteristic of other professions (e.g., state licensure and a legal monopoly in the provision of certain services), the movement toward professionalization among policy analysts is clearly evident and is a trend that will continue as policy expertise becomes more specialized and as evaluation techniques become more arcane. If this trend is in the cards, it raises some worrisome and unsettling questions all the same—especially ethical questions to which neither analysts nor the policymakers they serve can afford to be indifferent. The profession of policy analysis at the present time does not have a clear sense of what it professes; it does not have a clear sense of the civic and human values it embodies and is dedicated to serve.

To be caught up in a headlong drive toward prefessionalization without the concomitant articulation of a "profession" (a vocation or ethical mission) is to be in a no-man's land where the democratic legitimacy of policy analysis is suspect and where the moral justifications of various roles policy analysts might play are not easy to construct. When they find themselves thus exposed and challenged in this no-man's land, policy analysts commonly head for cover behind the sandbags of science and method. Although, as I shall argue later, this move is more complex and problematical than policy analysts often realize, it is not unreasonable. There is an important connection between the epistemic grounding of policy advice on one hand and the democratic legitimacy of policy analysis on the other. Policy analysts are, as the saying goes, properly in the business of speaking truth to power. By doing so they exercise a form of power of their own that is not arbitrary or illegitimate in democratic political system. But saying this does not resolve the normative problem of what the practice of policy analysis should profess; it merely formulates that problem in a new and potentially fruitful way. It suggests that we must pay close attention to the epistemological dimensions of policy analysis as a prelude to an investigation of its ethical dimensions. It may well be that policy analysts should speak truth to power, but how they should speak (and how power should use what it hears) depends upon the nature of the truth that is spoken as well as the motive behind the speaking of it.

To see more clearly what is involved in an attempt to sort out these issues, consider the following case:

An intelligence analyst under contract to the CIA submits a report on current economic and political conditions in Mexico to the director of the agency. At the time the director is engaged in an effort to convince the President to authorize a program of covert operations and economic pressure to induce the Mexican government to more actively support U.S. foreign policy objectives in Central America. To recommend this program he wants a report that will stress impending instability in Mexico as a threat to U.S. interests in the region. However, the analyst's report indicates that the evidence does not warrant such a policy and maintains that less coercive diplomatic options remain viable.

The director instructs the analyst to rewrite the report so that it will support the conclusion the director favors. The analyst refuses to do so, arguing that his version of the evidence is accurate and should be allowed to stand. The director then turns the report over to others who make the prescribed changes and subsequently dismisses the analyst by refusing to extend his contract when it comes up for renewal.

After leaving the agency, the analyst publicly criticizes the director's actions, arguing that the distortion of intelligence analysis for pre-determined policy objectives hampers the full discussion of issues among analysts and policymakers. He shares the belief, widely held among intelligence analysts, that intelligence estimates are supposed to provide a neutral base of information and analysis for policymaking and that intelligence analyses should be conducted on the basis of the best available facts, without political interference.[4]

This case raises several important and difficult questions about the ends served by professional policy analysis in the policymaking process, about the appropriate relationship between the analyst and the policy-maker, and about the guiding motivations of the participants in this encounter. Was the CIA director, the policymaker, justified in over-riding the professional judgment or expertise of the analyst and in seeing to it that the report confirmed his preconceived policy conclusion rather than the conflicting conclusion the analyst had reached? In doing so, was the policymaker violating his own ethical responsibilities as a public official and misleading his superiors? Or was he simply taking a "broader view" of the policy problem and remaining within the bounds of his legitimate discretion—or even his affirmative duty—by sub-ordinating the professional preoccupations of the analyst to more compelling political ends?

Was the analyst correct in refusing to comply with the order to change the report? Or should he have compromised on some interpretive language in the document (assuming that, and not the outright falsification of data, was what was at stake) so as to salvage his ability to speak truth to power, even though it would have been from his point of view a diminished truth?

And what, finally, are we to make of this entire incident? Was it a cynical abuse of policy analysis? Was it a straightforward clash between "science" and "ideology," a victory of rationalization over rationality? Or is the incident most accurately construed as a conflict between two types of advocacy that could not be reconciled in this case: a professional advocacy by the analyst on one hand and a political advocacy by the policymaker on the other?

Clearly, exploring all the issues raised here would take us too far afield. The question which I hope the reminder of this essay will help answer is this: How can the analyst in this case—and in many similar, if less dramatic, cases—most reasonably justify the stance he took, and to what normative conception of the policy analyst's role might he most reasonably appeal in mounting that justification?

POLICY ANALYSIS AS SCIENCE

Like other second-order reconstructions of policy analysis, policy analysis as science offers an account of the epistemological status of the type of knowledge the analyst contributes to the policymaking process and an ethical account of the role obligations of the analyst vis-à-vis other actors in that process. The Science Model was the animating force behind the development of the policy sciences and applied social science in the postwar years, and its roots go back to Enlightenment rationalism and nineteenth-century positivism and empiricism.

The quest for a systematic understanding of the nature and functioning of human society is a very old intellectual adventure. From one point of view, the history of the social sciences corresponds to the history of Western social and political philosophy. Plato in *Republic* and Aristotle in *Politics* established a tradition of discourse to which the modern social sciences still belong; they formulated interconnected and fundamental questions that social scientists still pose and attempt to answer. Nonetheless, to focus exclusively on the continuity of this Great Tradition is to overlook three things of equal, or greater, importance about the social sciences: (1) their overriding self-consciousness of their own modernity; (2) their founding sense of the inadequacy of traditional social theory; and (3) their attempt, in breaking with that tradition, to inaugurate a kind of social inquiry at once more solidly established epistemologically and more powerful as an instrument of social control.

These three elements of the modern orientation in the social sciences grew out of a more comprehensive reordering of knowledge that took place in the nineteenth century, for it was then that the social sciences began to coalesce into the disciplinary pattern still operative today.[5]

During this period a new cultural ideal of knowledge emerged and was called simply science. This ideal was based on the empiricist doctrine that sense perception is the basis of all human knowledge and that through controlled observation general laws of cause and effect could be discovered that would mirror in human language and thought the true structure of external reality itself. So conceived, science was placed at the top of the intellectual hierarchy, supplanting religious revelation, aesthetic imagination, and practical common wisdom and relegating them, as it were, to the epistemological dustbin. Moreover, as it was widely held that the natural sciences—preeminently Newtonian physics—came closest to realizing this ideal of science, many thinkers concluded that other disciplines must henceforth adopt the methods and stance of the natural sciences if they were to achieve a sound footing and discover the truth about their objects of study.

Debates surrounding this ideal of science and its relation to other modes of knowledge have been raging for the better part of two centuries. These debates pit positivism, a philosophical elaboration of the ideal of science, against its conservative and radical critics: traditionalists, literary romantics, philosophical idealists, and, most recently, proponents of a hermeneutic or interpretive philosophy of social science. It is in differing reactions to the intellectual challenge posed by science and by the complex industrial, technological civilization being produced by the applications of science that one finds the source of divergences in the social sciences and, by extension, in regulative ideals of policy analysis. In order to understand what is at stake here, we must take note of three general features of positivism having to do with the epistemological and the ethical stance of the knowing subject vis-à-vis the object of knowledge.

First, positivism is a deeply skeptical and antitraditional doctrine. Its first impulse is to sweep aside all received doctrines and all claims to truth based solely on the authority of canonical belief or established practice. In this its image of the knowing subject is highly individualistic and even heroic. If the human intellect could free itself from the fetters of accumulated belief and dogma, if, like Descartes in the *Meditations*, it could dig down to some bedrock of certainty and then logically and methodically rebuild a body of knowledge, it could know the truth.

Second, following from this demanding image of scientific discovery, positivism is equally severe in its demands on the mental discipline of the knowing subject. Not only must scientists avoid sources of error coming from outside, they must also control or suppress sources of bias within themselves. This does not mean that science, even according to the positivist account, must be a cold, passionless endeavor. But it does mean that the scientist qua scientist must establish an emotional distance from the phenomena he or she studies. For positivism, the first virtue is objectivity or value neutrality; the cardinal sin is to allow judgments of value or preference to influence one's analysis of facts.

Third, positivism externalizes the relationship between the knowing subject and the object of knowledge. That is, the activity of science is ontologically separated from the reality it studies; it observes that reality but does not in any important or essential way participate in it. This doctrine (which was derived from the seventeenth-century shift from a teleological and Christian cosmology to a mechanistic cosmology)[6] meant that the objects of scientific knowledge were things to be described, manipulated, and controlled. Scientists can have no human (or spiritual) relationship with their objects of study, for that would involve anthropomorphic projection and myth. Moreover, the practice of science does not, in and of itself, either depend upon or enhance the broadly human or spiritual qualities of the scientist. Pushed to its limit, positivism takes the individual scientist, with all his or her multifaceted characteristics as a human being, out of the practice of science and substitutes the almost faceless figure of the scientist as vehicle for the application of method.

Policy analysis as science applies these tenets of positivism to the practice of policy analysis. For it the policy analyst is the bridge between the growing corpus of objective, empirically confirmed social scientific laws of human behavior and the world of practical problem solving and policy formation. The policy analyst qua applied social scientist stands between the pure social scientist and the policymaker much as an engineer stands between the physicist and the layperson with a practical problem to be solved.[17] The policy analyst's usefulness and credibility are essentially derivative from the scientific validity of the stock of knowledge he or she offers the lay policymaker.

Similarly, the policy analyst's role is, according to the Science Model, essentially reactive and instrumental. The policy analyst's expertise is limited to the questions that science can properly answer; that is, to questions of empirical fact and practical means. As a scientist, the policy analyst has no special expertise or authoritative knowledge concerning questions of value or ends—in a democracy the values and ends of public policy can properly be determined only by politically accountable (elected or appointed) public officials, and policy goals must be set by politics and not by science. Hence, in the Science Model the role obligations of policy analysts are clear and narrowly circumscribed: The policy analyst must obey the canons of scientific honesty and objectivity; in advising the policymaker on viable options and effective means to achieve preset ends, the policy analyst must not permit private values (read: preferences, biases) or special interests to color his or her assessments, recommendations, or advice.

POLICY ANALYSIS AS ADVOCACY

This sketch of policy analysis as science highlights the principal features that make this model antithetical to policy analysis as advocacy. In the Science Model the policy analyst is an "advocate" only in a very special sense: an advocate for the triumph of disciplined, objective, scientific intelligence over subjective preference, utopian fantasy, and nonscientific understandings of social reality that are distorted by ideological commitments and narrowly partisan, economic, or bureaucratic interests. For the proponents of policy analysis as science, as for the early positivist and empiricist philosophers, epistemological realism—the notion that there is a world of brute facts "out there" to which our beliefs and activities must conform—provides the only basis for intersubjective rational agreement among policymakers, and it can lift policy decisions above the play of "politics" or ideological debate where outcomes are determined by superior power, influence, or persuasiveness.

Policy analysis as advocacy clearly does not provide for "rational" decision making—the lifting of policy above politics—in this sense.[8] On the contrary, it forthrightly politicizes policymaking, pointing out along the way that the purported ethical and political neutrality of the positivistic Science Model is an illusion masking the inherently value-laden character of any analytic method. Armed with this insight, but misconstruing its import, the defenders of policy analysis as advocacy then fall back on a procedural rather than a scientific rationality to guide policy decisions toward efficacy, justice, and the public interest.

In this respect policy analysis as advocacy belongs to a much older and broader family of arguments in political theory whose classic formulation can be found in James Madison's *Federalist* 10 and 51. Unwilling to rely on the rare occurrence of political rulers possessing true wisdom and genuine civic virtue, Madison proposed instead an adversarial structure of constitutional offices and powers that would serve the public interest and especially protect the rights of minorities by keeping unchecked governmental power from falling into the hands of one dominant group ("faction") or a majority coalition of groups. This leads by a short route to a system in which justice would be achieved through an adversarial process of give and take (in the legislature and the bureaucracy, as well as in the courts) among advocates representing particular social interests.[9]

Here, without stretching the point too much, I think we find in one tradition of political theory a paradigm for the connection one finds in policy analysis as advocacy between a skeptical or pessimistic view of the possibility of objective knowledge and disinterested (or, more accurately, *publicly* interested) motivation on one hand and a largely adversarial and procedural conception of legitimate processes of governance or policymaking on the other.

POLICY ANALYSIS AS COUNSEL

We are now in a position to see somewhat more clearly the dilemma of the intelligence analyst in the case presented earlier in this chapter. In justifying his refusal to alter his report, our analyst might appeal to the Science Model; but much of the force of that appeal is undermined by the epistemological flaws in the model. The truth our analyst must defend against manhandling simply cannot be the sort of truth envisioned by traditional positivism. If that is the case generally for policy analysis as a genus, then it is all the more so for intelligence analysis because the latter is one of the "softest," most interpretive analytic specialities. On the other hand, our analyst cannot justify his position by baldly appealing to the Advocate Model either, because that would play directly into the hands of the CIA director, who, after all, is operating on the basis of a highly politicized, advocacy conception of the policy process himself. The lower-level advocacy of the analyst must give way to the higher-level advocacy the director is engaged in at the White House.

To avoid this dilemma, what our analyst does do is try to have it both ways. He appeals both to the validity of his evidence and to the procedural notion that policymakers should have the benefit of a broad-ranging and unfettered debate on all the potential policy options. In defending this composite view of the value of "professional" (that is, methodologically competent and reasonably autonomous) policy analysis, he might well echo an argument recently put forward by Mark Moore: "Within the world of policy decisions that depend ultimately on judgment, experience, intuition, and guesses, decisions nonetheless differ in terms of how carefully and completely they are structured, how well informed they are, and how systematically alternatives have been considered."[10]

This provides, it seems to me, the beginnings of an adequate justification for our analyst in the case. But it is important to understand that this justification cannot be grounded or carried through on the basis of a patchwork conception of policy analysis stitched together out of a shred of the Science Model here and a swatch of the Advocate Model there. Our analyst, like so many harried real-world analysts today, may try to have it both ways, but he can't. What he needs is a third alternative, a profession with a different normative content and a different epistemological self-understanding to guide his practice. I believe that policy analysis as counsel provides that alternative. To flesh out the notion of policy analysis as counsel, we can begin by contrasting it with policy analysis as advocacy and by considering the different ways each of these models steps in to fill the normative void left by the decline of policy analysis as science.

Recall that policy analysis as advocacy begins with skepticism about the policy analyst's capacity to provide policy advice based on objective knowledge and disinterested motivation. From there it jumps to the conclusion that the only legitimate and honest solution is for a procedurally controlled, open advocacy; a system loosely analogous to the adversarial trial system of the courts. Just as political theorists, such as Madison, have argued that natural human selfishness cannot be transcended but can only be contained and channeled toward just ends, the Advocate Model holds that policy advice will inevitably be informed by some particularistic interests that can only be balanced but cannot be transformed into a more public-regarding *civitas*.

There is an irony here worth noting before we move on. The skepticism of policy analysis as advocacy suggests its underlying affinity with the positivistic Science Model, despite the apparent incompatibility of the two orientations. At the core of the Advocate Model there lies a disillusioned but unreconstructed positivism. For the positivists one either had objective knowledge or subjective opinion; there was no middle ground. Defenders of policy analysis as advocacy seem to believe in that either/or as well.

Policy analysis as counsel searches for some middle ground. Like the other normative models of policy analysis, it too posits a connection between the epistemological status of policy advice, the intentions, purposes, or commitments of the policy analyst, and the legitimate role of policy analysis in a democracy. For the Counsel Model the question is this: Can the analyst in fact provide the policymaker with a perspective that is broader, more public and objective (in some sense) than that which is provided by the policy analyst as advocate? The answer is yes. In order to see why, let us consider more closely the Science Model and its critics.

Recent criticisms of the Science Model, and the strong claims of positivistic objectivity and value neutrality upon which it rests, have come from several different sources. Work in the philosophy of science and the philosophy of social science has made it increasingly difficult to believe that the social sciences can ever provide the kind of knowledge base that scientific policy analysis presupposes. At the same time, descriptive studies of the relationship between policy analysts and policymakers and the dynamics of the policymaking process have shown that the instrumentalist, "engineering" conception of applied social science is untenable; it radically simplifies and distorts our understanding of the much more complex and nuanced interactions between decision makers and analysts in policy settings.

This is not the place to rehearse these rather sophisticated and well-known criticisms in detail.[11] But three general points merit our attention because they bear on the question of whether something like the Counsel Model provides a viable alternative to the Advocate Model.

First, social science does not provide the kind of objective knowledge that positivism has traditionally held to be the regulative epistemological and methodological ideal. (For that matter, neither does natural science.) Social scientific theories are not logically coherent structures of theoretical and empirical covering laws, and they do not generate deductive-nomological explanations (or predictions) of human behavior, at least not at a level of specificity that would make them useful to the policy analyst. Moreover, if social science does not provide a body of objective laws—that is, generalizations corroborated through controlled observation by numerous independent investigators—neither does it provide purely descriptive accounts of social phenomena. Even at the descriptive level social scientific observation is inherently selective and theory laden. The "facts" it reports are inevitably "artifacts" of particular conceptual schemes and theoretical presuppositions that are built into survey instruments, public records, and other sources of social information. In the face of these and other considerations, many social scientists are now coming to abandon positivism and to see themselves as engaged in a process of cultural interpretation rather than scientific or causal explanation.[12] This raises a host of new and still unresolved questions about the objectivity of social scientific knowledge and about the rationality of adjudicating among conflicting interpretations of human action.

Second, the more the theory-laden and interpretive character of social scientific inquiry is appreciated, the more untenable the traditional positivist separation of facts and values becomes. The value neutrality thesis always rests on the claim that it is possible to construct a theory- and value-neutral observation language within which to formulate empirical tests of conflicting hypotheses and to assess their results. Social scientists now largely recognize that this is not simply a practically unrealizable desideratum but a philosophically incoherent goal as well.

Social scientific interpretations and categories are superimposed on the culturally available interpretations and categories that human agents construct in the course of their ongoing social and institutional relationships. At the same time, especially in contemporary societies, social scientific discourse is appropriated into the broader culture and becomes a component of the self-understandings available to agents as they formulate their intentions, projects, and goals. Hence strict value neutrality is impossible in social science not only because social scientists' own idiosyncratic values enter into their thinking and analysis but also, and much more important, because the received categories that social scientists do and must use in their discourse already have a particular "value slope" built into their linguistic and cultural meanings.

Third, descriptive studies of the policymaking process have shown that analysts are not in fact merely reactive or instrumental handmaidens of policymakers. Policymakers do not often turn to analysts with clear instructions or firmly preset ends or goals in mind. (In this respect the case presented earlier is atypical and extreme.) They respond, rather, to much vaguer and more ambiguous signals and pressures in the political and bureaucratic environment. Policy analysts thus are in a position to shape and direct the agendas of policymakers to a much greater extent than the Science Model allows. Analysts define as well as assess policy options; they structure perceptions and negotiate the constraints that are placed upon them.[13]

These three considerations have dealt a body-blow to the Science Model of policy analysis. But they do not, in my estimation, suggest that the Advocate Model is the only viable alternative. To conclude that it is is to conclude that positivistic objectivity is the only meaningful or rational kind of objectivity possible. This, it seems to me, is a serious philosophical and political mistake.

While calling the positivistic notions of objectivity and value neutrality into serious question, the "interpretive turn" in contemporary philosophy of social science does not entail some kind of radical epistemological skepticism.[14] And, more to the point here, it does not even entail the more moderate skepticism central to policy analysis as advocacy. What it does suggest, however, is precisely that middle ground we have been searching for as a foundation for policy analysis as counsel. That is, recent philosophical accounts of interpretive social inquiry give us the basis for what I shall call "post-positivistic objectivity."[15]

To lay the groundwork for assessing this claim, we should consider more fully some of the features of interpretive social science upon which a conception of policy analysis as counsel can be based. As in our earlier summary of the tenets of positivism, the interpretive or hermeneutic philosophy of social science can be discussed in terms of the epistemological and ethical relationship it postulates between the knowing subject and the object of knowledge.

First, interpretive social science construes human behaviors, social relationships, and cultural artifacts as texts (or dramas or rituals) and then seeks to uncover the meaning that those texts have to the agents who constitute them and to others located spatially or temporally outside them.

Second, interpretive social science focuses on three key concepts: action, intention, and convention. It aims to make sense of (elucidate or explicate) individual actions in terms of the agent's intentions in (or reasons for) the action. And these intentions, in turn, are explicated in terms of the cultural context of conventions, rules, and norms within which they are formed. This second step in the explicative analysis is crucial, and it is important to understand how the notion of intention is typically construed in these studies. Intentions are not construed as internal mental events or private wants but rather as the purposes that an agent constructs or might in principle have constructed using the publicly available concepts and meanings of his or her culture. Thus in some instances we might say that an agent's intentions are conscious self-interpretations and conscious interpretations of the culture's judgment of the appropriateness of a given action. In other instances, however, it may be necessary to hold that the "intentions" ascribed to the agent in order to elucidate the action are not those of which he or she was (fully) aware at the time; rather they are the constructs of the social scientists, formulated on the basis of an assessment broader than the agent was able to make, of the overall cultural context within which the action took place. This is a perfectly legitimate move, and it suggests two additional points worth noting.

Interpretive social science does not rely, as has sometimes been charged, on some mysterious imaginative process whereby the social scientist (or historian) sees into the mind of the persons being studied. The categories of an interpretive analysis are publicly available concepts, drawn from the stock of intersubjective social knowledge. Concomitantly, interpretive analysis is not imprisoned in "the native's point of view"; it may—and usually must—go beyond the agent's own limited comprehension of this situation, filling out and correcting that comprehension with a broader, more critical perspective.

In addition, the logical form of the accounts given in interpretive social science is teleological rather than deductive-nomological. Another way of putting this is to say that interpretive explications offer an account that purports to make sense of the action by reconstructing the reasoning process leading up to it in terms of a practical syllogism.[16] In order to do this the analysis must contain (1) an empirically accurate description of the factual circumstances surrounding the action and (2) an understanding of the norms and values operating in the cultural context to make the action "appropriate." Thus interpretive analysis is committed, by the internal logic of its method, to treating both facts and values as rationally comprehensible entities with specifiable public, intersubjective meanings.

Accounting for an action by reconstructing the practical reasoning it instantiates is particularly instructive when the action in question is atypical and for that reason especially puzzling. The fact that interpretive social science provides a way of comprehending these cases of what J. W. N. Watkins has called "imperfect rationality"[17] suggests one of the most important ways in which it can contribute to policy analysis. Policy analysis is often motivated in the first place by policy failures, and these failures, in turn, are usually a function of the fact that some significant actors did not respond as it was assumed they would. Ideally, a good policy analysis must identify these anomalous responses, explain them in some coherent way, and provide policymakers with more realistic expectations about the behavior of those with whom they must deal and to whom the policy will apply. The question of whether positivistic or intepretive social science provides a more useful basis for policy analysis is really the question of whether a deductive-nomological causal explanation/prediction or a reconstruction of processes of practical reasoning can most adequately perform these tasks. In many instances, at least, it seems clear that the latter is a more promising approach than the former. Indeed, the interpretive reconstruction of practical reasoning also seems to be closer to the kinds of political, psychological, and sociological judgments that policymakers and most experienced policy analysts actually make. Like so many *bourgeois gentilhommes* who speak prose without knowing it, policymakers think in interpretive social scientific terms without calling their thoughts by that name.[18]

The third basic feature of interpretive social science is that it stresses the notion of coherence in the explications it offers. Its aim is to demonstrate the interconnections among the various conventions that make up the cultural context within which actions take place and to show how the agent's intentions in any particular action are related to the overall pattern of projects and roles that make up his or her self-identity. In this respect as well the structure of an interpretive analysis differs from that typically found in positivistic social science. In the connections it looks for, positivistic social science moves from the specific to the general, the aim being to subsume particular events under general laws. In interpretive social science the analysis does not move up and down a ladder; it spins a web. That is, it seeks to place a particular event in an ever-widening network of relationships; it seeks to transform thin particularity into thick particularity.

From these methodological orientations follow three broader points about the practice of policy analysis as it would be construed by policy analysis as counsel. In the first place, interpretations are inherently value laden and essentially contestable. The evaluative criteria for selecting among competing interpretations are much more imprecise than those proposed in the positivistic conception of science and are more closely akin to the evaluative criteria operative in certain disciplines in the humanities. Also, success in interpretive social analysis depends heavily on the personal, intellectual characteristics of the analyst, his or her insight and creativity. Finally, interpretive social analysis is largely a rhetorical or persuasive medium. Literary, figurative, and stylistic considerations and skills play a much more important role in this genre than in positivistic social analysis. This will inevitably affect the dynamics of the interaction between the interpretive policy analyst and the policymaker and will require a reorientation in the latter's expectations and capabilities if the material supplied by the interpretive policy analyst is to be useful.

The sort of postpositivistic objectivity that the Counsel Model requires comes from the fact that the concepts and categories employed in social inquiry (or policy analysis) are "publicly available" concepts— that is, they are drawn from a common, intersubjectively meaningful set of cultural norms, traditional values, and serviceable commonsense understandings of what human beings need and how they react in various circumstances. As such no singular, regulative use of these concepts can be prescribed, but alternative uses of them—alternative interpretations—can be rationally debated and assessed. Social analysis that survives an open and undistorted process of collective deliberation can be said to be "objective" in the relevant sense. This sort of objectivity will not give policymakers an understanding of the policy options that is based on science, but it will give them one based on *phronesis*— prudence and practical rationality. And that is the understanding that policy analysts as counselors aim to provide.

THE PROFESSION AND
DEMOCRATIC PROMISE OF POLICY ANALYSIS

This brings us finally to the ethical profession that policy analysis as counsel offers for the practice of policy analysis, and its democratic implications. The Counsel Model maintains that policy analysis should strive for the kind of objectivity mentioned above; in so doing it will strive to fashion an interpretation of what the public interest requires that can survive a collective process of rational assessment and deliberation. No individual analyst's specific policy advice will achieve this fully, and hence it will represent only one of several plausible perspectives on the public interest. But though limited and essentially contestable in this way, each policy analysis or assessment will at least be a perspective on the public interest rather than a self-conscious articulation of some particularistic or group-specific interest. In this sense policy analysis as counsel offers a more acceptable ethical profession than policy analysis as advocacy and is more in keeping with an ethos of democratic citizenship that aspires to transcend the Madisonian liberal politics of self-interest. When policy analysis offers counsel rather than advocacy, when it involves an interpretation that self-consciously attempts to provide a perspective on the public interest that can withstand the test of rational public deliberation, then bringing a number of different policy analyses together in the process of policy formation and debate amounts to a process of adjudicating among multiple perspectives on the public interest and fashioning a policy on the basis of the complementary "fit" among these perspectives.

If this assessment of what professional policy analysis can achieve in principle is correct, then it seems that the ethical superiority of policy analysis as counsel over policy analysis as advocacy is clear. If the analyst can offer social knowledge that is objective or intersubjectively rational in the senses I have defined, then it seems *prima facie* wrong for him or her deliberately to articulate an interpretation of social reality and an assessment of policy options that are based on a more partial, interest-based perspective. This is not to say that individuals who are clearly designated to represent specific and narrow interests do not have a legitimate role to play in the policymaking process in order to ensure that the special interests of those affected by the policy are given a fair hearing. These individuals are accurately called lobbyists. But as public officials, policymakers (legislators and executive branch officials alike) clearly have an ethical responsibility to serve the broader public interest and not simply to serve as arbiters and brokers of the particularistic interests lobbyists represent.[19] Blurring the distinction between the policy analyst and the lobbyist—as the Advocate Model does—will undermine the policymaker's ability to discharge that responsibility. Thus it is important to retain some notion, as policy analysis as counsel does, of the special role of the analyst whose obligations parallel those of the policymaker. That is, the policy analyst should serve as an ethical enabling agent vis-à-vis the policymaker, one whose responsibility is to provide the policymaker with a perspective that transcends the particularistic perspectives offered by lobbyists or advocates.

An additional democratic implication of interpretive policy analysis is that it can lead to the formulation of new objectives and social goals for public policy and to a deeper, more sensitive comprehension of the sociological, cultural, and psychological ramifications of governmental actions. This promise grows not so much out of the epistemological or methodological aspects of the interpretive approach as out of its characteristic themes and emphases and, more fundamentally, out of its underlying conception of the nature of human beings. For interpretive social inquiry human beings are essentially makers of meaning; they are purposive agents who inhabit symbolically constituted cultural orders, who engage in rule-governed social practices, and whose self-identities are formed in those orders and through those practices. These are the reasons why the interpretive approach maintains that a social scientific explanation of human action must involve the placement of that action in its specific cultural context. And although it does not always come out explicitly in the work of interpretive social scientists, a certain ethical commitment is entailed by this underlying philosophical anthropology as well. In this view the well-being—indeed, the very personhood and humanness—of human beings depends on the integrity and coherence of these cultural orders and social practices; the structures of social life provide the context for moral agency and for human self-realization.

Here it is possible to discern some of the policy implications to which the characteristic themes of the interpretive approach might lead. With its stress on purposive agency and transformation of self-identity through practical activity, the interpretive approach would provide policy analysis with an impetus to investigate the effect that a given (or contemplated) policy had (or would have) on such things as the vitality of civic life in a particular area, opportunities for participation, the creation and preservation of neighborhood organizations, incentives for the establishment of cooperative projects of mutual aid, the encouragement of voluntary social service provision, and, finally, the delegation of authority and the distribution of decision-making power under the programs implemented by the policy. Similarly, given its stress on both the functional and the normative importance of stable social practices and cultural traditions (i.e., they provide a sense of meaning and belonging, the experience of which is an intrinsic human good), the interpretive approach would raise the question of a policy's effect on community and would take the fostering of community and the mitigation of alienation and anomie to be fundamentally legitimate and important policy considerations.

To be sure, the notions of decentralization, civic voluntarism, empowerment, and community are perennial concerns, but they have never played a central role in our thinking about public policy; often in the past they have been totally eclipsed by other values and considerations. The history of American political and social thought is composed of two major and largely antithetical traditions: (1) a dominant liberal, individualistic tradition that views society as a field of separate, conflicting interests and human beings as essentially egotistic monads caught up in a competitive struggle for material resources and personal gratification and (2) a communitarian tradition that stresses the organic linkages between the individual and society.[20] Many of the intellectual forerunners of contemporary interpretive social science were theorists who rejected the abstract individualism of nineteenth-century liberalism, and it seems clear that in the American context, interpretive policy analysis would occasion a revitalization of the older communitarian tradition.

If I am correct in maintaining that the interpretive approach is to be located broadly within the communitarian tradition, it seems clear that it will inevitably stand in some tension with liberalism on substantive grounds, in much the same way (and for many of the same reasons) that it conflicts with positivism on methodological grounds. What, then, are its ideological dimensions? I do not think that any unequivocal answer to this question can be given. Whether the import of interpretive policy analysis is "conservative" or "radical" depends, it seems to me, on empirical judgments about the viability and workings of particular cultural contexts at particular times. If an interpretive analysis shows that these contexts do, in fact, provide the conditions necessary for the genuine exercise of moral agency and meaningful sociality, then its policy implications will be conservative in the sense that, like Burke, it will counsel a respect for those "little platoons" of community life. But there is no reason a priori why an interpretive analysis must show this. To be sure, interpretive policy analysis will look for coherence in the situations it studies and will insist upon the proposition that no human situation is devoid of agency and meaning, but this does not preclude its offering a critique of existing social structures and the effects of previous or proposed social policies.

A third democratic promise of interpretive policy analysis involves not the content or goals of policy but the process by which policy decisions are made and implemented. The characteristic concerns and perspectives of interpretive policy analysis would inject a new kind of style or ethos into the policy-making process. Let me try to spell out more fully what I mean by this. It has frequently been argued, persuasively I think, that positivistic policy analysis and highly bureaucratic and rationalistic forms of public administration tend mutually to reinforce one another.[21] There is a symbiotic relationship between a mode of social scientific explanation that defines human agents as objects whose behavior is determined by causal forces and a form of governance that relies on the instrumental manipulation of those forces for the achievement of social objectives and the maintenance of social order.

If the practice of policy analysis were to conform to the regulative ideal of policy analysis as counsel, policy analysts would take it to be their professional responsibility to enable policymakers to look in different ways at the nature of the social problems they have to address and to be more democratically responsive in conducting their political and administrative activities. The reasons for this are pragmatic rather than simply moral or ideological.

If there is one dominant leitmotif of interpretive social inquiry, it is this: Human beings are self-monitoring and self-directing agents who invariably seek to pursue life plans that they find subjectively meaningful. From this conception of the human being as an active, self-interpretive being, it follows that if the incentives used by a given policy to restructure activity in a certain way are to function as the policymaker intends, these incentives will have to be construed by the individuals toward whom they are directed as an integral part of their own sense of meaningful self-identity. If these incentives are not so construed, if they are perceived as alien constraints externally imposed, experience shows that they will be resisted and subverted in various ways so that either the policy will not have its intended effect or an unacceptable and impractical degree of coercion will have to be used to achieve the desired restructuring of activity. The question then becomes how to facilitate this acceptance and internalization of policy incentives. The answer, again implied by the interpretive social science perspective, is that the individuals toward whom the policy is directed must be actively brought into the deliberative process in which the goals and values of the policy are formulated; they must come to understand the connection between these goals and the incentives they are being asked to accept.

Assuming that one effect of interpretive policy analysis would be to get policymakers to see their situation in something like these terms, I think it is reasonable to conclude that interpretive social science would tend to reorient the style and ethos of governance so that the relationship between policymakers and citizens would take a more participatory or dialogic form.

The notion of policy analysis as counsel provides a value orientation and a civic commitment that the practice of policy analysis can still profess, even in a chastened, postpositivistic season.

NOTES

1. On the growth of policy analysis see the special section on the "Policy Analysis Explosion," *Society* 16 (September/October 1979): 9-51. For interesting but uneven efforts to develop a theory of policy analysis see Aaron Wildavsky, *Speaking Truth to Power: The Art and Craft of Policy Analysis* (Boston: Little, Brown, 1979) and Martin Krieger, *Advice and Planning* (Philadelphia: Temple University Press, 1981).

2. See Edith Stokey and Richard Zeckhauser, *A Primer for Policy Analysis* (New York: W. W. Norton, 1978).

3. For discussions of the concept of a practice, see Richard E. Flathman, *The Practice of Rights* (Cambridge: Cambridge University Press, 1976), 1-10; and Alasdair MacIntyre, *After Virtue* (Notre Dame, In: University of Notre Dame Press, 1981), 175-189.

4. This case is adapted from Philip Taubman, "Analyst Reportedly Left CIA in a Clash with Casey on Mexico," *New York Times* (September 28, 1984).

5. I have glossed over otherwise significant differences between nineteenth-century positivism and the later, more specific philosophical schools of logical positivism and logical empiricism because a more fine-grained account is not necessary for my general purposes here. On the influence of positivism see Maurice Mandelbaum, *History, Man and Reason: A Study of Nineteenth Century Thought* (Baltimore: Johns Hopkins University Press, 1971); and Anthony Giddens, "Positivism and Its Critics," in *Studies in Social and Political Theory* (New York: Basic Books, 1977), 29-88. For a technical discussion of recent critiques of positivism, see Frederick Suppe, ed., *The Structure of Scientific Theories*, 2nd ed. (Urbana: University of Illinois Press, 1977), 3-241, 617-730.

6. See E. A. Burtt, *The Metaphysical Foundations of Modern Science*, rev. ed. (Garden City, NY: Doubleday, 1954); and Charles Taylor, *Hegel* (Cambridge: Cambridge University Press, 1975), 3-50.

7. For further discussion of the engineering model and others, see James S. Coleman, *Policy Research in the Social Sciences* (Morristown, NJ: General Learning Press, 1972); and Alvin W. Gouldner, "Theoretical Requirements for the Applied Social Sciences," *American Sociological Review* 22 (February 1957): 92-102.

8. See C. K. Leman and R. H. Nelson "Ten Commandments for Policy Economists," *Journal of Policy Analysis and Management* 1, 1 (Fall 1981): 97-117; J. M. B. Fraatz, "Policy Analysts as Advocates," *Journal of Policy Analysis and Management* 1, 2 (Winter 1982): 273-276; and John L. Foster, "An Advocate Role Model for Policy Analysis," *Policy Studies Journal* 8, 6, (Summer 1980): 958-964. Although little has been written on the advocate role in general, it is often endorsed in the context of discussions of specific policy areas. See, for example, H. Folk, "The Role of Technology Assessment in Public Policy," in A. Teich, ed., *Technology and Man's Future* (New York: St. Martin's Press, 1972), 246-254.

9. Sheldon S. Wolin, "The American Pluralist Conception of Politics," in Arthur L. Caplan and Daniel Callahan, eds., *Ethics in Hard Times* (New York: Plenum, 1981), 217-259.

10. Mark H. Moore, "Statesmanship in a World of Particular Substantive Choices," in Robert A. Goldwin, ed., *Bureaucrats, Policy Analysts, Statesmen: Who Leads?* (Washington, DC: American Enterprise Institute, 1980), 26-27.

11. I have discussed these issues at more length in "Interpretive Social Science and Policy Analysis," in Daniel Callahan and Bruce Jennings, eds., *Ethics, the Social Sciences,*

and Policy Analysis (New York: Plenum, 1983), 3-36, from which some of the discussion in the last two sections of this essay is drawn.

12. See Clifford Geertz, "Blurred Genres: The Refiguration of Social Thought," *The American Scholar* 49 (Spring 1980): 165-179.

13. See Carol H. Weiss, "Ideology, Interests, and Information: The Basis of Policy Positions," in Callahan and Jennings, *Ethics, the Social Sciences, and Policy Analysis*, pp. 213-145; and Martin Rein, "Value Critical Policy Analysis," in ibid, pp. 83-112.

14. See Paul Rabinow, *Reflections on Fieldwork in Morocco* (Berkeley: University of California Press, 1977); and Hilary Putnam, *Reason Truth, and History* (Cambridge: Cambridge University Press, 1981).

15. Richard J. Bernstein, *Beyond Objectivism and Relativism* (Philadelphia: University of Pennsylvania Press, 1982).

16. See George H. von Wright, *Explanation and Understanding* (Ithaca, NY: Cornell University Press, 1971); and Charles Taylor, "The Explanation of Purposive Behavior," in Robert Berger and Frank Cioffi, eds., *Explanation in the Behavioral Sciences*, (Cambridge: Cambridge University Press, 1970), 49-79.

17. J. W. N. Watkins, "Imperfect Rationality," in Berger and Cioffi, *Explanation in the Social Sciences,* pp. 167-217.

18. See Charles E. Lindblom and David K. Cohen, *Usable Knowledge: Social Science and Social Problem Solving* (New Haven: Yale University Press, 1979); and Wildavsky, *Speaking Truth to Power*, pp. 1-19, 109-141, 385-406.

19. For an extended treatment of the ethical responsibilities of public officials and their public trust, see The Hastings Center, *The Ethics of Legislative Life* (Hastings-on-Hudson, NY: The Hastings Center, 1985).

20. See David E. Price, *The "Quest for Community" and Public Policy* (Bloomington, In: The Poynter Center, 1977).

21. Laurence H. Tribe, "Policy Science: Analysis or Ideology," *Philosophy and Public Affairs* 2 (Fall 1972): 66-110.

6

ANTICIPATING IMPLEMENTATION: NORMATIVE PRACTICES IN PLANNING AND POLICY ANALYSIS

JOHN FORESTER
Cornell University

What do planning and policy analysts do? What must they know to do their work well? What strategic and normative judgments must they routinely make? This essay seeks to answer these questions by empirically assessing the practice of a city planning analyst at work. Presenting a quasi-ethnographic account, this essay assumes that the practical problems that city planners and policy analysts share may far exceed those that distinguish them.[1] Despite their differences, policy analysts and city planners alike may learn about the opportunities and requirements of their practice by assessing an example of a metropolitan planner's work in some detail.

The argument proceeds as follows. The first section presents a partial transcript of a working meeting in which a city planner in New England

Author's Note: *For comments on earlier drafts, thanks to Simon Neustein, Frank Fischer, Lawrence Susskind, Aaron Fleischer, Alan Mandell, and Rick T. I am especially indebted to Lloyd Rodwin for prompting me to expore further the difference between analysts' work of "prediction" and practical "anticipation."*

begins the process of "project review." Listening to a real estate developer's proposal to put two office buildings on a large parcel near a major arterial street, the planner does much more than record the developer's intentions or the project's specifications. The second section proposes a way to understand the richness of what in this case the planner actually does. Facing a complex environment and an uncertain future, the analyst needs less to predict and evaluate project consequences than *pratically to anticipate* possible implemented outcomes and respond accordingly, taking steps early on not only to foresee potential consequences but to shape them as well. This work is inescapably normative; but how is it to be done?

Section three explores the structure of such practical anticipatory analysis and its requirements. Notice here that ordinary language suggests that "to anticipate" and "to expect" do share meanings but that they diverge as well. Fowler points out the distinctiveness of anticipation by telling us that "to anticipate a crisis" (or a project, a policy) is not simply to foresee or expect it but to *take steps beforehand* to meet it.[2] But how is this possible in analysts' practice? Before steps can be taken to deal with potential outcomes, strategies must be prepared. And surely before strategies of action and analysis can be organized, possible implemented futures must first be imagined. What are the practical requirements to do this work?

The third section seeks to answer these questions in two ways. First, it shows what types of working theories analysts must have if they are to envision (a) policy or project consequences, (b) the normative and political world in which implementation is to occur, and (c) the interorganizational world of actors who must be involved for project review, analysis, and implementation to proceed. Second, the section assesses the necessity for analysts to be strategic managers of arguments within the decision-making process. A brief recapitulation of the argument as a whole brings the essay to a close.

THE TRANSCRIPT:
INITIAL PROPOSAL AND PLANNING ANALYSIS

Consider a local urban development case. Tom Johnson is in his early 30s; he has moved to the Planning Department after spending ten years in the city's Community Development Office. Gerald Sullivan is in his mid-50s, a ruddy-faced real estate developer. He proposes to tear down an existing warehouse and erect two office towers in its place. The existing parking lot would remain, drainage would be maintained, and landscaping would be provided.

Developer Sullivan and his engineer, Bert James, have come to Planning Director Johnson's office for advice. Next they will apply for a building permit; then they will go before the city's Planning Board for a decision about any special conditions that may need to be attached to the permit. On paper the process is straightforward: Johnson will write up an analysis of the project. He will submit it to the Planning Board, which will decide about conditions to attach to Sullivan's permit.

The Planning Board, however, may or may not read Johnson's analysis and may or may not care much if they do, Johnson's recent experience suggests. "Powerful" is not an adjective that Johnson would use to describe his distinctly advisory role in the decision-making process. Decisions are made by the Planning Board—even though the board may not be inclined, with their pro-growth sentiments, to attach any impact-mitigating conditions to the requested building permit. Consider the case.

After initial greetings and a reference to their prior telephone conversation, Sullivan says to Johnson, "We wanted to review the city's criteria with you, to look at the process, to get your advice about whether we're going in the right direction or not." This sounds quite cooperative and even deferential, but at the end of the conversation to follow, Sullivan will surprise Johnson with, "Well, we'd like to submit the plans next week . . ." Such surprises notwithstanding, the developer and planner are friendly, cooperative, and attentive to each other. They are wary of each other too, though, keenly aware of the potentially adversarial relationship between them.

By looking closely at how this meeting progresses, we can study planning analysis not simply as the frozen content of a static document (Johnson's recommendations to the Planning Board) but as actual practice. We can assess what the planning analyst really does when faced with the developer's proposal. From the meeting transcript we can assess a range of practical judgments that the analyst must make. We can explore quite concretely what the planner's analysis involves. In particular, it will be important to notice how much the planner does *before* presenting "an analysis" to the relevant decision makers. The meeting continues:

Planning Analyst: What's your timetable?

Developer: We'd like to break ground next fall with the first phase. All together there'll be half a million square feet of office space.

PA: Ok, how about showing us what you've got?

D: Let me introduce Bert, our engineer. He'll show you what we have.

Engineer: Yes, these plans are very incomplete, but they'll let us get started. They're at 40 scale; do you need 20?

PA: The Planning Board can waive that; it looks like it'll all fit at 40.

E: (Pausing over the site plan) Do we need a separate application for the parking lot?

PA: No, since the new ordinance was passed, the forms haven't been done yet.

D: The new review process supersedes the old parking application, but not the traffic review, right?

PA: Right.

PA: (Looking at the plans) The only thing missing is the indication of the existing buildings nearby. . .

D: Let's write that down (as much to himself as to Bert)

PA: The way most people do that is by taking the assessor's plans. . .

D: As far as this is concerned, should this include existing or proposed buildings as well?

PA: Proposed as well.

E: (Motioning over the site plan) So this is the site. This shows the amount of paving, and the coverage by the buildings. We'll be reducing the present footprint. We'll have data on this with the new stats about footprint area, amount of landscaping, . . .

PA: (nods at each point)

E: . . . and the plans for the drainage—we propose maintaining the existing outlets . . .

E: So let's go on to the parking. This pavement would be maintained; the existing access would remain; we show two loading docks here—the Zoning by-laws say that's required, . . . 12 by 25, right?

PA: Right. (Then, moving from the question of access to the broader transportation issues) Do you know about what the state is doing with the Route 3 improvements nearby?

D: What are they doing? Can you brief us?

Here the planning analyst describes the three phases of the road improvement project that the state has initiated near the developer's site. Phase 1 is 100 % designed and due to begin construction in the coming year. Phase 2 is 75% designed, but Phase 3 is hardly on the drawing boards. Even with these improvements, though, the large intersection close to the site will still rate an "F" (over capacity at peak periods) on the state's rating system—it will have improved from 160% (over) capacity to "only" 110% (over) capacity after the Phase 1 improvements are made. Getting this intersection below 100% capacity would require a major commitment of funding that no jurisdiction was willing to consider.

D: I've never heard of an "F." What about Phase 3's schedule?

PA: Depends on Phase 2. By the way, do you know about [the regional shopping center's] plans?

D: No. (Wondering again what information the planner might have)

PA: They'll impact the transportation situation in a couple of ways, but if you stick to your timetable you'll be in the ground long before they make their changes; they have lots of environmental problems.

E: (Joking) We don't have any runoff problems, it's all paved! (They all laugh) So let's get back to the plans here . . .

They go on to review the parking layouts, required dimensions, and the way the plans should look to be reviewed by the Planning Board.

PA: (Pointing to the edge of the site) Is this going to be the principal access?

D: Yes, (He explains that the other entrance would be used less frequently; it lies at a steeper grade but will be altered too. The engineer continues to present plans for drainage and landscaping.)

E: (Probing) We haven't seen any problem with drainage in that area (right?)
PA: Not in that area, no.

After this initial review of the site, the conversation turned to the review process itself. The developer and engineer went item by item through the steps listed as recommended or required in the city's documents describing the project review process.

E: On this Development Impact Statement—we're ready to go to the state for a new driveway . . .

PA: A curb cut permit, yes.

D: The impact statement seems to cover air, water, traffic on the site. How deep do we really have to go into all this?

PA: Let's take it one by one. On traffic it should be a full-blown analysis. This is like what you'd do under NEPA.

D: Oh, don't give me those monograms—or whatever they are! (He then laughs at what he's said)

PA: For environmental impact assessments, what we've accepted before is a short narrative, or even an outline—unless you think there's a real problem. For example, because of that intersection, you'll probably need an air quality study for the state; so when you file it with them, just give it to us too.

PA: (Moving through the other items to be considered in the application process) Talk to Joe Hart, the Director of Public Works, and make sure that he understands what you're going to do with the sewers and all . . .

PA: (Continuing with more general advice) Talk to anyone who has jurisdiction beforehand—Public Works is just one who will be reviewing this.

PA: (Turning to the question of fiscal impacts noted in the city's documents) A statement of fiscal impacts is recommended, not required . . . there are standard methods for calculating them; 1 can give you an example if you want.

E: I'd appreciate that. (Taking prodigious notes all the while)

PA: (After discussing other possible impacts) Do you know about the [regional planning association's] Growth Impact Study?

D: No. Are they part of the state?

PA: No, they're an organization of several of the municipalities here, without formal authority, but you might review their study . . .

D: How do we get it?

PA: Talk to Jeanne Wall on their staff.

E: Who else gets all these plans for review?

PA: (The planner lists several other city departments)

E: Would it behoove us to meet with all of these departments?

PA: Yes, especially with the City Hall departments.

D: After we've filed the plans?

PA: Better before, so you can incorporate their comments into your plans; we can set up a meeting and do it all together.

D: Is that a new process here?

PA: No, it depends on the size of the project and the site; we like to encourage it . . .

D: Well, that would really help—it could save several weeks. That's super; if we had to go to each one of them alone [it could get all tangled up]. So we go through you to do this?

PA: Yes, we'll try to set it up; we'll need a couple of weeks probably.

D: Well, we'd like to submit the plans next week . . .then let's meet with all the Departments. (Surprising the planner)

PA: Ok, sure, but the Planning Board won't want to schedule a hearing on this without hearing from the other departments . . .

E: (Drawing the obvious implication) So it'd be good to meet all together earlier.

PA: Yes.

This meeting continued to cover other questions of project consequences, relevant officials for the developer's team to contact, and requirements imposed by the city upon new developments of substantial scale. At the end of this project review session, it was not clear either when the developer would formally file his plans, how those plans might yet change, or just what analysis and recommendation(s) the planning analyst would forward to the formal decision makers, the Planning Board.

If Sullivan really intended to file his current plans for the project "next week," had this whole meeting been pointless, an empty ritual? Hardly, for three months later the plans had still not been filed. "Why?" the author asked Sullivan. "Well," he said, "the city changed the law on us. We're taking the new Site Plan Review process into account now; in another month or so, we'll file." In fact, the "new" site plan review procedure had been adopted by the City Council five months earlier but Sullivan apparently—and significantly—had only realized this in the course of meeting with Planning Director Johnson. Even so, that review procedure could be satisfied in a wide variety of ways, as Johnson knew only too well and regretted. It seemed to Johnson that Sullivan would try to push ahead quickly, but to Johnson's surprise once more, Sullivan did not.

This suggests that not only are project consequences uncertain, but the various elements of the review, decision making, and implementation process can be uncertain too. As we shall see, the work of analysis calls for attention both to "the project" and to the practicalities of "the process." Consider, on the basis of this transcript, just what the planning analyst has actually been doing in this case.

ANALYSIS:
ANTICIPATING IMPLEMENTATION (AND RESPONDING)

Notice first what the planning analyst is obviously not doing in this case. He is not solving a technical problem as an engineer or a statistician. He does not gather data with a formula or a set of equations ready at hand with which to generate an answer or a solution. Indeed, before the planner can think about solving anything, he needs first to find out—or, better, to formulate—what the problems might be.

Notice second that the planner is not simply trying to *predict* project consequences. Beyond attempting to forecast project impacts, the planning analyst actually calls the developer's attention to other actors' plans—to those of the state and of a nearby shopping center that may affect the current proposal. Here the analyst is indeed looking ahead to possible outcomes, but for the purpose of changing—potentially improving—the developer's proposal in light of shifting environmental and economic conditions. What the planner is doing in this case, then, is neither solving a technical problem nor simply predicting and evaluating the consequences of a proposal; the planner, rather, is working to *anticipate and respond* to future implementation possibilities—in which versions of the presently proposed project would actually be on the ground, implemented, inhabited, socially and functionally interdependent with the surrounding land, community, and organized public and private bodies. To anticipate and respond to development possibilities, the planning analyst must think politically as well as technically, probe political questions as well as functional ones, seek to learn not only about consequences but also about what is consequential and to learn not only about impacts but also about a wide range of political and community concerns. But how is such a practical anticipation possible?

The planner does not equate the problem at hand with the project or the site alone. He works both to find out what the developer is proposing and to construct a sense of the overall project context. He asks questions about the current proposal, and he suggests that the developer find out about both the state's plans to improve local traffic conditions and another developer's plans to enlarge a nearby shopping center—an expansion that could well affect the present project. The planner here tries to envision the developer's site as proposed but in conjunction with the developing physical and socioeconomic *context* encompassing it.

The planner places the proposal in institutional space as well as in geographic space, so he tells the developer about the growth impact study of the regional planning body, about the jurisdiction of other city agencies, and about the standard procedures of the planning board, which "won't want to schedule a meeting without hearing from the other departments." Surveying the institutional world that the project proponent must yet navigate, the planner can suggest, for example, what the Planning Board may waive—and what they might not waive.

Placing the project in institutional space, the planning analyst anticipates the official concerns that other agencies and public bodies are likely to have with traffic, air quality, water quality, and adjoining properties, and he acts beforehand to try to persuade the developer to address those concerns. So he recommends a "full-blown study" on traffic impacts, a study on air quality (that the state, he predicts, will likely require anyway), the inclusion of existing buildings near the site when the plans are to be forwarded to the Planning Board, and so on. Similarly, the planner anticipates the mandates, the official interests of other city departments, and he acts to respond to them. Therefore he encourages the developer, for example, to meet with the relevant city departments before filing plans, so that the plans to go before the decision-making bodies can incorporate the comments of the departments' staff reviewers.

Besides placing the proposal in its functional and institutional contexts, the planner also addresses questions of the relevant actors to be consulted or taken-into account. Notice that "Talk to Joe Hart . . . and make sure he understands what you're going to do" is politically and practically a piece of advice very different from "satisfy the standards of the Department of Public Works." In a similar way, without naming names or specifying a formal rule, the planner anticipates the Planning Board's reticence to act on a project without having letters of review from certain city departments. Here the planning analyst provides the developer with a practical analysis not of institutional rules or procedures but of the operative political *culture* animating the relevant institutions that will determine the proposal's future. The planner provides information not only about formal rules but about the informal ways in which such rules may be applied, interpreted, or waived by significant actors in the project review process: decision makers or "influentials."

At a basic level, then, the planning analyst listens to the developer and his engineer and seeks tentatively to answer three questions: What are the important *facts* about what's being proposed? What mandates, procedures, rules, and *official requirements* are relevant? And *who* are the actors that need to be involved; which particular social *relationships* count here? Because these three questions raise quite different concerns, I will consider at greater length how planning and policy analysts might pursue these issues in practice as they anticipate possible project or policy implementation.

Notice that the planner in this case acts more like a practical participant, anticipating future implementation and seeking to shape it, than like a disengaged observer or spectator looking ahead to problematic consequences, violated standards, or disgruntled actors. The planner wants to make a difference, not just to make an analytical argument (as essential as that is). What does he do?

First, the planner provides counsel about the navigation of the application process (e.g., "the Planning Board can waive" the scale requirement). Second, the planner helps the developer to prepare (and perhaps improve) the project proposal by suggesting tools to use ("most people do that by using the assessor's plans"). Third, the planner shares his knowledge of contextual changes with the developer to allow or even to encourage the developer to fit the proposed project more appropriately (if perhaps opportunistically as well) into its physical, functional, and social contexts (thus the planner describes the state's road improvement plans and the plan of the nearby shopping center). Fourth, the planner directs the developer's attention to real problems, to the critical issues (not drainage but traffic, air quality, and perhaps fiscal impacts as well). Fifth, the planner refers the developer to other agencies and actors whose "comments" about the proposal may be important— to the developer or to the planner and Planning Board. Sixth, the planner manages the review process; he details and interprets requirements, suggests particular staff to contact, proposes a follow-up meeting with the other departments, and generally organizes the tasks to be performed before the proposal is to be decided upon (in this case first by the Planning Board).

What ties these six activities together? Throughout, the planner seeks not so much to make an argument about the proposal but to *manage the process of argumentation* concerning it. The planner is concerned both with getting the developer's proposal in shape and up-to-date and with attending to the arguments ("comments," "concerns," "feedback") of other agencies, actors, and departments whose word(s) will make a difference. Indeed at the early stages of project review the analyst is more attentive to managing the process of argumentation than to formulating his own argument (the "analysis," "report," or "recommendations"). Seeking to manage these arguments is no act of altruism, for only by doing so can the planner in turn get sufficient information for his own "analysis" to be sent to the Planning Board and ultimately, perhaps, to other decision makers as well, such as the Zoning Board of Appeals.

Thus the work of analysis involves far more than performing calculations and writing the analysis; it requires not only the work of making reasonable judgments about likely futures but the prior work of attending to and indeed shaping a range of other actors' arguments and "inputs" to the process. In the meeting that the transcript reflects, notice that the analyst's attention was focused first on the proposal, the site and its environment, then on a range of other actors whose comments might be relevant, and only then on the actual moment of decision before the Planning Board.

THE STRUCTURE OF ANTICIPATORY ANALYSIS

The planning analyst, then, is involved in at least three phases of anticipatory analysis. First, the analyst must *envision* possible futures of the (implemented) project in its physical, institutional, and cultural contexts. Second, the analyst must *prepare and manage* arguments both supporting the proposal (the analyst thus seems to assist the developer) and seeking to modify the proposal (the analyst thus sets the stage for the comments of the Public Works director and others). Third, the analyst must seek effectively to *present* (and perhaps *negotiate* with) his or her own formal analysis of a final proposal and alternatives to it. Within the limited space of the present chapter, we consider only the first two, if the most neglected, phases of analytical practice.[3]

If analysis involves these three components (envisioning, managing, and presenting), notice that neither of the images of "technical problem-solving" or "prediction and evaluation" captures adequately what analysts actually do. The work of planning and policy analysis can no longer be narrowly equated with the calculation and presentation of results. Instead, this empirical, micropolitical look at an analyst's practice suggests a different understanding of what planning analysis and, by extension, policy analysis really involves.

Planning and policy analysis can be understood not solely as the work of calculation but as the *practical anticipation of potential project (or policy) implementation*. Analysts must thus in part formulate the very problems that they face; prepare, solicit, and manage the arguments evaluating those problems; and then present synthetic arguments (an analysis) proposing one or more courses of action. Before an analysis is *presented* it must be *prepared,* its complex and potentially conflicting components *managed;* but before its component arguments can be prepared and managed, the scope of the project (natural, social, political-economic) must be first *envisioned.* How is this envisioning possible? Consider each requirement in turn.

ENVISIONING POSSIBLE IMPLEMENTATION: IMPLICATIONS FOR PROBLEM FORMULATIONS— ANALYSTS ARE PRACTICAL THEORISTS

This analysis extends and refines the familiar argument that in planning and policy analysis problems must be formulated before they are solved.[4] Consider what distinguishes the planning or policy analyst's formulation of a new growth policy, for example, from that of a social scientist or a journalist interested in the same problem. The social scientist typically wishes to explain behavior and so looks for a causal account, or wishes to understand action and so looks for an interpretive account. The journalist typically seeks to report the facts, perhaps to comment upon them as well. What distinguishes the planning analyst's formulation of the same proposal is its character of practical anticipation and response. The planning or policy analyst is engaged with a prospective project; the analyst must not only present the facts of what may happen, not only interpret and explain what is likely, but he or she must try to respond practically to anticipated problems and so seek directly to influence, alter, and shape what will happen.

Thus, paradoxically, an influential planning or policy report might anticipate a transportation problem *and* prevent the problem from ever occurring. Notice that this can make success quite difficult to show: How does one measure something that never happened? Showing what a project or policy does (housing units or inoculations or jobs provided or regulated) can be difficult enough; showing the (nonexistent?) problem that has been averted is far more difficult. The planning analyst needs to be as interested in what should not be as in what should be, in what will never exist as in what does or will exist. For the analyst the *anticipated world,* including potential problems to be prevented, is every bit as real as the existing observable world—even though, if the analyst succeeds, this potentially problematic world might never exist! No wonder these professions have been difficult to define: They are as much about preventing worlds as they are about creating them—but what is prevented does not exist, cannot be observed, is difficult to measure, and is perhaps still more difficult to appreciate!

The planning or policy analyst's work may nevertheless affect proposals by refining them before decisions are made, influencing the decisions about them, or affecting the conditions ("mitigation measures," "contingent contracts," etc.) that may attach to implementation. The analyst must respond to the problems that he or she can envision *were* the project at hand to be implemented. This work of anticipating problems—envisioning hypothetical futures and responding to fashion desirable ones—is interventionist through and through.

Such analysis is far from conventionally technical or rule-bound; it appears instead to involve an intimate mixture of descriptive and normative elements. Problem-formulation was always understood to be a value-laden, selectively descriptive activity, but now we are in a position to understand that problem formulation is not just arbitrarily but rather *systematically normative*. The work of analysts' anticipation of implementation and response requires that a series of normative choices be made. In addition, as we shall see, the work of planning and policy analysis is inescapably and practically theoretical—for without a range of substantive theories, the analyst could never (1) envision future implementation situations and their consequences, (2) prepare and manage the arguments exploring implementation alternatives, or (3) present either a cogent analysis of several alternatives or a recommendation specifying "what ought to be done."

Consider briefly, then, the theoretical competence that the planning analyst in our case must have to envision and shape the future as he listens to the developer and engineer present their plans.[5] He works from experience, to be sure, but from the experience of what? How does he learn from that experience and draw implications prospectively about this particular project? Facing a new and arguably unique situation, the analyst must use the rough theories he has. Three types of theories come into play: behavioral or functional, normative, and moral-cultural.

Behavioral Theorizing

Imagining the site in question, the analyst sees that drainage has been adequate, that the paving on the site will not expand, and that the building footprint will shrink. Without further changes, he infers, the existing drainage system should work and present no new problems.

Traffic is a different matter. The road system in the surrounding area is already overstressed; this project will only add to these problems by requiring employee trips to and from work, unless a strategy can be devised to reduce such peak-period trips through use of carpools, vanpools, staggered work hours, and so on. The projection of 500,000 sq. ft. of office space translates silently into numbers of likely employees and then numbers of trips to work generated daily. The planning analyst easily predicts aggravated traffic congestion, and so he moves directly to call for a full-blown traffic impact study.

To envision such functional problems at the site, then, the analyst relies in this meeting on relatively simple physical and behavioral theories: a change in paving will change drainage requirements; an increase in office space will generate jobs that will in turn generate traffic in the immediate vicinity (whether the increase in jobs is net to the region or not). Through further studies the analyst can explore and begin to specify these problems and then suggest solutions or mitigation measures; but first the planner needs basic behavioral theories—if only rules of thumb—to begin to envision and imagine the problems that will need further attention.

Normative Theorizing

Yet the analyst's basic behavioral theories only help when they are joined with the normative political theories that he brings to bear on the case. In this meeting he interprets and formulates a whole series of requirements, obligations, and needs that he asks the developer to respect: The Planning Board may waive a procedural requirement but they may not consider it proper to review the full proposal before considering the evaluations of other city departments; the applicant should "talk to anyone who has jurisdiction beforehand"; the developer is encouraged to review the study of the regional planning association; he is assured that the air quality study done for the state will be good enough for the city; and so forth. Here the planning analyst uses elements of quite practical normative theory: He recognizes discretion and not just the "letter" of the regulations; he points to the normative (not just functional) interdependence of the Planning Board and the city departments, and he thus invokes the legitimacy of the departments' reviews; he invokes the legitimate authority of "anyone who has jurisdiction" and encourages the developer to seek them out early, or risk surprise, the normative arguments we call "opposition," and subsequent delays; he appeals to the legitimacy of the regional planning associations's concerns (without making an argument to take those concerns seriously).

The analyst's normative political theorizing here is also conspicuous for what it lacks: He makes no mention of a broader public, or of active citizens' groups concerned with regional growth, or of the strongly pro-growth attitudes of the Planning Board itself. Given those latter attitudes, the analyst's silence on this point reflects part of a deliberate political strategy: to push the project toward as much analysis of potential impacts as possible in the hope that other actors' arguments for mitigation measures might then arise. For lacking that, the Planning Board might just pass the project along with its blessing, leaving future city residents to pay for its neglect. The analyst's silence about the decision makers' real attitudes, then, reflects a normative political theory and a series of calculated judgments about the limited power and lack of legitimacy of certain official bodies, and the proper ethical and professional role of a planning analyst.[6]

The point here is neither that the analyst is right to make these judgments in this case or that his performance is exemplary. The point, rather, is that such normative judgments, and more fundamental normative political theories, are *necessary* to planning and policy analysis practice at the level of *detail,* not simply at the level of broad generalities and homilies pledging allegiance or resistance to democratic capitalist regimes.

The still stronger point to be made is this: In the existing literature discussing planning and policy analysis, little seems to be known about the day-to-day work of analysts, and still less seems to be known about the variety of normative judgments they must perpetually make, the normative political theories of all sorts they employ to make and defend such judgments, the ways in which such judgments might be *rationally* criticized and refined, and the ways in which such normative theories might also be criticized and improved.[7] Can practitioners, researchers, teachers, and students afford to continue to ignore these questions, pay them lip-service as barely discussable value judgments, and suppose that in the thoroughly evaluative professions of planning and policy analysis the work of valuation must then be either strictly utilitarian or irrational?

The simple case discussed here suffices to show both that analysts need normative theories to make the judgments necessary to do their work, and that those judgments are poorly rendered as utilitarian. The planning analyst in our example makes arguments and gives reasons; only in a trivial sense is he calculating benefits and costs and reporting the results.

Cultural Theorizing

In addition the analyst in our case brings to bear practical cultural theories that he has tacitly developed in the course of building and maintaining working relationships with many others over the years. He knows that Joe Hart at Public Works is someone who will want to be consulted early on. He knows that Jeanne Wall of the regional planning body hopes to be helpful in such cases. He knows that different participants in the planning process have different values and concerns: The developer may be interested in trading design improvements for assurances of speedy review; the majority of the Planning Board may be interested only in growth; and so on.

The analyst's cultural theories that come into play focus attention upon the webs of local political culture and morality in which the planner operates; these are working theories of political culture and morality writ small, not large. The analyst's practical theorizing concerns particular people's personal identity and reputations, their concerns, interests, sensitivities, quirks, and biases, any special characteristics of people (e.g., having fought past turf battles) with whom the developer and analyst alike might work. Will last year's Planning Board scandal lead anyone to be more conscientious this year? Will Peabody push for more information when Tuttle wants simply to approve the works, or will Peabody just shrug and defer again? Practical cultural and moral theories allow analysts not just to fantasize but to imagine ahead of time what it might be like to work with particular people in a wide range of possible situations.

In every meeting that a planning or policy analyst has with others, such practical theories of identity, culture and morality, come into play as the analyst must make judgments about the likely candor, duplicity, support, reliability, cooperation, opposition, interests, or commitments of other participants in the planning or policymaking process. Is it even possible to work with others and not have such questions arise? Planning analysts, then, need to gauge not only behavioral consequences of possible courses of action and the normative mandates and procedures shaping possible alternatives, but also the realistic character and identity of other participants in the planning and policy process.

Consider, then, the lessons to be derived about problem formulation from this case. What do analysts initially require to do their work before writing their reports—to anticipate and respond to the range of practical futures that can be envisioned? First, in order to envision consequences, analysts need behavioral theories. Second, in order to envision mandates, procedures, obligations, and their own legitimate roles, analysts need normative political theories. Third, in order to envision the character of those they must listen to, watch out for, and build durable working relationships with, analysts need cultural and moral theories of their institutional worlds.

Turn now to the second requirement of anticipatory analysis. After envisioning potential futures, analysts must prepare and manage arguments strategically.

MANAGING ARGUMENT STRATEGICALLY

Notice that as the analyst brings these three types of working theories into play, the analysis is just beginning. How are these practical theories to be built upon? How may analysts work to prepare the initially embryonic analysis, to *explore* the substantive grounds for the arguments to be made, and to *manage* the process of analysis and review? These questions of the preparatory or management aspects of analysis unfortunatey have been widely neglected. Two common academic views of analysis distract attention from what analysts actually do. Analysis has been considered either as a purely cognitive problem-solving activity or as one of structured social interaction.[8] The problem-solving view of analysis reduces the practice of analysts to essentially mental processes such as calculation (and guesswork); the interactionist view focuses upon processes such as voting or market exchange but so may ironically finesse the question of an individual analyst's practice altogether.[9]

Yet insightful alternatives stand out. Peter Szanton's book, *Not Well Advised,* for example, neglects political and normative questions that haunt policy analysis, but it shows the essential significance of the analyst's relationships to others with whom he or she must work.[10] Analyses must not only be thought, they must be argued. Then, as practical arguments, they must be managed in the form of strategies as well.

Notice how much the transcript shows us about what the planning analyst does. He asks, suggests, explains, checks, agrees, refers, warns, and promises. His words matter. Failing to respond, or responding inconsistently or too brusquely, he might be held responsible later—say, if the developer adds one such complaint to others in front of the Planning Board or the City Council. So the analyst chooses his words carefully. He seeks to be clear and responsive but also at other times not altogether clear—for very specific reasons—as we shall see. He does not want to be held to predictions (e.g., about timing) whose validity he cannot assure; he wants to promise cooperation but also to be professionally critical without being (overly) threatening. Thus in speaking the analyst is acting. His actions are "speech acts," actions that are not only purposive but more practically communicative, conveying meaning and shaping expectations as well.[11] What the analyst's communicative actions add up to are practical arguments. But what is the role of such arguments?

In this case the analyst manages practical arguments in several ways. He directs attention to issues (is this the principal access? Show the existing and proposed buildings . . .). He also manages the developer's perception of the review process: He makes an argument providing potential roles for representatives of the state, other planning bodies, local agencies and departments, and neighboring developers. The analyst manages arguments not only about participation but about the timing and sequence of the process. He recommends early reviews by other city departments, and he backs up that recommendation with the conjecture that the Planning Board will not move ahead until such reviews are completed. He suggests a process for the review, for the development of the project itself ("so you can incorporate comments"), and for the analysis that will follow. He suggests not only the joint review but a series of consultations—with Joe Hart, Jeanne Wall, and perhaps a representative of the neighboring shopping center. The analyst offers to provide an example of a fiscal impact analysis; he suggests, in effect, that the developer do the analysis (even if it is "recommended," not "required") rather than risk delay later should someone become concerned about the possible fiscal consequences of the project for the city. Here the analyst seeks to manage (and even perhaps to create) uncertainty: Is the risk of delay sufficient to get the developer to submit an analysis for public scrutiny? In sum, then, the analyst here manages arguments that direct attention to issues, shape participation and involvement by affected parties, gauge the timing of the process, and fit this project into the larger context of local and regional development as well.

Actions fit together into arguments. Arguments fit together—are managed—into larger pieces that we can call strategies. In this case the analyst's strategy in part is to involve other established bodies and focus their analytical attention upon this proposal before the Planning Board ever sees it. That strategy consists of a set of related arguments: "Check with the regional planners because they might help you do the impact analysis"; "Check with Joe Hart because he's central to the process"; "Traffic's a real problem here, so do a full blown impact study of it"; and so on. Perhaps, this analyst hopes, if other established city departments raise concerns about potential project impacts, the Planning Board might (have to) listen—something their pro-growth sentiments would likely prevent were the lone analyst to raise exactly the same concerns. Managing argument strategically here, then, the analyst seeks to enhance his own limited influence—and resist the Planning Board's pro-growth ideology as well.

Recall now the developer's move that surprised the planner: "Well, we'd like to submit the plans next week . . ." The planner's strategy in the meeting had been designed, of course, to forestall just such a quick submission that might push the project through. Three months later, it turned out, the developer had not yet submitted the plans; he was preparing the documents required by the public review process. "In another month or so," he then told the author, "we'll file . . ."

To assess and study analysts' strategies of working on project or policy proposals, then, we must study the arguments they fashion in *practice*. This means, of course, studying not simply the content of their arguments, *what* they claim, but the pragmatic force of their arguing, *how* they make persuasive arguments in real time. Studying arguments practically, in turn, will mean studying actions, the communicative actions of analysts in practice.[12] Understanding that actions may add up to arguments and that arguments can be managed as strategies should make vitally clear that "the social construction of policy and planning problems" is not simply a matter of academic sociological interest. This social or communicative construction of problems is deeply political, for it is necessarily selective, allocating attention and concern to some issues but not to others, shaping the agendas of consideration (and participation) for a range of actors and decision makers.

Analysts, then, must both argue and manage. Without an argument to consider, we have process without content. Without a strategically managed process, the most lucid and insightful analysis may be altogether ignored, produced too late to be useful, or manipulated for extraneous ends. Planning and policy analysts must thus learn not only to explore substantive issues, they must learn strategically and ethically to manage the process of analysis and public scrutiny as well.[13]

CONCLUSION

Several lessons can be derived from this consideration of a project review conversation between a real estate developer and a metropolitan city planning analyst. First, the work of the analyst is not simply to solve the problem at hand but to formulate initially just what the problem (traffic? scale?) might be. Second, the analyst wishes not merely to formulate the problem but to intervene to meet it ahead of time: to *anticipate* implementation and so respond to the particular opportunities and problems presented, by involving other city departments, for example.

Third, this work of anticipation has a logical structure. If analysts are to anticipate implemented projects or policy outcomes and seek to shape them, the analysts must do several things. They must envision the functional, normative, and cultural worlds in which proposed projects or policies will have meaning. They must then prepare and manage the arguments, and the process of argumentation, available to consider potential outcomes. In this process analysts might devise arguments as technicians just as they simultaneously manage those arguments strategically as political organizers. Analysts might then present their analyses to decision makers.

Fourth, to anticipate project implementation, analysts must make a wide variety of normative judgments, ranging from their interpretations of mandates, rules, regulations, and procedures to their strategic choices about information or arguments to offer or to withhold. Fifth, and finally, to understand planning and policy analysis as deeply anticipatory encourages further research clarifying how skilled practitioners' actions can fit together into arguments, and how those arguments can in turn fit together into normative strategies of effective planning and policy analysis.

NOTES

1. See Rachelle Alterman and Duncan MacRae, Jr. "Planning and Policy Analysis," *Journal of the American Planning Association* (Spring 1983): 200-215.

2. H. W. Fowler, *A Dictionary of Modern English Usage*, 2nd ed. (New York: Oxford University Press, 1965).

3. For a parallel exposition, see John Forester, "Learning From Practice," *Journal of Planning Education and Research*, (Winter 1987).

4. See John Seeley, "Social Science: Some Probative Problems," in Maurice Stein and Arthur Vidich, eds., *Sociology on Trial* (Englewood Cliffs, NJ: Prentice-Hall, 1963), 53-65. Compare with Donald Schön, *The Reflective Practitioner* (New York: Basic Books, 1983).

5. See Richard Bolan, "The Practitioner as Theorist: The Phenomenology of the Professional Episode," *Journal of the American Planning Association* (Summer 1980): 261-274.

6. For further discussion of this point, see Rosemary Tong's essay in this volume (chapter 8).

7. See, for example, Frank Fischer, "Critical Evaluation of Public Policy: A Methodological Case Study" in John Forester, ed., *Critical Theory and Public Life* (Cambridge: MIT Press, 1985), 231-257; Ralph H. Johnson and J. Anthony Blair, "Informal Logic: The Past Five Years 1978-1983," *American Philosophical Quarterly* 22, 3 (July 1985): 181-196; and Richard J. Bernstein, *Beyond Objectivism and Relativism* (Philadelphia: University of Pennsylvania Press, 1982).

8. See Charles Lindblom and David Cohen, *Usable Knowledge* (New Haven: Yale University Press, 1979).

9. For a partial exception, see Aaron Wildavsky, *Speaking Truth to Power* (Boston: Little, Brown, 1979).

10. See Peter Szanton, *Not Well Advised* (New York: Russell Sage Foundation, 1981).

11. For an examination of the role of speech acts and communicative action in policy analysis, see John Forester, "The Policy Analysis-Critical Theory Affair: Wildavsky and Habermas as Bedfellows?" in John Forester, ed., *Critical Theory and Public Life* (Cambridge: MIT Press, 1985); and John Forester, "Toward a Critical Empirical Framework for the Analysis of Public Policy," *New Political Science* (Summer 1982): 33-61.

12. See for example, John Forester, "Critical Theory and Planning Practice," *Journal of the American Planning Association* (Summer 1980): 275-286; "Understanding Planning Practice: An Empirical, Practical, and Normative Account," *Journal of Planning Education and Research* (Summer 1982): 59-71, and other essays in *Planning in the Face of Power* (under review).

13. See John Forester, "What Do Planning Analysts Do? Planning and Policy Analysis as Organizing," *Policy Studies Journal* (Winter 1980-1981): 595-604; and "Bounded Rationality and the Politics of Muddling Through," *Public Administration Review* (Winter 1984): 23-31.

7

POLICY SCIENCE AND RATIONAL CHOICE THEORY: A METHODOLOGICAL CRITIQUE

TIMOTHY W. LUKE

Virginia Polytechnic Institute and State University

Over the past generation many policy scientists enthusiastically have embraced the deductive paradigms of rational choice theory. "While the analysis of public policy," as Tullock and Wagner suggest, "has . . . been dominated by empiricism, deductive approaches to policy analysis maintain a vigorous . . . presence in the literature."[1] With its formal operationalization of decision making in efficient means-ends terms, rational choice methodology has helped to nurture the administrative application of the "economic principles' of choice, particularly as embodied in cost-benefit analysis. By adopting the conceptual and methodological assumptions of economic rationality, policy scientists have aspired to formalize the ethical, moral, or political relations of policymaking in terms of costs and benefits. Such cost-benefit analyses of public policy start with "the enunciation of some first principles of human action, followed by a logical analysis of how this action will manifest itself differently in alternative institutional frameworks. Taken in conjunction with certain presumptions as to the ends to be achieved

AUTHOR'S NOTE: *Some portions of this chapter originally appeared in* Social Research, *Vol. 52, No. 1 (Spring 1985), pp. 65-98.*

through policy, it then becomes possible to evaluate alternative policies."[2] In the context of complex policy decisions, the hope is to emulate the technical advances made in economic theory.

Yet these movements toward applying choice-theoretic or cost-benefit models to the value-charged problems of policymaking seem somewhat misbegotten. Indeed, these aspirations are good examples of what Kenneth Boulding calls "economics imperialism," which is the attempt being made by social scientists trained in economic methods to take over all the other social sciences.[3] These "imperial" ventures, however, are ill-considered. Behind this empire building, policy scientists must recognize rational choice theory as a scientistic ideology, seeking to colonize all forms of social analysis with its managerial mode of discourse and hiding administrative decision making in the language of democratic public choice.[4]

For example, the theory of public goods and its intrinsic logic of cost-benefit analysis has been invoked as a factual challenge to the political "values" of obligation and participation. Olson has argued that rational, self-interested individuals, in contrast to the moral injunction that people are obliged to provide and work for the common good of their state or political group, will not discharge these obligations when such collective action provides only a commonly shared or public good because it is irrational, or inefficient, for individuals. The costs of participating are seen as exceeding the benefits derived from their contributions to participation. He operationally assumes that individuals in society are analogous to individual firms in the marketplace because both are engaged in "atomistic" competition with each other. Thus it is in the interest of a rational individual to work only at those tasks which ensure that their benefits exceed their costs. Otherwise it is rational for the individual to become a "free rider"[5] with respect to public goods by taking advantage of the economy of scale intrinsic to supplying public goods. The efforts, or costs paid, exerted by a few ensures enough benefits for the enjoyment of all, including those who do not contribute.[6]

Obviously, rational behavior contradicts the implicit moral precept of individual obligation to collective activities and group values. Individual obligation is reduced, then, to a cost-benefit calculation tied to the actual enjoyment of private incentives. An individual is not obliged to aid others because he or she feels bound by collective purpose or civic duty; rather, the individual fulfills his or her obligation selectively to enjoy economic, social, or psychological incentives—that is, "individual, noncollective goods."[7] All of Olson's observations about individuals and collectives may be quite accurate empirically, but even if Olson is correct about how rationally, self-interested individuals usually behave, these factual insights do not weaken or disprove the absolute value of various political obligations. At best Olson's individual (as well as Olson) totally misunderstands what obligation to the public is as a valued end in itself; it is not merely a cost-benefit calculation. At worst Olson's individual—from a normative theorist's vantage—abides by a private rule of individual gain as he or she immorally insists that the "public" or "common" good serve his or her personal goal maximization without making a personal contribution toward that end.

Here, then, I will ask what exactly a rational choice theory can contribute to the activity of normative decision making in policy science. This reassessment of rational choice theory indicates where critical conceptual failures can develop as policy scientists turn to collective choice theorists, particularly if they ignore the methodological boundaries between normative and empirical theories. By marking some of the limits imposed by the philosophical foundations of collective choice theory, then, this investigation hopes to point out new problems that the policy sciences productively might research and detect old preoccupations that its research program legitimately might leave behind.

THE NORMATIVE CONNECTION IN
RATIONAL CHOICE THEORY

Given these conceptual limitations, what can rational choice theory contribute to the practice of normative reasoning in the policy sciences? A vast amount of controversy surrounds this question. The debate arises because, as Riker and Ordeshook note, rational choice theory ambivalently deals with "what choices ought to be made—the class of the desirable."[8] In the policy sciences many practitioners would agree with Blair and Maser that "axiomatic models are more conducive to normative analysis of public policy than empirical approaches" inasmuch as "rigorous deductive models have been remarkably successful at generating policy relevant statements based upon fairly weak normative criteria."[9] Actually, as Downs asserts, choice-theoretic political analysis occupies "a twilight zone between normative and descriptive models. It is not normative, because it contains no ethical postulates and cannot be used to determine how men should behave. Nor is it purely descriptive, since it ignores all the non-rational considerations so vital to politics in the real world."[10] Here one must cast more light into this "twilight zone" between theories of the politically possible, or rational choice theory, and theories of the politically desirable, or normative political theory, in policy science by illustrating how these two activities differ in both their theoretical operations and practical intentions.

If normative reasoning is considered to be largely the intellectual activity of constituting first-order moral principles for guiding political action—that is, of articulating the rationality of political *ends*—then it seems clear that rational choice theory has not and cannot contribute to the practice of normative thinking. With regard to economics and ethics, Lord Robbins has suggested that "economics deals with ascertainable facts; ethics with valuation and obligations."[11] The same holds true for empirical and normative political theory. Rational choice theory, as a science of "subjective rationality" dealing in the facts of efficient means, is logically unsuited to discovering basic political norms that involve the valuation of ends. Such normative ends must be explicated with a different "science" of values dealing in and expressing what could be called the "objective rationality" of moral ends.[12] The rational choice analysis of politics "can explain what people will do *given their beliefs and knowledge* of alternatives," yet it seems unable to explain "how people come to think up new beliefs or appreciate that new alternatives exist."[13] If the differences between the two types of theorizing, however, are as easily drawn as these points suggest, then why all the confusion?

Ultimately, what is confused and held subject to question in the choice-theoretic program is the distinction made by normative and choice theorists between different orders of theoretical judgments, or judgments between "is" or "ought" as well as judgments between varied levels of "ought." Many choice-theoretic policy scientists would conflate these two separate theoretical orders by reducing fact and value to "axioms." As Plott asserts,

> If processes can be decomposed into axiomatic parts, we can then compare them by comparing the parts. Similarities among processes can be identified in terms of the parts they share, the axioms they have in common. Such comparisons may help us pin down the particular aspects of processes which cause us to accept or reject them.[14]

Unlike chicken, however, "parts is not parts" when it comes to normative thinking. Yet many policy scientists recognize and respect the distinction between "is" and "ought" judgments as one enforced by the demands of logic. The real controversy, however, arises with further distinctions between distinctly separate levels of "ought" judgments. Here, after conceding moral absolutes to normative theory, choice theorists assert that choice-theoretic analysis might have practical normative applications or may be a conditionally normative form of judgment. Thus, although many choice theorists would agree with Shepsle that such models "may be put to normative use,"[15] rational choice models still are not "normative models" in the traditional sense of the term. To ascertain what rational choice theory can contribute to normative decision making in the policy sciences, then, the following section outlines concretely the limits of choice-theoretic judgment with regard to the "is-Ought" and the "ought-Ought" problems.

THE "IS-OUGHT" QUESTION

As the issues have been posed historically in political science by the choice-theoretic program, rational choice theorists and normative theorists are said to differ in that the former study facts whereas the latter attend to values; the former analyze empirical data scientifically whereas the latter scrutinize normative imperatives philosophically; and the former deduce rigorous, testable lawlike predictions about how politics "is" whereas the latter adduce reliable practical prescriptions about how politics "ought to be." These rigid formal dichotomies overly exaggerate the differences between these two modes of theorizing. Nonetheless, these differences should underscore the fact that the two theoretical subcultures follow their own unique decision rules "about what is worth studying, how it shall be studied, and what shall be accepted as knowledge."[16] Plainly, choice theory and normative theory do differ profoundly over what a theory is, what rules theories are formed by, what kind of rationality they embody, and what purposes they serve.

In the twilight zone allegedly dividing positive from normative theory, many choice theorists have ignored or forgotten the distinctions between these two modes of theorizing. Believing that such disciplinary frontiers are solely the artifacts of tradition, choice theorists have sought, under the banner of "economics imperialism," to apply their methods to any and all political questions, especially to normative problems in politics.[17] In fact, Fiorina suggests that

the structure of a normative theory looks no different from that of a positive theory. Sometimes it is claimed that the premises of a normative theory contain imperatives, whereas the premises of a positive theory

contain only declaratives. But I suggest that such distinctions do not lie in
the theory or the model itself, but rather in the mind of the theorist, in his
attitude towards the theory.[18]

From this vantage point of structural identity, "theories are theories"
and vary only in the theorist's subjective attitude toward the world.
Consequently, "for the positive theorist" as Fiorina continues, "the
model must accommodate the world. For the normative theorist the
world must conform to the model."[19] Both intellectual practices simply
but mistakenly merge as ways of doing "behavioral science" given that
political science, "normative or positive, is a science of human action."[20]
Unfortunately, this perspective seriously distorts the actual differences
by confusing the dissimilarities of theoretical type with one of subjective
intention.

In other words, positive and normative theorists actually are seen as
working on the same conceptual plane, using the same methodological
tools on the same empirical material, in order to form only somewhat
different statements due to subjective intentions, which actually com-
plement rather than contradict each other. Hence it seems only natural
for choice theorists to assert, as Downs does, that normative theory
might be "tested" by a positive theory. "Our model," Downs maintains
with regard to democratic politics, "can thus be used to test normative
theories, we will employ it for this purpose only when there is a striking
difference between rational behavior and some well-known precept for
good behavior."[21] As long as "is" assertions about efficient means in
politics do not contradict "ought" assertions about ethical ends, positive
and normative theories may coexist for choice theorists on the same
subjective plane. Yet in the clash of ethics with efficiency, the inefficient
normative rule is tested before the efficient positive model and can be
found wanting against the standards of rational behavior.

In crossing these frontiers choice theory ignores distinctions between
"facts" and "values" as well as differences in theoretical forms. Arrow,
for example, confuses "values," or moral ends, and "tastes," or factual
whims. He maintains that "one might want to reserve the term "values"
for a specially elevated or noble set of choices. Perhaps choices in
general might be referred to as 'tastes'. . . . I believe, though, that the
distinction cannot be made logically, and certainly not in dealing with a
single isolated individual."[22] Somehow this position does violence to the
notion of values; a single individual can value freedom but not necessarily have a "taste" for freedom. Likewise, one can have a "taste" for
pineapples, but one does not "value" pineapples. The two choices—the

wanting of freedom as a "value" and the taste for pineapple as a "fact"—and the ways they are made are quite different. However, choice theorists maintain that between positive investigations of taste and normative determinations of value the distinction is solely one of subjective attitude.

Initially the twilight zone buffering positive political theory and normative political theory was respected as an inviolate frontier by many choice theorists. Eventually, however, increasingly softer criteria used in delimiting choice from normative theorizing have led many rational choice theorists to confuse the "is" and the "ought" orders of analytical judgment. Thus a number of choice theorists from Downs to Fiorina have reasoned that if the practical distinction is purely one of attitude, and if both choice and normative theorists build basically the same theoretical structures on their respective sides of the "is-Ought Gulf,"[23] then why not fill in and abolish the gulf in the name of scientific progress? For Buchanan and Tullock, the "is-Ought" distinction "has separated the moral philosopher on the one hand from the scientist on the other, but the dichotomy so achieved is too simple in relation to the problems that arise in political theory and philosophy."[24] And in practice most policy scientists simply ignore the ethical issues posed by the "is-ought" gulf.

Believing that scientific analysis of the facts can test and thereby improve normative political theorists' value assertions, these choice theorists contend, "normative theory must be erected upon and draw its strength from the propositions of positive science, but it is only when this extension of normative theory is made that 'reform' in existing institutions can be expected to emerge from specialized scholarship. Indeed the only purpose of science is its ultimate assistance in the development of normative propositions."[25] Thus a group of choice theorists—sorely confused about the limits of "is" and "ought" statements in positive and normative science—enjoin both positive theorists and policy scientists to break down the barriers between "facts" and "values," "empirical" and "normative," and "is" and "ought" in order to improve society by rationalizing social choice and eliminating "a lot of nonsense about 'is' and 'ought.' "[26]

Yet these two modes of theorizing and orders of judgment *do* diverge radically. Their divergence does not derive simply from the subjective intentions of the theorist. To paraphrase Fiorina, theories are *not* theories, nor should choice and normative theories of politics be seen as methodologically identical when, in fact, they are unlike in logical structure, dissimilar in ontological approach, distinct in epistemological basis, and different in practical intention. Furthermore, "is" and "Ought" judgments follow unique logical guidelines that preclude theories from being "interpreted normatively or behavioristically"[27] at the subjective whim of the analyst intent upon applying economic categories to normative decisions.

To reinforce these points one need only return to a Kantian perspective, which stresses that positive/empirical science and normative reasoning discuss different realities, aim at formulating dissimilar kinds of knowledge, use distinct modes of theorizing, and serve diverse practical intentions. On one hand a *normative mode* of thought searches for articulations of moral will formulated in terms of practical knowledge derived from *transcendental* ideas about a transphenomenal world of values, ends, goals. A *positive mode* of thought, on the other hand, seeks certain, theoretical knowledge, or empirical understanding, by testing and verifying *analytical propositions* about the phenomenal world of facts, means, and policies.

Normative political thinking in the last analysis boils down to a mode of reasoning rooted in *reasonable belief* rather than *factual knowledge* per se. Clearly moral knowledge or categorical imperatives are discoverable within human belief and activity "as it were a fact."[28] This recognition, however, is one of an unequivocal a priori and not that of a given empirical fact. The moral will remains a fact of human activity, but it can be realized for practice only through the speculations of normative reason, not by scientific analysis. Normative dictates, in turn, are proven in ethical practice and are tested in terms of the unremitting human conscience that appraises the degree to which such absolute ethical or political values can become moral activity.

Obviously, choice theorists have attempted to circumvent the grasp of this "objective rationality" by admitting to its existence while asserting, despite its well-known illusiveness, that it still is merely a preference ordering that requires an "interpreter—judge or bishop, philosopher or monarch"—and thus "the social choice is his preference as expressed in his interpretation."[29] This position represents a gross error in analysis. A moral intuition is not a preference ordering, nor can it be rightly reduced to such a status. It is not simply a fact, nor is it only data for an individual's subjective taste to prefer over an alternative moral intuition. Rather, it is an *end*, not a means, which demands adherence or enactment because of its "objectively rational" quality as a moral or ethical good. An "interpretation," especially by some political authority figure, could as easily rob the ethical judgment of its moral quality by bending the interpreter's preference into the social choice.

Another choice-theoretic tactic in dealing with moral intuition has been to follow Arrow and claim "that each individual has two orderings, one which governs him in his everyday dealings and one which would be relevant under some ideal conditions and which is in some sense truer than the first ordering."[30] Individuals have "subjective preferences," or their interests, which are orderings in accord with completely personal considerations, and "ethical preferences," or their conscience, which are orderings expressing rare moments of impartial and impersonal judgments that account for other individuals' economic orderings.[31] This second position commits an equally serious analytical mistake. In fact, normative judgments aim not at divorcing kinds of preferences but rather at displacing everyday subjective preferences with reasonable belief in moral intuitions. Normative political thought unfolds by educating individuals to follow their moral will in practical activity. It does not relegate ethical ends because of their inefficiency to the status of "relevant under some ideal conditions." Instead normative theorists work toward a politics in which the moral will of ethical ends governs the individual "in his everyday dealings." An absolute moral standard for political activity is reasonable in itself as a valued end, under real or ideal conditions. Hence its impact on everyday political or social practice should not be confined by individual subjective preferences that have proven "factually" efficient in everyday actions.

Choice theorists, then, must not indiscriminately mingle the orders of "is" and "ought" judgments. The break between them is not one of subjective attitude; rather, it is one of both theoretical operation and practical intention. A wholly divergent approach in logical structure (verified factual lawlike statements versus reasonable but practical moral belief), in ontology (the experiential phenomenal plane as opposed to the transcendental valuative dimension), to epistemology (testable empirical reasoning against disciplined conscientious intuition), and in intention (the description and manipulation of subjective rationality in contrast to the prescription and enactment of absolute ethical standards) precedes the choice and normative theorists' simple division of "is" and "ought" judgments. Despite what rational choice theorists argue, all theories are *not* alike in operation, structure, or purpose.

Granted the preceding comments, it appears clear that rational choice theory cannot "test" the conceptions of ethical political activity against the data of economically rational activity. Yet because rational behavior quite often clashes with normative imperative, some rational choice theorists claim that their findings might "improve" the scope of normative judgments and render "assistance in the development of normative propositions."[32] As Downs remarks with respect to such value testing, "though our model can thus be used to test normative theories, we will employ it for this purpose only when there is a striking difference between rational behavior and some well-known precept for good behavior."[33] In fact, the apparent intention of many choice theorists has been to engage in exactly these kinds of tests to evince the superiority of positive over normative political theory.

By way of example, choice theorists often insist that there is a "paradox of participation." That is, it is rational for a "rational, self-interested individual" to participate in political activity to the extent that his vote or say decisively affects political outcomes, thereby providing him incentives to participate. As the number of participants increases, choice theorists argue, each individual's probability of decisively effecting outcomes diminishes, as does his incentive to participate. "Thus, a citizen," according to Riker and Ordeshook, "evaluates his opportunities for political action and concludes that because his acts are of little consequence, a failure to participate does not greatly diminish his welfare."[34] Once again, however, choice theorists reduce a *valued end*—namely, that of participation—to the level of *efficient means*.

Because activity that fulfills the absolute moral standard of personal participation in public affairs does not also entail constant maximization of the individual's welfare, rational choice theorists assert that participation is not conducive to rational behavior. Nevertheless, this "fact" does not weaken the participation precept from the value-oriented perspective of normative political theory. In fact, political participation is an end in itself and remains a legitimate end for all citizens of a democratic polity. Participation may be economically inefficient, but this "fact" does not weaken the moral force of this political value.

Still, choice theorists such as Downs maintain that normative theorists "do not always consider whether the behavior they advocate as good is also rational in the economic sense." What is more,

a man who is good in their eyes may be unable to perform his function in the division of labor efficiently. In fact, good behavior as they define it may be so inefficient that its prevalence would disrupt the very social state they desire. If so, their normative prescriptions are really contradictory; hence their conception of good behavior must be reexamined.[35]

This position, basically, is nonsense. Normative political theorists usually do not take into account "economic rationality" because usually it is superfluous. What is morally "good" more than likely *is not* going to be economically rational. As Downs makes these points he fails to recognize that a good person *may not* perform well in an efficient division of labor because that may be the cost of attaining the political good. If normative prescriptions fail the test of social efficiency they need not necessarily be reexamined as disruptive, contradictory, or inefficient unless efficiency is made into a higher good than ethical precepts such as obligation, freedom, and participation.

Downs is incorrect for three reasons. First, as indicated above, "is" and "Ought" propositions are and must be separated by a logical gulf. "Oughts"—or reexamined conceptions of the good from Downs's position—cannot be derived from what "is"—or an efficient division of labor.[36] Although it is considered, reality should not be allowed to constrain moral will too strongly. If one remains in awe of the alleged empirical barriers against achieving full democratic participation, one will be unlikely to act so as to realize this moral value, because it is not politically realistic. Second, facts and theories are and must be distinguished by the logical gap between theory and fact as statements—that is, a theory of the politically good cannot be proven or disproven by claiming that a set of facts falsifies a statement of theory. In other words, with only the Downsian fact of "efficient labor" one cannot falsify the normative theory of the goodness of full democratic participation.[37] Third, normative theorists do not need to reassess their theories under the hard light of economic rationality because it is immaterial to propounding of first-order moral principles. Indeed, normative frameworks might well censure and sanction economic efficiency as amoral or immoral given the tendency of the efficient, or individually possible, to deny, destroy, or displace the good, or socially desirable. The fact of efficient choice is a judgment of a different order than the value of political goodness—unless, of course, the good is also efficient; yet this relation is always accidental, not essential, when seeking first-order moral norms. Choice-theoretic science as science has nothing to contribute to normative political theorists' definition of absolute moral standards and ultimate political values—unless, of course, efficiency itself becomes the ultimate political good.

THE "OUGHT-OUGHT" QUESTION

The confusion of the "is" with the "Ought" is one of the problems with which choice theorists must deal as they approach normative political theory. One cannot create "Ought" judgments from an "is" grounded science, at least, in a absolute first principles sense. But what of judgments made at different levels of "Oughtness?" Might not the qualified findings of choice theory be put to normative use as conditionally normative forms of "ought" assertions? Such questions suggest another possible contribution that choice theorists might make to normative political theory: framing situationally constrained "ought" judgments that might have limited "normative" implications.

Again, one must assume that "normative" denotes a first-order moral principle, or an "Ought" judgment as a categorical imperative usually stated as "Always do X"—for example, imperatives claiming, "One always should participate in public life" or, "One always should serve the collective good." When speaking as scientists, however, choice theorists err in advancing choice-theoretic propositions as normative judgments of this order or in using such formulae to disprove the social utility of first-order precepts.

Still, for many choice theorists the term "normative" often assumes a conditional or provisional judgment relating to the actual enactment of rules. The "ought" judgment is a partial imperative usually stated as, "To always do X, under conditions Y, then do Z." Here "is" and "Ought" do not ultimately merge. On the contrary; this order of "ought" judgments simply incorporates both factual and value premises to draw conditionally normative outcomes. This construction of normative as "ought" runs along a rather different track than the tight first-order notion of "Ought" as it concentrates on a third dimension sandwiched between "isness" and "Oughtness"—that is, on the question of implementation under limiting empirical conditions, or the question of "Can it be?" A basic ground rule in moral argument notes that "ought" implies "can"; to say that a moral principle "ought to be" requires also that it potentially "can be." If the ethical precept cannot be followed, no matter how difficult or inefficient its enactment, then it remains quite a hollow injunction. It fulfills its social or political value largely by becoming, as an ideal moral norm or an actual moral practice, incarnated in human activity. The conditionally normative, then, does not trade in categorical judgments but, rather, in operative imperatives that translate the first-order principles of "Ought" into the everyday "oughts" of real political action.

Using choice-theoretic propositions as conditionally normative judgments, then, relates choice theory to *policy craft* instead of to *moral philosophy*. Like welfare economics, this mode of choice theory necessarily makes limited value judgments and "is concerned with policy recommendations."[38] Friedman, in keeping with Lord Keynes, distinguishes between a *"positive science* . . ., a body of systematized knowledge discussing criteria of what is; a *normative* or regulative science . . . , a body of systematized knowledge discussing criteria of what ought to be . . . , and *art* . . . , a system of rules for the attainment of a given end."[39] Thus the normative forms that choice theory properly can deal with are those which relate to the attainment of a given moral-political end or those required in crafting means for artfully attaining, predetermined goal. But to admit these points one need not argue that the "is" and "Ought" ultimately merge.[40]

Kant and his classification of imperatives—those of skill, those of assertorial practical principles, and those of categorical principle—are useful for exploring this problem.[41] He states,

> all imperatives are formulations determining an action which is necessary according to the principle of a will in some respects good. If the action is good only as means to something else, then the imperative is *hypothetical*. If the action is conceived as good *in itself* and consequently as necessary being the principle of a will which of itself conforms to reason then it is categorical.[42]

Both imperatives of skill and assertorial imperatives are hypothetical in that they are created as means to something else. Categorical imperatives, on the other hand, are notions of absolute moral standards that are ends in themselves. The positive science and choice theories focus largely on imperatives of skill—purely technical injunctions—in part, on imperatives of assertorial principles.[43] Normative political theory, although it also historically has operated with assertorial imperatives—mixed technical and normative injunctions—mainly concentrates on the "Oughts" of categorical imperatives in its intellectual practice.

Rational choice theorists, then, are caught in a paradox. For the "Ought" judgments of normative political theory, choice theorists as such are unable to contribute from the choice-theoretic paradigm.[44] Likewise, the conditionally normative statements, which are possible for choice theory, actually are propositions for policy. Hence these formulas do not add to the essence of normative political theory. Choice theorists cannot, as scientists, propound statements like this one: "Always do X because X Ought to be done." Still, choice theorists, such as Arrow, have outlined useful hypothetical imperatives, such as, "To always do X, under conditions Y, then do Z," which aid in specifying the "moral intuition" of X by indicating the structural conditions under which policies might practically enact as everyday "oughts" the moral will of the original "Ought." Nevertheless, to confound the categorical and hypothetical level of imperatives within the "Ought" dimension of normative judgment, as most choice theorists do, continues to be a major intellectual failing, especially in a research program than prides itself in its practitioners' deductive thinking and formal mode of argument.[45]

Ultimately, policy science must keep positive and normative political thinking on their respective sides of the "is-Ought Gulf" to preserve the logical and practical integrity of each activity. Positive political theory cannot specify scientifically ultimate moral ends; moreover, policy scientists must accept this theoretical fact of life. Using weak normative assumptions leads to even weaker policy science. Still, as a means of blending factual premises, value judgments, and a specific logic of conditionally normative judgment, the practitioners of rational choice theory in policy science can make a modest contribution to policy craft. By inquiring systematically into how a given moral precept "can be" attained, once its normative importance has been determined, choice-theoretic constructs can explicate certain operative imperatives that translate normative judgments into effective practice. Beyond this limited role, however, axiomatic choice theory has little to contribute to normative thinking in the policy sciences. Its practitioners, in turn, must renounce their imperial ambitions for claiming the normative theorist's territory in the policy sciences as their own.

NOTES

1. Gordon Tullock and Richard E. Wagner, "Introduction: Symposium on Deductive Models in Policy Analysis," *Policy Studies Journal* 5, 3 (Spring 1977): 280. Also see Vincent Ostrom, *The Intellectual Crisis in American Public Administration* (University: University of Alabama Press, 1974); and William Mitchell and Joyce Mitchell, "Comparative Policy Analysis: A Public Choice Paradigm" (Paper delivered at the annual meeting of the International Political Science Association, Paris, July 1985), 15-20.

2. Ibid.

3. Kenneth Boulding, "Economics as a Moral Science," *American Economic Review* LIX, 1 (March 1969): 1-2. For comprehensive overviews of rational choice theory, see Brian Barry, *Sociologists, Economists, and Democracy* (London: Macmillan, 1970); Anthony Heath, *Rational Choice and Exchange Theory: A Critique of Exchange Theory* (Cambridge: Cambridge University Press, 1976); Charles R. Plott, "Axiomatic Social Choice Theory: An Overview and Interpretation," *American Journal of Political Science*

XX (August 1976): 511-596; Ronald Rogowski, "Rationalist Theories of Politics: A Mid-Term Report," *World Politics* XXX, no. 2 (January 1978): 296-323; and V. C. Walsh, "Axiomatic Choice Theory and Values," in Sidney Hook, ed., *Human Values and Economic Policy,* (New York, 1967), 193-195.

4. For some examples of rational choice theorizing in Western democracies, see Kenneth J. Arrow, *Social Choice and Individual Values* (New Haven, CT: Yale University Press, 1951): Albert Breton, *The Economic Theory of Representative Government* (Chicago: Aldine, 1974); James M. Buchanan, *The Demand and Supply of Public Goods* (Chicago: University of Chicago Press, 1968); idem., *The Limits of Liberty: Between Anarchy and Leviathan* (Chicago: University of Chicago Press, 1975); James M. Buchanan and Gordon Tullock, *The Calculus of Consent: Logical Foundations of Constitutional Democracy* (Ann Arbor: University of Michigan Press, 1962); Anthony Downs, *An Economic Theory of Democracy* (New York: Harper & Row, 1957); W. A. Niskanen, *Bureaucracy and Representative Government* (Chicago: Aldine, 1971); Mancur Olson, Jr., *The Logic of Collective Action: Public Goods and the Theory of Groups* (Cambridge, MA: Harvard University Press, 1965); Alvin Rabushka and Kenneth A. Shepsle, *Politics in Plural Societies: A Theory of Democratic Instability* (Columbus, Ohio, 1972); William H. Riker, *The Theory of Political Coalitions* (Westport, CT: Greenwood Press, 1962); Amartya K. Sen, *Collective Choice and Social Welfare* (New York: Elsevier, 1970); and Gordon Tullock, *Towards a Mathematics of Politics* (Ann Arbor: University of Michigan Press, 1968). A small sample of works applying rational choice theorizing to administration and management issues would include Buchanan and Wagner, eds. "Symposium on Deductive Models in Policy Analysis," *Policy Studies Journal* 5, 3(Spring 1977); R. L. Ackoff with S. K. Gupta and J. S. Minas, *Scientific Method: Optimizing Applied Research Decisions* (New York, 1962); C. West Churchman, *Prediction and Optimal Decision: Philosophical Issues of a Science of Values* (Westport, CT: Greenwood Press, 1982); Peter C. Fishburn, *Decisions and Value Theory* (New York, 1964; 1984 reprint: Melbourne, FL: Krieger); R. D. Luce and Howard Raiffa, *Games and Decisions: Introduction and Critical Survey* (New York: John Wiley, 1957); and Howard Raiffa and R. Schlaifer, *Applied Statistical Decision Theory* (Boston: Harvard Business School Press, 1961).

5. Olson, *The Logic of Collective Action,* pp. 5-52.

6. Ibid.

7. Ibid., p. 61.

8. William H. Riker and Peter C. Ordeshook, *An Introduction to Positive Political Theory* (Englewood Cliffs, NJ: Prentice-Hall, 1973), 6.

9. John P. Blair and Steven M. Maser, "Axiomatic Versus Empirical Models in Policy Studies," *Policy Studies Journal* 5, 3 (Spring 1977): 282-288.

10. Downs, *An Economic Theory of Democracy,* p. 31.

11. Lionel Robbins, *An Essay on the Nature and Significance of Economic Science* (London, 1932; 1981 reprint: Darby, PA: Darby Books), 132.

12. To paraphrase Downs in order to draw out the assumptions of absolute moral standards, one might say that when speaking of "objective rationality," the term "rational" is always applied to an agent's *ends.* This follows from the definition of "rational" as ethical, i.e., acting always to fulfill the values and ends of a reasoning being which conforms to objective reason—a force felt not only in each individual but also in the overarching order of the world. Here, to be sure, "objective reason" stands for those social ideals of "some Platonic realm of being" that Arrow claims are "meaningless" to "the nominalist temperament of the modern period." See Arrow, *Social Choice and Individual*

Values, p. 22. Yet their "meaninglessness" is *not* necessarily a widely accepted belief, except perhaps among choice-theoretic political theorists. Actually, once one assumes the presence of "objective reason," it can be seen as a force, an order, and a mode of thought. As Horkheimer asserts, "objective reason" has been "thought of as an entity, a spiritual power living in each man. This power was held to be the supreme arbiter—any, more, the creative force behind the ideas and things to which we should devote our lives." Consequently this force enforces an order in existence: "The term objective reason thus on one hand denotes as its essence a structure inherent in reality. . . . On the other hand, the term objective reason may also designate this very effort and ability to reflect such an objective order." Ultimately, "objective reason" stands for the "human process of discovering and the social embodiment of the relation between means and ends: it was regarded as the instrument for understanding the ends, *for determining them*." Max Horkheimer, *The Eclipse of Reason* (New York: Continuum, 1973), 9-12. Of course, one also might suspend Horkheimer's ontological construction of "objective reason" in favor of a perspective, following Habermas, that defines it in terms of a "world-maintaining interpretative system" (*Legitimation Crisis*, pp. 118-119). In this sense, "objective reason" is a set of social conventions, or a "contextual rationality," that prescribes ultimate ends and values for human action in contrast to a more "strategic rationality" of "subjective reason."

13. Heath, *Rational Choice and Exchange Theory*, pp. 159-160 (emphasis added).

14. Plott, "Axiomatic Social Choice Theory," p. 555.

15. Kenneth Shepsle, "Theories of Collective Choice" (mimeo, 1976), 10.

16. Sheldon Wolin, "Political Theory: Trends and Goals," *International Encyclopedia of the Social Sciences* 12 (1968): 327.

17. Gordon Tullock, "Economic Imperialism," in James M. Buchanan and Robert D. Tollison, eds., *Theory of Public Choice: Political Applications of Economics* (Ann Arbor: University of Michigan Press, 1972), 321.

18. Morris P. Fiorina, "Formal Models in Political Science," *American Journal of Political Science* XIX (February 1975): 149.

19. Ibid.

20. Buchanan and Tullock, *The Calculus of Consent*, p. 308.

21. Downs, *An Economic Theory of Democracy*, p. 33.

22. Arrow, *Social Choice and Individual Values*, p. 4.

23. Arnold Brecht, *Political Theory: Foundations of Twentieth-Century Political Thought* (Princeton, 1959; reprint: Ann Arbor, MI: University Microfilms), 127. Brecht states, "In logic there is, as some have expressed it, an 'unbridgeable gulf' between Is and Ought."

24. Buchanan and Tullock, *The Calculus of Consent*, p. 307.

25. Ibid., p. 308.

26. Churchman, *Prediction and Optimal Decision*, p. 150.

27. Martin Shubik, *Game Theory and Related Approaches to Social Behavior* (New York: Wiley, 1984), p. 30.

28. Brecht, *Political Theory*, p. 377.

29. Riker and Ordeshook, *Positive Political Theory*, p. 3.

30. Arrow, *Social Choice and Individual Values*, pp. 82-83.

31. John C. Harsanyi, "Cardinal Welfare, Individualistic Ethics, and Interpersonal Comparisons of Utility," *Journal of Political Economy* LXIII, 4 (August 1955): 315.

32. Buchanan and Tullock, *The Calculus of Consent*, p. 308.

33. Downs, *An Economic Theory of Democracy*, p. 33.

34. Riker and Ordeshook, *Positive Political Theory*, p. 57.

35. Downs, *An Economic Theory of Democracy*, pp. 31-32.

36. Brecht, p. 126. He records that "inferences of what 'ought' to be, therefore, can never be derived deductively (analytically) from premises whose meaning is limited to what 'is': they can be correctly made only from statements that have an Ought-meaning, at least in the major premise."

37. See Imre Lakatos and Alan Musgrave, eds., *Criticism and the Growth of Knowledge* (New York: Cambridge University Press, 1970), 99. Or, as May Brodbeck notes, "Explanation, therefore, is always of statements by means of other statements." "Methodological Individualisms: Definition and Reduction," in May Brodbeck, ed., *Readings in the Philosophy of the Social Sciences* (New York: Macmillan, 1968), 287.

38. Sen, *Collective Choice and Social Welfare*, p. 56.

39. Milton Friedman, *Essay in Positive Economics* (Chicago: University of Chicago Press, 1953), 3.

40. To be sure, some persons still maintain that "is" and "Ought" should merge. See, for example, Max Black, "The Gap Between 'Is' and 'Should,' " *Philosophical Review* LXXII (April 1964); and John Searle, "How to Derive 'Ought' from 'Is,'" *Philosophical Review* LXXIII (October 1964).

41. Carl J. Friedrich, ed., *The Philosophy of Kant* (New York: Modern Library, 1949), 160-164.

42. Ibid., p. 163.

43. See G. von Wright, "Practical Inference," *Philosophical Review* LXXII (April 1963): 159-179. This brief consideration of "technical imperatives" details the conditions and limitations binding judgments pitched at the level of a purely technical criterion.

44. Here even Harsanyi, who has tried consistently to introduce a strong normative dimension into his works on rational choice theory, admits that choice theory cannot adduce categorical imperative judgments. Instead, one must deal with ethics on the level of hypothetical imperatives, given an initial statement of first principles. See John C. Harsanyi, "Ethics in Terms of Hypothetic Imperatives" *Mind* LXVII, 267 (July 1958).

45. For some choice theorists, John Rawls's *A Theory of Justice* represents an attempt to use rational choice theory in a work that *is doing* "normative political theory." For the most part, however, I must disagree. Rawls's notions of rationality, justice, the good, and the state are all framed in terms of subjective reason rather than some explicit and consistent notion of objective reason. As Barber observes, in Rawls's theory "reason itself totters in its meaning between a consequentialist Hobbesian ratiocination and a deontological Kantian 'practical reason.'" See Benjamin R. Barber, "Justifying Justice: Problems of Psychology, Politics, and Measurement in Rawls," in Norman Daniels, ed., *Reading Rawls: Critical Studies of A Theory of Justice* (New York: Basic Books, 1976), p. 315.

PART IV

Professional Responsibility

8

ETHICS AND THE
POLICY ANALYST:
THE PROBLEM OF RESPONSIBILITY

ROSEMARIE TONG
Williams College

Policy analysis is at present undergoing a turbulent period of self-examination. Although this makes the philosopher's attempt to analyze it more difficult, it also makes the attempt more necessary and compelling. This chapter is intended to contribute to the somewhat sparse literature on the specifically ethical questions raised by the rapid development of policy analysis as a profession.

Since the late 1960s, the number of natural and social scientists at every level of government (local, state, and federal) has been increasing steadily. Today scores of policy analysts help elected and appointed policymakers (legislators, executives, and members of the judiciary) to research, formulate, implement, evaluate, and terminate alternative public policies. As society grows in complexity as well as magnitude, policymakers are becoming more, rather than less, dependent on policy analysts for information and advice. Aware of this trend, graduate schools of public policy are multiplying and think tanks are proliferating. Academics are taking time off to serve as policy analysts, and they are

Author's Note: *Portions of this chapter are adapted from Rosemarie Tong,* Ethics in Policy Analysis *(Englewood Cliffs, NJ: Prentice-Hall, 1985).*

introducing courses aimed at encouraging their students to do likewise. Today's political science, economics, political economy, sociology, psychology, anthropology, environmental studies, urban affairs, bio-chemistry, mathematics, computer science, engineering, educational research, or statistics major is likely to spend some time working as a policy analyst, if only as a part-time researcher or as an intern. Given this it is important to prepare not only today's but tomorrow's policy analysts for the ethical as well as technical challenges that await them.[1]

Unfortunately, policy analysis' adherence to a value-free view of inquiry and its failure to stake out clearly its own professional identity effectively narrowed its examination of ethical problems for decades. Until relatively recently policy analysts simply conceived of themselves as scientists whose work was governed by the predictable professional norms of objectivity, impartiality, thoroughness, and precision. The more "scientific" a policy analyst was, the more "ethical" (in the sense of competent) he or she was presumed to be. Significantly, this situation changed dramatically when policy analysts joined social scientists in questioning many of the traditional verities underlying the positivistic approach. As policy analysts came to understand just how subjective, partial, and imprecise policy analysis can be, they began to construct an expanded ethics for themselves, an ethics based on their position as dispensers of "knowledge" to public officials possessed of "power."

Reading through the new literature on the emerging ethics of policy analysis, it becomes clear that the main topic of discussion so far has been the conditions under which policy analysts can be either excused (although I did wrong, certain conditions were present that made me less than fully blameworthy) or justified (although my action seems wrong, certain conditions make it right) for their apparent moral failings.[2] Three excuses/justifications have been offered to date: Dirty Hands, Many Hands, and No Hands. I shall argue that the Dirty Hands excuse/justification, traditionally invoked by policymakers who find that they sometimes have to sacrifice individual rights for the sake of aggregate utility (Walzer) or to trade a lower right for a higher right (Goldman), does not really fit the situation of policy analysts who rarely, if ever, are asked to make the kind of lonely decisions policymakers (e.g., chief executives) must make. I shall also argue that the Many Hands (Thompson) and No Hands excuses/justifications better fit the realm of policy analysis because they at least recognize the ways in which bureaucratic structures and collective decision making make it difficult for policy analysts to assume personal responsibility for their actions.

Nevertheless, these two excuses/justifications are not as developed as that of Dirty Hands because they lack an explicit analog for the concept of rights and utilities that helps us appreciate just how difficult it is for a policymaker to do the right thing. This lack may be more apparent than real, however. An analog may be present in the twin concepts of what Alasdair MacIntyre terms a "practice" and its correlative "institution." Thus what I finally argue is that to the extent that policymakers must learn to balance or choose between two values they treasure—rights and utilities—policy analysts must learn to balance or choose between two sets of values they treasure—the external goods (power, prestige, money) of the institution that employs them and the internal goods (the satisfaction that comes with doing the best job possible) of the practice that absorbs them.

DIRTY HANDS

As I have pointed out elsewhere,[3] political philosophers have recently been preoccupied with the classic problem of "dirty hands," the possibility that public life may require people who deal in the policy arena to act in ways that would be wrong in private life. In *The Prince*, written in the sixteenth century, Machiavelli argues that a monarch cannot afford to be good. If not naturally inclined toward evil, the prince must make a deliberate effort to learn how to overcome his moral inhibitions and scruples. In particular, the prince must come to define "vice" as that which, if followed, would contribute to the state's ruin and "virtue" as that which, if followed, would lead to the state's glory.[4] Although some of us may be repelled by a prince whose good ends justify his evil means, it is difficult to ignore the benefits he provides: a flourishing economy, military might, law and order. Writing three and a half centuries after Machiavelli, Max Weber further defends "princely" types by articulating a full-fledged two-moralities worldview. According to Weber, the political realm is characterized by power interpreted as coercion, violence, and/or force. Because politicians live, move, and have their being in this ugly world of power, the ethical standards that rule their professional activities are not likely to send sugar plums dancing in their heads. Indeed, claims Weber, politicians are ruled by an "ethics of responsibility" that simply asks about the "foreseeable results of one's action." Given the irrationality of human history, the complexity of human psychology, and the enormous effort it takes to keep the human enterprise afloat, politicians cannot afford to be ruled by the competing "ethic of ultimate ends" that cares only about the purity of one's intentions. When the common good is at stake, those who are steering the ship of state must overcome their moral scruples and "pay the price of using morally dubious means or at least dangerous ones" in order to safeguard the lives of those who depend upon them.[5]

The significance of Weber's claims cannot be overemphasized. If some version of the two-moralities worldview is correct, then we are all moral schizophrenics who wear one moral persona to the office and another one home, never quite knowing which one of ourselves is doing right and which one of ourselves is doing wrong. Apparently Michael Walzer is willing to concede that even if all of us are not divided moral selves, certainly the public servants among us are:

> A particular act of government . . . may be exactly the right thing to do in utilitarian terms and yet leave the man who does it guilty of a moral wrong. The innocent man, afterwards, is no longer innocent. If on the other hand he remains innocent, chooses, that is, the 'absolutist' side . . ., he not only fails to do the right thing (in utilitarian terms), he may also fail to measure up to the duties of his office (which imposes on him a considerable responsibility for consequences and outcomes).[6]

Walzer provides two examples to illustrate this dilemma: (1) In order to win an election, a candidate must make a shady property deal with a dishonest ward boss. Convinced that his opponent, a totally incompetent moral nerd, will win the election unless he gives in to the ward boss, the candidate reluctantly makes the deal. (2) In order to find out where a terrorist has hidden a bomb that will probably kill scores of people a public official, known as a defender of human rights, reluctantly orders the terrorist tortured so that innocent lives may be spared.[7] To Walzer's examples we may add the case of the policy analyst who fudges her data in order to secure funding for a worthy project or the case of the policy analyst who betrays his client's confidence in order to prevent a probable harm from befalling an innocent third party.

As Walzer sees it, the candidate, the public official, and our two policy analysts have done the right thing in the sense that all of them have acted so as to produce the greatest ratio of good to evil for everyone. Nevertheless, assuming the kind of moral education most of us have received, all of these public servants are likely to feel guilty, for in another sense they have also done the wrong thing by lying, torturing, or betraying as the respective case may be. The most immediate way to resolve this paradox would be to exclaim: "Utilitarianism is the moral point of view. Not only public servants but everyone at all times and in all places should abide by the Principle of Utility." But Walzer refuses to take the easy way out. Rather, he argues that even if we cannot justify the actions of public servants who choose aggregate utility over individual rights in the sense of loudly affirming that they have clearly done *the* right thing, we should forgive them provided that they not only feel regret for their wrong actions but also are willing to accept responsibility—and even punishment—for them.[8]

Despite the appeal of Walzer's analysis—its attention to the complexities of the moral universe in particular—it is not without flaws. The greatest problem with Walzer's schema is that it could easily lead public servants—be they veteran policymakers or beginning policy analysts—to think that if only they "love" the public, they are above not only statutory law but common morality. In a major critique of Walzer, Alan H. Goldman argues that the same ethics governs us in both the public and the private realm. Opting for an ethics in which individual rights serve to trump aggregate utility, Goldman claims (1) that Walzer's candidate may not make the shady property deal unless "he is convinced that his opponent, if elected, will fail to honor rights more precious than economic rights to fair bidding"and (2) that Walzer's public official may torture the terrorist because the terrorist's right not to be tortured is not as sacred as innocent citizens' rights not to be blown away.[9] Using Goldman's analysis, it is also safe to conclude both that an analyst may not pass fudged data to her policymaking client unless she is convinced that a right, more important than her client's right to truthful information, is in jeopardy; and that an analyst may not betray his client's confidences unless a right greater than that of privacy is at stake.[10]

The advantage of Goldman's analysis is that it forcefully answers the question of when rights take precedence over utility. "Always," announces Goldman. But the more we reflect on Goldman's announcement, the more we must wonder whether his resolution of the Dirty Hands dilemma is any more satisfying than Walzer's or, for that matter, the utilitarian who would let utility trump rights in the private as well as the public realm. In particular, we must ask ourselves whether Goldman's analysis is any more helpful to the public official who would be moral than Walzer's is. Goldman gives the politician *nonutilitarian* reasons for torturing the terrorist. There exists, we are told, a scale of rights, and the right of one individual not to be tortured stands lower on that scale than the right of many individuals not to lose their lives. Thus terrorists who threaten to deprive people of their very existence may be tortured. Walzer gives the politician *utilitarian* reasons for torturing the terrorist. "The day you took office you agreed to serve all of your people. You have no right to sacrifice aggregate utility—the happiness of the many—to serve the individual rights of a terrorist who does not care a bit about the lives with which you have been entrusted. It is a shame, but you have no choice in this matter." Of course, there are even more ways to confuse the public official, who is by now perhaps convinced that all abstract moral points of view lead to the same concrete conclusions. It has always bothered me, for example, that John Stuart Mill suggests in Chapter Five of his *Utilitarianism* that justice (respect for individual rights) is the highest form of utility.[11] Thus apartheid is an immoral institution not simply because it constitutes a violation of Blacks' rights but because it is a nonutilitarian institution. Apartheid is, in Mill's analysis, wrong because it will fail to maximize aggregate utility in the long run. The Blacks will rebel and there will be a blood-spilling from which South Africa is unlikely to recover. But, we must ask Mill, if no such rebellion occurs in the long run, will this mean that apartheid was a moral institution after all?

What is ultimately disappointing about Walzer's and Goldman's respective analyses of the problem of Dirty Hands is neither Walzer's moral schizophrenia nor Goldman's magical ability to pull rights out of a hat full of utilities; it is their oversimplification of the policy process. For centuries Western moral philosophers have been fighting a battle that pits the Categorical Imperative against the Principle of Utility, justice against utility, intentions against consequences and they have fought this battle assuming that only one moral point of view is permitted to emerge triumphant. But why should we assume that the same side has to win all the time? If the moral universe is part of the human universe, then tragedy is no stranger to it. Sometimes rights must be sacrificed for utility and sometimes utility must be sacrificed for rights. And, as I shall argue later, the moral genius knows when to sacrifice which value, how, and why. Furthermore, why should we believe, as Walzer and Goldman seem to, that moral agents make all their decisions solo? To be sure, moral agents must each assume their separate moral burdens, but there are many moral decisions that are complicated enormously simply because people are often required to work together. Nowhere is this more true than in the public policy arena. Anyone who has ever worked as a policy analyst knows how many analysts are involved in a given project; how vested are the interests of policymaking clients; how quickly policy analysis is done; how work is chopped up and then pulled back together by the use of loosely ruled teams, groups, or task forces; how great is the pressure to please superiors; and how easy it is to have an analysis excluded if it does not follow the orthodox "prayer book." All these bureaucratic factors inhibit ethical reflection and cause policy analysts to seek if not society's blessing then its forgiveness, in either the excuse of Many Hands or that of No Hands. The excuse of Many Hands is invoked whenever so many cooks are stirring the policy pot that it is difficult even in principle to identify who is morally responsible for what. The excuse of No Hands is invoked whenever the belief in free will begins to give way to the doctrine of determinism—whenever, that is, we are told that not concrete men and women but abstract institutions shape public policy. The readiness with which both of these excuses are summoned forth tend to erode traditional notions of personal responsibility and thus both of them must be laid to rest along with the Dirty Hands excuse.

MANY HANDS

Depending on the size and complexity of the bureaucracy in which they work, policy analysts may feel that they are responsible for too little or too much. Looking back at his Office of Management and Budget team's efforts to balance the budget, David Stockman, Reagan's chief economist, confessed,

> The defense numbers got out of control and we were doing that whole budget-cutting exercise so frenetically. In other words, you were juggling details, pushing people, and going from one session to another, trying to cut housing programs here and rural electric there, and we were doing it so fast, we didn't know where we were ending up for sure. And it didn't quite mesh. That's what happened. But, you see, for about a month and a half we got away with that because of the novelty of all these budget reductions.[12]

Even if we overlook Stockman's delight in having gotten away with something he should not have, we must wonder what his OMB team was thinking as they performed radical surgery on the budget. Did it ever occur to them that their cuttings would be translated into no food stamps for some women with dependent children into no school lunches for some hungry children, and into no health care for some sick and needy retirees? If so, how did the team perceive their moral responsibility to these women, children, and retirees? Did they blame someone else, no one, or themselves for the consequences of their actions?

In situations such as that one described above, there are two standard models for ascribing responsibility: the hierarchical model and the collective model. Those who view the moral universe in hierarchical terms would see in Stockman and his team a single chief with many Indian braves at work. The person on the top makes the decisions; the persons at the bottom, among whom are situated most policy analysts, simply rubber-stamp and/or carry them out. In sum, policy analysts are merely the agents of the policymaking clients who employ them. Their job is to work assiduously to achieve whatever objectives they are told to achieve. It is not their job to reflect on the worth or value or morality of these objectives. One policy analyst, who served as a high-ranking science adviser, takes a pragmatic attitude toward this state of affairs:

> If a Science Adviser is going to count, he must be a foot-soldier marching to the program of the President, not the company chaplain. The Science Adviser is recruited into a policy management system that is committed to a political agenda. His job, basically, is to use his wits and expertise to inform the choices of a President and to carry his share of the President's burden. . . . He can do this in a straightforward way as long as he is seen to be supporting the main directions of the administration and not obstructing them. It is not a clear line of sight, and it is not unheard of for a willful President or one of his purely political henchmen to grind his teeth over the conscientious staff advice he is given, and to murmur, "Who will rid me of this troublesome priest?"[13]

In return for not nagging their bosses, policy analysts are absolved of moral responsibility for their immoral actions. At very least their guilt is shouldered by the person in charge who, in all fairness, to his or her subordinates assumes that the head of the body must take responsibility for the movements of its hands and feet.

Although the person at the top of the hierarchy seemingly gains in moral stature by letting the little fish off the hook, in point of fact better theatrics than ethics are so achieved. Nixon may have scored a point or two when he assumed total responsibility for Watergate on the grounds that only a "cowardly" leader would pin the blame on the low men on the totem pole,[14] but in so doing he treated his underlings as something less than full moral agents. When top policymakers take full responsibility either for the moral failures or moral successes of their policy analysts, they deprive these men and women of a measure of disapprobation or approbation. In order to develop as moral agents, as persons who view ourselves as accountable for the things we make happen to ourselves and to others, we need both positive and negative feedback. Thus if other people take the credit or blame for our actions, they retard our moral development.

In order to remedy the obvious defect of the hierarchical model—its division of the moral universe into a few giants who carry their own and everyone else's responsibilities on their shoulders and many midgets who are encouraged to think of themselves as mere cogs in a machine—another model of responsibility, the collective model, has been forwarded. According to this model, everyone on Stockman's OMB team, for example, is responsible for the consequences—good or bad—of the budget slashings. No policy analyst, no matter how new on the job, is absolved from his or her part in producing a study, report, analysis, or policy statement. Clearly this model is on the right track in that it provides everyone with plenty of approbation or disapprobation as the case may be.

Nevertheless, as the saying goes, there can be too much of a good thing. Consider, for example, the recent tendency to compare disfavorably American business' reliance on a hierarchical model of responsibility with Japanese business' reliance on a collective model of reponsibility. Because Japanese organizational structures adapt to the conditions of homogeneity, stability, and group consciousness prevalent in Japanese society, the notion of collective responsibility—interpreted to mean that state of affairs in which each individual is accountable for every decision and action of the collectivity—takes root and flourishes. In contrast, because American organizational structures adapt to the conditions of heterogeneity, mobility, and individualism characteristic of American society, the notion of hierarchical responsibility (interpreted as above) is dominant. Supposedly a concept of collective responsibility, unlike that of hierarchical responsibility encourages each and every person to accept his or her share of moral responsibility. Thus if my company pollutes, I see myself as partially to blame. But even if the collective model of responsibility avoids the major problem with the hierarchical model, it has its own serious pitfall. William Ouchi, author of *Theory Z*, a comparison of Japanese and American business practices, points out that Japanese employees are comfortable "in not knowing who is responsible for what" since "they know quite clearly that each of them is completely responsible for all tasks, and they share that responsibility jointly."[15] In theory this sounds ideal. In practice it falls short of our expectations. Not only does this approach sometimes leave things undone because everyone thinks that "George is doing it," it frequently leads people to adopt the psychology of the contented committee member who is able to assuage any pricks of conscience with the balm, "It must be okay because the group says it is okay." "We're in this together" is a consoling motto, but it can cause individuals to ignore just how much or how little they have contributed to a collective decision. After all, not every person on Stockman's OMB team was equally responsible for the outcomes of the administration's budget reduction program. Our intuitions tell us that the more knowledgeable and powerful a member of a group, the more he or she is to blame or praise for the group's decisions and actions.

NO HANDS

Unable to invoke the Many Hands excuse easily, policy analysts invoke the No Hands excuse instead: "The structure of this bureaucracy is such that it precludes me or anyone from making a real decision. I put in my two cents' worth and so does everyone else. Somewhere along the line, all these strands of responsibility get woven together and a decision emerges for which no identifiable person is responsible." Not persons but the "Impersonal It" is the "bad guy" or, less likely, the "good guy." That such sentiments should be voiced so frequently is not surprising. At least three aspects of bureaucratic structures tend to convince policy analysts that they are not in charge of anyone's moral destiny including their own: (1) the rational/technical ethos of bureaucracy, (2) the tendency of bureaucracy to separate agents from the consequences of their actions, and (3) the growing belief that individual choice is no match for institutional coercion.

According to Robert Jackall, the rational-technical ethos of bureaucracy is constituted by three elements—goal orientation, calculated planning to achieve those goals, and abstracted language.[16] Because bureaucracies are goal-oriented organizations, they set for themselves specific targets. Once these targets are set, they are rarely challenged. Everyone becomes so absorbed in achieving the target that they question neither the means used to secure the target nor the worth of achieving the target. Jackall provides an excellent example of this bureaucratic obsession. When Richardson-Merrell, the American company that produced MER/29, received reports that their miracle anti-cholesterol drug had such unfortunate and serious side-effects as reduced libido, loss of hair, partial blindness, and cataracts, the managerial response was strangely stubborn. Rather than temporarily stopping the distribution of MER/29, the managers of Richardson-Merrell developed ever "more aggressive marketing strategies to overcome the drug's tarnished image and to continue its high sales."[17] The company's policy analysts redoubled their efforts to find or even to manufacture the data that would support the company's goals with respect to the sale of MER/29. Like crossword puzzle devotees, confronted with a challenging maze, the policy analysts sought to surmount whatever evidentiary "obstacles" presented themselves.

The goal orientation of the typical bureaucracy is furthered by the techniques of rational decision making in bureaucracies—operations research, systems analysis, cost-effectiveness analysis, cost-benefit analysis, risk-benefit analysis—and, even more significantly, by a style of discourse best termed "technics." The language of technics is the language of speed, efficiency, and productivity. For some policy analysts this modality of speech and thought and the instruments that facilitate it are veritable ends in themselves. Policy analysts cannot imagine doing their work without computers. After all, with these instruments they are able to collect, sift through, and organize data incredibly swiftly. So enamored are some analysts of the tools of their trade that they claim that these tools can change our whole way of thinking. Perhaps they can. But "can" does not imply "ought," and it may be a mistake for us to abandon our current worldview, especially if it encourages us to reflect on the worth of the goals we are told to pursue.

Finally, bureaucracy's trivialization of moral values is reinforced by vocabularies that screen out morally resonant words. Policy analysts have their own language that tends to obscure certain unpleasant realities. Once again Jackall provides an excellent example. He reminds us that during the Vietnam war Pentagon analysts called bombs "ordnance," bombing "interdiction," and defoliation "a resources control program."[18]

Not only does the rational-technical ethos of a bureaucracy militate against a sense of personal responsibility, so too does its tendency to separate agents from the consequences of their action. This separation is easily achieved because of the two bases of any bureaucracy's efficiency: specialization and segmentation. Segmentation is the breaking of tasks into small parts to obtain speed and is typical of work at the bottom of bureaucracies, where most policy analysts reside. A supervisor, commenting on his analysts' work, observes the following:

> One analyst is responsible for one input (the effect of the credit on the automobile industry); another for another type of input (the effect on steel industry investment); etc., until the problem reaches me. I do not contest these previous assumptions. They are accepted as gospel. For one thing, I usually know the individuals involved and trust their work; but more important, I don't have time to rework other people's estimates. Therefore, the outcome is a composite work.[19]

Specialization, which also characterizes the work of most analysts, is the demand for exhaustive but narrow expertise on some aspect of a problem. Although both segmentation and specialization separate people from their work, they effect this cleavage in different ways. Whereas segmentation separates workers from a final product, specialization separates experts from the use to which their knowledge is put. Gradually the workers—in this case the policy analysts—find it difficult to visualize the people whom their products affect. Even worse, they slowly find it easy to view people as numbers or as anonymous ciphers. This point was brought home to me during a conversation I had with some policy analysts. One of them actually claimed that because he never came into direct contact with the people who had been negatively affected by his policy recommendations, he was somehow not responsible for the harm that had befallen them as the result of his work. In short, he seemed to believe that you cannot harm what you cannot see.

What further contributes to this feeling of No Hands is the sense that there is no controlling "the Institution." It will have its own way no matter what. It will coerce all its members to do its bidding. Among others, radical feminists have made good use of the concept of institutional coercion in the course of arguing that in our culture women are made to feel compelled to have sexual intercourse with men—something they would not automatically do in a less male-dominated culture. Coercion, these feminists claim, is not confined to instances of *individual coercion* ranging from a particular man's deliberate threatening of a woman to his plying her with drugs or alcohol. Rather, coercion also embraces cases of *institutional coercion* that proceed from the systematic organization of heterosexual relations in this culture—a culture that discourages women from asserting themselves both in the

private and public spheres, that encourages women to submit to all of
men's demands but especially to their sexual demands, and that
convinces men that women are always able, ready, and especially willing
to have sex even when women indicate that sex is the farthest thing from
their minds.[20]

That many men think women are saying "yes" to sexual intercourse
when in fact they are saying "no" to rape is apparent. Nevertheless, to
suggest that the forces of institutional coercion make it impossible for
men ever to get women's signals straight may be to overstate the case.
Patriarchal institutions may narrow, limit, impede, constrain, and
constrict women's choices as sexual beings without totally determining
them. There is, after all, a significant difference between claiming that
women's sexual wants and needs are shaped by their culture and
insisting that no individual woman can ever break the mold culture
initially imposes upon her sexual wants and needs. In other words, if the
notion of institutional coercion is overemphasized, all real choice is
impossible—including the choice of women to change the status quo.
Therefore, if women wish to think of themselves as agents who can make
a difference, it may be in their best interests to regard the forces of
institutional coercion as surmountable in ways that the forces of
individual coercion are not.[21]

The point of this digression is to agree with those who have pointed
out that the culture of any bureaucracy is antiethical but to disagree that
nothing can be done about this sad state of affairs. According to Arnold
J. Meltsner, bureaucracies are a pathological environment. There is
much pressure on analysts to conform to bureaucratic norms, to join in
the general scramble for prestige and power and to manipulate people
(and, in worst-case situations data and analyses) in order to gain access
to those empowered to make the decisions. This is part of the
bureaucratic structure, where "knowledge" in the form of the analysts
speaks to "power" in the form of the policymaker, and where analysts
must of necessity concern themselves with gaining access to power if
they are to have any assurance that their studies or reports will do more
than gather dust on a bookshelf. In addition, the desire for influence and
access to power may lead to an analyst's becoming (either consciously or
unconsciously) a mere "hired brain," gearing analysis and conclusions
toward the prejudices of the policymakers. Bureaucratic pressures such
as these often turn the analyst into a passive supporter of the status quo
or the latest political trend.

The problem with pinning the blame for one's personal actions on "the Institution" is that it overlooks what is obvious: People act in the context of ongoing institutions, and they "may be culpable for creating the structural faults of the institution, or for making efforts to correct them."[22] To the degree that institutions shape people, people shape institutions. In this connection, B. F. Skinner argues in *Beyond Freedom and Dignity* that even though the environment does indeed control us, it is, after all, a manmade environment:

> An experimental analysis shifts the determination of behavior from autonomous man to the environment—an environment responsible both for the evolution of the species and for the repertoire acquired by each member. Early versions of environmentalism were inadequate because they could not explain how the environment worked, and much seemed to be left for autonomous man to do. But environmental contingencies now take over functions once attributed to autonomous man, and certain questions arise. Is man then "abolished"? Certainly not as a species or as an individual achiever. It is the autonomous inner man who is abolished, and that is a step forward. But does man not then become merely a victim or passive observer of what is happening to him? He is indeed controlled by his environment, but we must remember that it is an environment largely of his own making.[23]

Policy analysts need not be passive victims of their bureaucratic environment. They can, if they so choose, respin the bureaucratic web within which they are entangled.

PRACTICE VERSUS INSTITUTION

Prevailing institutional structures do indeed militate against some of our most treasured notions of personal responsibility. But the solution is not to destroy our institutions, which, after all, make possible a quality of life most of us are not prepared to forsake. Rather, it is to reshape our institutions so that their structures can, as much as possible, support our efforts to achieve the good life. In this connection, Alasdair MacIntyre makes a helpful distinction between what he terms a "practice" and what he terms an "institution" and it is my view that policy analysts can assess their moral progress in terms of their ability to engage in their practice or profession without succumbing to those aspects of the institutional or bureaucratic framework that are, in some way or another, always going to be in tension with their desire to be good in both a moral and a nonmoral sense.

A practice, according to MacIntyre, is a cooperative human activity that has its own standards of excellence. These practices include everything from game playing (chess, football, tennis) to professional activities such as medicine, law, and business to personal activities such as parenting and praying. They also include policy analysis. One feature that is common to all practices is that if they are to flourish, their practitioners must appreciate those satisfactions or goods internal to them. Most of us realize that one of the satisfactions internal to chess is thinking of the strategic move, that one of the satisfactions internal to medicine is healing a body that seemed destined to die, and that one of the satisfactions internal to parenting is the joy of sharing in the development of a new human person. But because policy analysis is a relatively new practice, most of us do not realize that it too has internal satisfactions—for example, what Aaron Wildavsky describes as the pleasure in making "a little knowledge go a long way by combining an understanding of the constraints of the situation with the ability to explore the environment constructively." What makes doing policy analysis worthwhile for the analyst is the intellectual challenges it provides and the sense that he or she is solving a policy problem that needs to be solved if people are to have a better life.

It is, of course, not easy to achieve the goods internal to policy analysis. It is a process, claims MacIntyre, that involves standards of excellence and obedience to rules.[24] When a person decides to become a policy analyst, he or she will be judged by a set of performance criteria established by authorities in the field of policy analyzing, advising, and consulting. Quickly the novice analyst will realize both that a certain degree of conformity to "the way things are done" is required and that certain idiosyncratic notions both of public policy and of analysis must be given up if he or she is to become a recognizable member of the community of policy analysts.

As difficult as it is to submit to the transforming process of becoming a first-rate policy analyst, it is even more difficult to persevere in the process. According to MacIntyre, none of us can persevere in a practice long enough to achieve its internal goods without the requisite virtues or acquired human qualities that enable us to keep striving on those days when the goal does not seem worth all the effort. Anyone engaged in a human practice knows not only how hard it is to become excellent at that which one has chosen to do, but also how hard it is to do this alongside and along with others. Among other things, we have to learn how to be just, courageous, and honest in the context of our chosen practices.[25] Thus insofar as policy analysis is concerned, justice consists both in fulfilling all of one's obligations—to clients, to colleagues, to affected third parties, and to the public in general—and in giving credit to whom credit is due. Courage consists in articulating a new idea or devising a novel method of analysis even if such innovations go unrewarded or are penalized. And honesty consists in realizing one's own limits as an analyst as well as the limits of others. (The honest analyst has in other words proper self-respect. He or she neither overestimates his or her value [arrogance] or underestimates his or her value [servility].) In addition to exhibiting such basic virtues as justice, courage, and honesty, the good analyst is also candid, competent, and diligent. If the analyst is going to provide policymakers with the kind of information they need to shape policies that will serve the public best, then the analyst must strive to present all the facts, to master the tools of the trade, and to work at a task until it is done to the satisfaction of one and all. Finally, if the analyst is going to be trusted by the policymakers for whom he or she works, then the analyst must be loyal and discreet, a person with whom sensitive information can be shared. As simple as all this may seem, any policy analyst who has tried to meet all of his or her obligations, some of them conflicting, without cutting any corners or inflicting any unnecessary pain, to submit an innovative analysis of a complex policy process only to have it rejected, to accept his or her own limitations as an authority, to tell his or her client unwelcome but true facts, to work overtime day after day, and / or to stand by his or her client under adverse circumstances knows just how difficult it is to become a *good* analyst.

Virtuous practitioners are, as I have just observed, a necessary condition for a practice's survival. But they are not a sufficient condition because practices cannot be sustained without institutional support systems.[26] Although some of us may identify practices such as teaching, business, medicine, tennis playing, and policy analysis with institutions such as colleges, corporations, hospitals, tennis clubs, and the multiplicity of government agencies and departments that dot the Washington D.C. landscape, such identifications are to be resisted. Practices are characteristically concerned with what we have described as internal goods and they are held together by the cement of human cooperation. In contrast, institutions are necessarily concerned with external goods such as money, power, and status and they are energized by the fragmentary fires of human competition. But this is not necessarily a sad state of affairs provided both that "the ideals and the creativity of the practice" do not succumb to "the acquisitiveness of the institution"[27] and that the notion of service to the human community is not lost as one climbs up the ladder.

In other words, provided that the policy analyst tries to provide the best possible information to his or her clients so that they can serve the common good, the analyst need not be embarrassed by the fact that he or she responds to certain institutional carrots on sticks—praise or a higher salary, for example. What is welcome about MacIntyre's analysis of institutions is that he recognizes that they have positive as well as negative features. Teachers would still be peripatetic intellectuals were it not for the advent of the academy. Business persons would still be trading trinkets were it not for the creation of the corporation. Doctors would still be letting leeches loose on patients were it not for research institutions. What an institution provides a practice with are the material means and psychological framework within which people can gather together and challenge each other to achieve their common goals. To be sure, institutions are not unalloyed blessings for practices. The external goods of the institution do not always sit well with the internal goods of the practice. And sometimes when a practice is weak its practitioners succumb to the blandishments of the institution not so much because they are evil men and women who care only about power and prestige as because they do not have a clear sense of professional mission.

If the distinctions made earlier reflect reality, then policy analysis is a practice generally embedded in the bureaucratic or institutional structure we sometimes call "government." Significantly, policy analysis is different from many other practices in that its institutional framework seems to have predated it. Whereas most institutions have postdated the practices they currently envelop—medicine predates hospitals, teaching predates the academy, business predates the corporation—policy analysis has been absorbed into long-established government institutions. Thus policy analysts must not only develop the practice of policy analysis, which, according to most accounts, is still in its adolescence,[28] they must also simultaneously modify the institutions that currently house them. Otherwise the practice of policy analysis will not mature, for a practice cannot mature if its institutional support system militates against it. For example, if the government bureaucracy is structured in ways that encourage policy analysts not to take personal responsibility for their decisions and actions, then the practice of policy analysis will wither away. The only way the practice of policy analysis can survive, let alone thrive, therefore, is if policy analysts develop a set of institutional structures that will prompt them to raise their hands whenever they are responsibile for a decision or action.

The notion that practices and institutions exist in creative tension is a helpful one for policy analysts. Policy analysts who would be good need to ask themselves questions such as these: Am I giving my client this advice because it reflects reality or because it is what he or she wants to hear? Am I using a certain methodology because it is accepted by those who wield the power in my professional association or because it provides the most accurate results? Do I keep my clients' confidences simply because doing so can promote my career? Does getting ahead mean more to me than doing my job as well as possible?

Asking concrete questions like these may not enable policy analysts to resolve any better the problems Walzer and Goldman tried to resolve through a complicated ordering of abstract rights and utilities, but they will force policy analysts to reflect upon the ways in which institutional structures and systems of reward and punishment can either help or hinder their efforts to serve the public's best interests. In the 1960s, academics realized the ways in which the external goods of the university or college were detracting from the internal goods of teaching and scholarship. Professors seemed to care more about their grants, book contracts, salaries, tenure, and promotion than their students. Distressed by their own behavior, many professors abandoned the Ivory Tower for the streets, where they set up free universities and universities without walls. For a short time the practice of teaching flourished, but soon students and professors alike realized that without some sort of institutional support they would not be able to sustain themselves on energy and enthusiasm alone. It is hard to keep up standards without any external measures of approbation such as grades for students and promotions for professors; it is hard to teach without remuneration if one is not independently wealthy; and it is hard to study only for studying's sake. Gradually, professors and students went back to the university with walls, which, however, had been structurally changed for the better as a result of the rebellion.

Policy analysts face a similar challenge today. They have to strike the mean between blind or obsequious loyalty to "the Institution" on one hand and a quixotic or overly romantic do-goodism on the other. Neither extreme will do. Although this balancing act is not likely to satisfy the policy analyst who was hoping for the security of a revised version of the Ten Commandments, it is the most honest guidance that an ethicist can provide. Policy analysts, like the rest of us, are condemned to make some tough moral calls, to figure out when an institutional framework, intended to further the goals of a practice, is actually subverting them. Fortunately, ever since Adam and Eve were cast out of the Garden of Eden, none of us fallible human beings is expected to make the right decision each and every time. If the practice of policy analysis is not only to survive but to thrive, it is enough for its practitioners to take the challenges of morality seriously. To know the good may not be to do the good, but it certainly takes a person some distance in the right direction.

NOTES

1. Donald P. Warwick and Thomas F. Pettigrew "Toward Ethical Guidelines for Policy Research," *The Hastings Center Report, Ethics and Social Inquiry: A Special Supplement*, 13, 1 (February 1983):9.

2. See especially Dennis F. Thompson, "Moral Responsibility of Public Officials: The Problem of Many Hands," *The American Political Science Review* 74, 4 (December 1980).

3. Rosemarie Tong, *Ethics in Policy Analysis* (Englewood Cliffs, NJ: Prentice-Hall, 1985).

4. Niccolo Machiavelli, *The Prince*, trans. George Bull (Baltimore: Penguin, 1961), 96-98.

5. Max Weber, "Politics as a Vocation," in Hans H. Gerth and C. Wright Mills, eds., *From Max Weber: Essays in Sociology*, (New York: Oxford University Press, 1946), 125-126.

6. Michael Walzer, "Political Action: The Problem of Dirty Hands," *Philosophy and Public Affairs* 2, 2 (Winter 1973): 161.

7. Ibid., pp. 165-167.

8. Ibid., p. 179.

9. Alan H. Goldman, *The Moral Foundations of Professional Ethics* (Totowa, NJ: Rowman & Allanheld, 1980).

10. One problem with Goldman's analysis is that it requires us to describe as rights many interests that may not have the status of rights either in law or in ordinary morality. In other words, Goldman frequently asks us, without much of an argument, to accept his revisionist analyses of what does and does not constitute a right.

11. John Stuart Mill, *Utilitarianism* (London: Everyman's Library, 1863).

12. William Greider, "The Education of David Stockman," *Atlantic Monthly* (December 1981): 40.

13. William D. Carey, "The Pleasures of Advising," in William T. Golden, ed., *Science Advice to the President* (New York: Pergamon, 1980), 97.

14. Thompson, "Moral Responsibility of Public Officials," p. 907.

15. William G. Ouchi, *Theory Z* (New York: Avon, 1981), 56.

16. Robert Jackall, "Structural Invitations to Deceit: Some Reflections on Bureaucracy and Morality," *Berkshire Review* 15 (1980): 51-54.

17. Ibid., p. 52.

18. Ibid., p. 53.

19. Arnold J. Meltsner, *Policy Analysts in the Bureaucracy* (Berkeley: University of California Press, 1976), 151.

20. Rosemarie Tong, *Women, Sex, and the Law* (Totowa, NJ: Rowman & Allanheld, 1984), 109-110.

21. Ibid., p. 110.

22. Thompson, "Moral Responsibility of Public Officials," p. 908.

23. B. F. Skinner, *Beyond Freedom and Dignity* (New York: Bantam/Vintage, 1972), 205.

24. Alasdair MacIntyre, *After Virtue* (Notre Dame, IN: University of Notre Dame Press, 1981), 171.

25. Ibid., p. 178.

26. Ibid., p. 181.

27. Ibid.

28. Arnold J. Meltsner, "Creating a Policy Analysis Profession," *Society* (Sept./Oct. 1979): 51.

9

UNWITTING HUMAN SUBJECTS AND
THE ARMY'S BIOLOGICAL WARFARE TESTS

LEONARD A. COLE

New School for Social Research

Experimentation often provides a basis for policy evaluation. Testing a hypothesis through an experiment involving human subjects raises questions about social values as well. The questions largely arise from the tension between the rights of subjects and the potential benefits from an experiment. Provisions for safety and informed consent by prospective subjects are seen as requirements for most research. Yet some experiments, if they are intended for the good of the subject or the larger society, may be considered appropriate even if they do not fulfill these criteria.

In this chapter I assess the conditions for such research, with an emphasis on ethical considerations. Heightened sensitivity in recent years has led to enhanced protection for human subjects in general, though at least one area appears to be an exception. There is increasing evidence that the U.S. Army might wish to conduct biological warfare tests that would expose unwitting citizens to chemicals and bacteria. This recalls a period after World War II when the Army was spraying bacteria over populated areas to assess the nation's vulnerability to a germ warfare attack. I shall discuss the likelihood of renewed open-air testing in the latter portion of the chapter, after reviewing the development of protective mechanisms for human subjects.

ETHICS AND CHANGING VALUES

Some research characteristically involves deception and poses risks to a subject's physical or psychological well-being. New drugs, for example, are often administered to human subjects in an effort to assess their safety and efficacy before making them available to the public. The subjects presumably are informed of the known risks before taking the drugs. Yet the research may also involve deception insofar as one group of subjects receives active drugs, the other receives placebos, but subjects do not know which category they are in. Such a protocol is intended to enhance the validity of results and is commonly considered appropriate.

Deception is sometimes employed as well in social science experiments, particularly in social psychology. Among the best-known, and much criticized, are the "obedience to authority" experiments performed by Stanley Milgram in the early 1960s.[1] Subjects were instructed to press keys on a shock board, thereby administering painful shocks to an individual when he or she answered questions incorrectly. The real purpose of the experiments was to determine if people would inflict pain simply because an authority figure instructed them to do so. In fact, most people did.

Only afterward were the subjects informed that the shock board was a fake involving no electric current, and that the person receiving the "shocks" feigned pain and anguish. The Milgram experiments were initially applauded as a brilliant demonstration of the willingness of people to perform heinous acts in obedience to authority. In recognition of his work Milgram received a prize from the American Association for the Advancement of Science in 1965, and soon after was elected a Fellow of that association as well as of the American Psychological Association. Controversy about the experiments later began to surface, however. Some critics thought that subjects may have experienced severe anxiety reactions and that on that basis alone the experiments were inappropriate.[2] While Milgram continued to defend his work, by the late 1970s,[3] many doubted that such experiments could be conducted any longer because of prevailing social values.

The Milgram experiments place into dramatic relief the issues that are framed by all experimentation involving unwitting human subjects. What are the limits of harm to which a subject may be exposed? Under what conditions may informed consent be waived and deception or secrecy employed? When are such experiments, in a word, unethical?

Seeking absolute answers to these questions would be futile. Standards are affected by the changing values of society over time, as the reactions to the Milgram experiments demonstrate, as well as different views among individuals during any particular period. A review of society's attitudes in recent decades to such research helps to clarify these points.

THE NUREMBERG CODE

No event concerning experimentation with human subjects is more important than the trial of German doctors at Nuremberg in 1948. At the end of World War II evidence emerged that Nazi researchers had performed medical experiments on Jews and other concentration camp inmates. As the trial revealed, subjects were not voluntary participants, and many of the experiments were gruesome and sadistic. Among more than 3,200 human subjects used in the experiments cited at Nuremberg, about 1,100 died as a result; survivors commonly suffered physical and mental disabilities. "In every one of the experiments the subjects experienced extreme pain or torture, and in most of them they suffered permanent injury, mutilation, or death, either as a direct result of the experiments or because of lack of follow-up care," said the Nuremberg chief prosecutor.[4] Although only 23 physicians and scientists were defendants at the trial, evidence was presented that hundreds participated or had firsthand knowledge about the experiments and that thousands more had inferential knowledge.

The verdict rendered by the Nuremberg tribunal included a list of ten basic principles regarding human experimentation that, according to the judges, "must be observed in order to satisfy moral, ethical, and legal concepts."[5] The principles became known as the Nuremberg Code and were the first norms specified by an international body that pertained to the protection of human subjects. The code remains a basic statement of subjects' rights and has influenced virtually all subsequent efforts to formalize rules for the treatment of human subjects.[6]

The first principle sets the tone for the entire code. It holds that a subject should be fully informed about the nature and risks of the experiment, and that voluntary consent is "absolutely essential." Subsequent principles specify that the experiment should be for the good of society, that it be justified by anticipated results, that it avoid unnecessary suffering, that it be conducted only by scientifically qualified persons, and that it be terminated if it "is likely to result in injury, disability, or death." The principles, if breached sometimes in practice, have remained the ideals of properly conducted research involving human subjects.

AFTER NUREMBERG

Since issuance of the Nuremberg Code, policies in the United States concerning the protection of human subjects have been marked by two periods. The first existed through the mid-1960s, when governmental directives or regulations aimed at protecting subjects were nonexistent. Only in 1966 did a governmental agency announce a formal policy. The U.S. Surgeon General issued limited regulations concerning the use of human subjects by scientists working with funds from the National Institutes of Health.[7]

Impetus for further governmental involvement came from the disclosure a few years later that the U.S. Public Health Service had been conducting unethical experiments. Beginning in 1932, public health service doctors administered placebos to hundreds of black men in Tuskegee, Alabama under the pretense of treating them for syphilis.[8] During the next 40 years the naive subjects returned periodically for purported treatment. In fact they were being observed in an effort to determine the effect of untreated syphilis on physical and mental health.

By 1952, 40% of those who went untreated had died, compared to 20% who had received treatment. Nevertheless, the study continued. Not until 1966 did a public health adviser question the ethics of the experiment. His inquiries were shunted aside, and he later spoke to a journalist about the study. Following press reports the study was ended in 1972. Soon after, an investigative panel that was appointed by the secretary of Health, Education, and Welfare repudiated the study. The panel concluded that the research had been "ethically unjustified" and "scientifically unsound."[9] The disclosure of the Tuskegee experiment prompted the beginning of an effort on the part of the government to formulate codes for all agencies involved with human subject research.

The first federal legislative effort was included in the National Research Act of 1974.[10] The act required that any "entity" receiving federal funds for human subject projects establish an institutional review board (IRB) "in order to protect the rights of human subjects." The IRB was to review all biomedical and behavioral research involving human subjects "conducted at or sponsored by" that institution (usually a government agency, university, or research institute). The act also directed the Secretary of Health, Education, and Welfare to appoint an

11-member National Commission for the Protection of Human Subjects of Biomedical and Behavioral Research. The commission had no regulatory powers but was given a mandate to investigate, study, and make recommendations concerning "the basic ethical principles which should underlie the conduct of biomedical and behavioral research involving human subjects." Among the matters designated by the act as important for the commission's consideration were "appropriate guidelines for the selection of human subjects for participation in biomedical and behavioral research," and "the nature and definition of informed consent in various research settings."[11] Thus as in virtually all policy considerations about human subject research, the issue of informed consent was emphasized. This takes on central importance when considering research involving unwitting subjects, as will be discussed.

During its four-year existence the commission issued reports on a variety of concerns dealing with its overall assignment, including the use of children, prisoners, and the institutionalized mentally infirm as research subjects. The activities of the commission helped to broaden public understanding of the issues, but by the end of its tenure in 1978, little had changed in terms of establishing a coherent national policy for protecting human subjects.

New legislation provided for a successor agency, called the President's Commission for the Study of Ethical Problems in Medicine and Biomedical and Behavioral Research.[12] This commission was charged with considering a wider range of issues than was the earlier commission. Like its predecessor, the president's commission had no regulatory powers. Nevertheless, the new 11-member body, appointed by the president, could make inquiries of and recommendations to federal agencies, who were then required to respond in writing within a prescribed period.

Several areas to be studied were specified in the enacting legislation. Their scope was far greater than that covered by the national commission and included issues as diverse as defining death, testing and counseling for genetic diseases, and examining the influence of social background on the availability of health care. But the first duty of the new commission, according to the law, was to consider "the requirements for informed consent to participation in research projects and to otherwise undergo medical procedures."

The president's commission went out of existence in March 1983.

During its tenure it addressed the matters mentioned in the enacting legislation as well as others, such as the ethics of genetic engineering. Of particular interest here is the commission's attention to the protection of human research subjects. It issued periodic reports on the matter, including a comprehensive assessment entitled *Protecting Human Subjects*.[13] Dealing with the requirement of informed consent proved to be one of the commission's most challenging tasks, as its reports make clear. The commission's work, along with that of other scholars, has helped to point out the complexities of the issue.

INFORMED CONSENT

Soliciting informed consent from a prospective subject seems at first glance to be an uncomplicated task. Levine devotes 24 pages to discussing why this is not true.[14] He describes 16 "elements of information that should be communicated to the prospective consenter." From the initial invitation to become a subject through the responsibility of explaining how information gleaned from the research will be disclosed, Levine offers a formidable list of elements. Included are a statement of purpose of the research, the basis for selection of the subjects, explanation of procedures, description of discomforts and risks, available help in case of injury, description of benefits, disclosure of alternatives, assurance of confidentiality, and provisions to answer questions and for consultation. Levine amplifies on these and other elements. He grants that not all must enter into information provided about every experiment—in certain cases some are irrelevant. Those that apply, however, "should be communicated."

Even Levine's list is not exhaustive. The president's commission mentions other information that "must be provided, when appropriate," such as anticipated circumstances in which the subject's participation may be terminated without his or her consent, additional costs to the subject that may result from participation, and the consequences of a subject's decision to withdraw from the research.[15] The requirements for providing the subject with "information"—only the first half of the informed consent formula—are thus striking. Then there is "consent."

The notion of consent, properly conceived, also involves different components. Comprehension is obviously essential, and its realization depends on several determinants. First is language. The researcher must be able to communicate in nontechnical language all the appropriate information if an informed judgment is to be made. Additionally, the potential subject must be able to understand the language. For some, even nontechnical explanations may not be fully comprehensible, especially if a project is complex. The reliability of informed consent may rest less on the communications skills of an investigator, in the words of Peter Brown, and more on "how rational, informed, and self-interested the consenter is."[16]

This suggests another element: the subject's level of interest. A prospective participant may simply not be interested in explanations yet be willing to sign a consent agreement. A variety of motivations might account for this: financial reward, a sense of altruism, or peer pressure, for example. Whatever the reason, a consenter might be uninformed because he or she paid no attention to explanations.

Finally, the question of autonomy enters into the matter of consent. Some people who seem to be voluntary agents may not in fact be so. Prisoners who agree to participate as research subjects may do so only because they are institutionalized. Several have indicated that in addition to financial remuneration, they believe that they receive better treatment as a result;[17] nor can the opportunity to break the monotony of prison routine be discounted. For others, such as children or mentally infirm people, the question of informed consent is virtually meaningless. Some observers contend that individuals who cannot exercise free choice should never be subjected to nontherapeutic research.[18]

DECEPTION

Deception in human subject research is, of course, the antithesis of informed consent. Apart from abstract ethical questions about a person's rights, deception research may bear on matters of physical or psychological damage. Thomas Murray tells of the unsettling reactions of subjects in a social psychology experiment that he helped to conduct.[19] The subjects were asked to sit in a small booth and watch a TV monitor. Soon after they would witness the "experimenter" in another room apparently receive a shock and collapse on the floor. Murray would then see if the subjects would seek aid for the victim. If after six minutes a subject made no move, Murray would retrieve the subject from the booth and inform him or her of the true nature of the experiment.

Many who failed to seek help were not merely embarrassed, says Murray, but "I saw individuals whose faces were drained of color, who were reduced to stuttering, or who could barely force words through their clenched teeth."[20] Murray soon joined those whom he called the "unknown number of would-be social psychologists who quietly retired from the field because they were unable to put their wholehearted efforts into deception research."[21] He and others believe deception research may harm the researcher no less than the subject. As a consequence of such work, they think a researcher can become callous, manipulative, and cynical about fellow human beings.[22]

Deception research may be assessed on a continuum between extremes. One extreme involves subjects who are entirely unaware of the true reasons for their participation, whether in the realm of biomedical or psychological research. This includes experiments that lead to anticipated physical consequences, such as the Tuskegee study, and one conducted in a San Antonio, Texas, clinic where women who thought they were receiving contraceptives were given placebos.[23] Milgram contends that such biomedical research is distinct from experiments such as those he conducted, which are "of a psychological character" and therefore atraumatic.[24] Apart from disagreement among scholars about whether social psychological research can be traumatic, for categorical purposes these deception experiments are identical. They share the characteristic that the experimental subjects have no idea about the true nature of the experiment.

At the other end of the deception continuum is the person who is frankly told that he or she is taking part in research involving deception. The most benign situation might involve telling a subject that some participants in the experiment will receive active drugs and some will receive placebos, but that neither the subjects nor the examining doctors know who is receiving which. At what point on the continuum deception research becomes unethical is problematic, involving in large measure the attitude of the community at a particular time. The Tuskegee study, which seems abhorrent today, would not have been viewed so harshly by the public in the 1930s when the experiment was begun. This was pre-Nuremberg Code, and at a time when national mores were more receptive to racial discrimination.

The most literal guide to understanding contemporary standards should lie with the regulations most recently adopted by governmental agencies. Yet even here inconsistencies abound, as the president's commission reported. Although all federal agencies involved with research on humans now have IRBs, regulations regarding protection vary from agency to agency. Some, like the Department of Health and Human Services (HHS), provide sanctions in case of noncompliance, including suspension of individuals from further financial assistance within the department. Others, like the Department of Agriculture, do not specify any sanctions for noncompliance.[25] Moreover, agencies are inconsistent in applying their regulations. Several agencies, according to Alexander Capron, former executive director of the president's commission, do not "really do much of anything to know how well their regulations are working."[26]

The president's commission viewed the HHS regulations as a model code that all agencies should adopt. Many have done so, including the Department of the Army. Yet in the matter of informed consent the HHS rules are not entirely comforting. After offering a rigorous list of requirements for informed consent, including several of the elements cited earlier, a qualifying clause appears to weaken the protective machinery. Under certain conditions "an IRB may approve a consent procedure which does not include, or which alters, some or all of the elements of informed consent set forth above." These include the requirements that "the research could not be practicably carried out without the waiver or alteration," and that "the research involves no more than minimal risk to the subjects."[27] Thus the "model" HHS regulations cited by the president's commission allows for waiving the requirement of informed consent. This clearly applies to drug research, where deception is considered legitimate. Yet the rules provide a loophole that can lead to abuse.

As we turn to consideration of the Army's biological warfare tests over populated areas, this assumes particular significance. Regulatory machinery to protect human subjects has been enhanced in recent years, and several experiments that were conducted 20 years ago would be impermissible today. Germ warfare testing, however, appears to be an exception.

BIOLOGICAL WARFARE TESTING

Readers of *The Washington Post* must have been uneasy about an article on December 5, 1984 headlined "Army Sprayed Germs on Unsuspecting Travelers." The article described a recently unclassified report about a secret Army test 20 years earlier at Washington National

Airport. Supposedly harmless bacteria were sprayed at passersby from specially constructed suitcases to assess whether an enemy could do the same with more lethal germs. (Conclusion: It could.) Critics contended that the bacteria used in the test were themselves dangerous.

The experiment was part of a "vulnerability test" program involving millions of unwitting citizens. At Senate committee hearings in 1977, the Army acknowledged having released germs throughout the 1950s and 1960s over hundreds of populated areas including San Francisco, Panama City, Key West, parts of Alaska and Hawaii, onto the Pennsylvania Turnpike, and into the New York City subway system.[28] Army witnesses contended that the bacteria used in the tests—usually Bacillus subtilis and Serratia marcescens—were harmless. But testimony indicated that in some areas where testing took place, pneumonia-like illnesses tripled. Dr. J. Mehsen Joseph, Director of Laboratories Administration of the Maryland State Department of Health and Mental Hygiene, called the tests "unconscionable." Like other health experts who testified, he regarded the research as an "unjustifiable health hazard for a particular segment of the population."[29]

The Army admitted that it never monitored the health of the exposed population but maintained in any case that the tests caused no harm. A Pentagon witness declared, moreover, that although such tests were not then taking place, they would be resumed when the Army felt a need to assess an "area of vulnerability."[30]

By the mid-1980s the Army seemed to be feeling the need. Although the United States, like the Soviet Union, signed the 1972 Biological Weapons Convention that prohibits the development or stockpiling of biological weapons, the treaty permits research for "protective" purposes.[31] This means that defensive research has not been prohibited, and the United States has continued to maintain programs, such as the development of vaccines and protective gear, and what Susan Wright calls "research into 'offensive' aspects of biological agents . . . for defensive reasons."[32] Prompted by concerns that the Soviets have been developing a biological warfare arsenal in violation of the treaty, the Reagan administration's budget for defensive research ballooned. Overall chemical-biological warfare expenditures rose from $160 million in 1980 to over $1 billion in 1985.[33] Precisely what percentage went to defensive biological research is unclear, although the chief of public affairs at Fort Detrick, Maryland, America's biological warfare headquarters, said that the amount was "very generous."[34] Vulnerability testing is considered defensive research.

Suggestions about how open-air testing could help in defense preparations have been raised with increasing frequency. In assessing how an enemy might attack with germs, proposals were made to test with new realistic simulants. A report prepared under Army contract urged open-air testing to evaluate "meteorological variables" and "detection devices."[35] Elsewhere the possibility was raised of protecting the public against germ warfare agents by spraying clouds of vaccine over populated areas, which presumably would first require outdoor testing.[36]

Other events also pointed to the surge of interest in research activity. Secret intelligence reports cited in columns by Jack Anderson and in *Wall Street Journal* articles indicated near panic that the Soviets were developing supergerms through genetic engineering. Anderson quoted a National Security Council document that warned that the Soviets had mastered "gene-splicing techniques as ominous as the atom-splitting discoveries that led to the nuclear bomb."[37] Evidence for this seemed flimsy, and many molecular biologists think the Soviets are years behind American gene-splicing capabilities.[38] Yet Secretary of Defense Caspar Weinberger said "there is an apparent effort on the part of the Soviets to transfer selected aspects of genetic engineering research to their biological warfare centers."[39] This view has fueled interest in assessing the nation's vulnerability and in devising better instruments for detecting biological agents through open-air testing.

Just such a proposal was made in 1984 by a committee of the National Academy of Science's Board on Army Science and Technology. Under contract from the Army, the 12-member committee published a report that proposed open-air vulnerability testing.[40] The committee urged that "field tests" be carried out using "realistic, nontoxic simulants." Nowhere in the report is there an indication that testing should be confined to unpopulated areas, nor is the question of exposing unsuspecting citizens mentioned.

After the report was issued, two scientists who served on the committee were asked about this omission. Neither could recall any discussions about the subject during committee deliberations.[41] One member, Dr. F. James Primus, an immunologist at the University of Medicine and Dentistry of New Jersey, doubted that the committee intended that testing be conducted in heavily populated areas, though "field tests would be done presumably where there are people." Indeed, the report's admonition that "nontoxic" biological and chemical simulants be used implies an understanding that people would be exposed.[42]

How the Army interprets the proposal to test under realistic conditions may only be surmised, but based on past performance there is reason for concern. Previous vulnerability tests were conducted among people because the Army wanted to simulate realistic conditions, as Army reports make clear. An enemy is unlikely to spray its germs over unpopulated areas, so field testing over remote desert terrain would not offer as much information as testing among buildings in cities.

Statements by Defense Department spokesmen have been ambiguous. At a symposium on Biological Research and Military Policy sponsored by the American Association for the Advancement of Science in May 1984, Thomas Dashiell, director of environmental and life sciences in the Office of the Secretary of Defense, was asked about resumed testing with microorganisms and chemicals over populated areas. "I would hesitate to guess on whether there will be a resumption or not," Dashiell said. He tried to reassure his audience by explaining that "any open-air testing at this point in time requires the completion of a complete and detailed environmental impact statement which is made public. We hold public hearings on all of those."[43] Subsequent behavior by the Army was not reassuring, however.

THE DUGWAY ISSUE

Three months after Dashiell's statement, the Army was trying to expand its testing program at the Dugway Proving Ground in Utah without an environmental impact statement. A new facility was proposed that would have no apparent bearing on open-air spraying. But the manner in which the Army sought approval raised further suspicions about its approach to the whole program. Before Congress adjourned in August, an acting assistant secretary of the Army sent a note to the House and Senate appropriations committees requesting a routine reallocation of $66 million. The funds were to be taken from existing programs and used for several apparently minor projects. The list included new military housing in Europe, a parking garage in upstate New York, and a physical fitness center in Pennsylvania. Tucked among such items was an aerosol test facility in Utah.

The request was reviewed by the chairmen and ranking members of the subcommittees on military construction. As is customary, upon their assent the reallocation was authorized. Two months later, Senator James Sasser, the ranking minority member of the Senate subcommittee and one of the four members who signaled assent, reversed his position. In a letter to Secretary of Defense Weinberger he explained that after reviewing the planned expansion of the test facility, he determined that it could be used "to test offensive biological and toxin weapons, a capability which is prohibited by a 1972 Treaty."[44]

Despite Pentagon statements that the expanded program would not violate the treaty, Sasser remained skeptical. On December 6 the Senate subcommittee decided to approve the $8.4 million project over Sasser's objection. Meanwhile a public interest group filed a suit to stop the project. The group, called Foundation on Economic Trends, is headed by Jeremy Rifkin, who has successfully filed other suits to prevent the introduction of genetically altered bacteria into the environment.

Rifkin's suit focused on concerns that toxic material might escape from the laboratory "and cause human disease." It contended that the project would impose risks on the health of people in the area, and noted that Salt Lake City was less than 90 miles away. The plaintiffs said further that the Defense Department had "wantonly disregarded the federal statute governing environmental risk assessment."[45] In response to the suit the Defense Department suspended the start of construction and issued an environmental assessment of the project. The assessment maintained that toxic materials would be contained within the new facilities and would therefore have no effect on the environment. Rifkin returned to court. In May 1985, Federal Judge June Green determined that the Army must produce an environmental impact statement, which by law requires public hearings and consideration of alternatives.[46]

IMPLICATIONS OF DUGWAY ON OPEN-AIR TESTING

The series of events should concern anyone worried about unwittingly breathing Army germs during open-air tests. The manner in which the Army sought to implement its project—with no formal votes, no hearings, no debates—is disturbing. There seemed to be an effort to avoid deliberate consideration of "an unprecedented expansion of the army's biological weapons research program," in the words of a writer for *Science* magazine.[47] Only when threatened with legal action did the Army agree to undertake an environmental assessment. This was all the more troubling in view of Dashiell's assurances a few months earlier that such programs would be preceded by an environmental impact statement and public hearings. Confidence that the Army would inform the public before spraying it with bacteria was scarcely inspired by the Dugway experience.

Ironically, several scientists who supported the Rifkin suit lent support to such spraying. Concerned about the use of toxic agents, they endorsed the suit's plea that simulants be used as alternatives. Roy Curtiss, a molecular biologist at Washington University, said typically that instead of pathogenic organisms, "one can easily choose non-pathogenic or avirulent agents with the same size and molecular properties."[48]

However unintentionally, critics of the Army's proposed facility at Dugway were promoting the idea that spraying "nonpathogenic" organisms would be safe—the army's very argument to justify vulner-ability tests over populated areas. Yet as Dr. George Connell of the Center for Disease Control testified at the Senate hearings in 1977, "there is no such thing as a microorganism that cannot cause trouble." Speaking of the supposedly harmless bacteria used in the germ warfare tests, he emphasized that "if you get the right concentration at the right place, at the right time, and in the right person, something is going to happen."[49] Similarly, Dr. Stephen Weitzman, an expert in infectious diseases, has pointed out that among elderly people, newborn babies, and people who suffer from debilitating diseases, "so-called non-pathogenic bacteria commonly cause illness and death."[50]

Nevertheless, the Army's long-standing position, which was endorsed in the 1984 report urging more field tests and implicitly by scientists who have criticized the Dugway project, is that "nontoxic" simulants are harmless and may be used over populated areas.

PROTECTING UNSUSPECTING CITIZENS
FROM ARMY TESTS

Apart from questions of safety, the right of citizens not to be unwitting guinea pigs should be at issue. Yet here too protection falls through the cracks of institutional safeguards. On the surface, protection of an unsuspecting public from Army germs would seem assured insofar as targeted citizens should be informed and give consent. "Not necessarily," says Alexander Capron, who had been the executive director of the President's Commission for the Study of Ethical Problems in Medicine and Biomedical and Behavioral Research. Capron says the Army's definition of research seems different from other people's. "If they develop a new battle plan or a new weapon, the army does not regard that as coming under the regulations on human experimentation."[51]

Another complication, according to Capron, involves the question of whether people who are sprayed during a germ warfare test should be considered experimental subjects. "To me it would be pretty clear that they are," Capron continues, "but to others, when you deal with widely dispersed testing, there may be some question as to who are the subjects." An army official involved in interpreting the Defense Department's human-subject regulations concurs that people exposed in open-air tests "would not, in fact, be experimental subjects"[52]

Thus between the Army's position that its test bacteria are harmless and that exposed citizens may not be viewed as experimental subjects, spraying could take place and no one would know. Present policy does not adequately protect the rights and safety of citizens who may be exposed during vulnerability tests.

CONCLUSION

While writing about social experimentation, Peter Brown provided insights concerning the responsibilities of citizens and society to each other. His remarks are apt responses to the Army's justification of germ-spraying research as a requirement for national defense. Brown mentions two essential points about a citizen's relationship to the larger society: first, that "presence by choice in a political society amounts to an agreement to abide by its laws"; but second, that "such tacit consent is not sufficient justification for saturation experiments that may cause harm to nonparticipants [i.e., those who did not explicitly agree to participate]."[53]

By virtue of being a citizen, one accepts the need for national security. This does not, however, signify tacit agreement to participate in experiments toward that end. Nor does a citizen surrender his or her privilege to make such a decision to elected representatives.

Perhaps this point may be seen more clearly by imagining the following absurd use of tacit consent arguments. The city council of X municipality permits the Air Force to test a new atomic device by dropping it on the city. One of the few survivors staggers up to a city council member and blurts: "What happened?" The city council member replies that the council authorized the test on the basis of the "tacit consent" of the

citizens of the city. Since nothing in the charter prohibited such author-
ization, it was presumed that the citizens consented to it. Clearly, such a
reply would be absurd.[54]

Brown summarizes: "The point is that tacit consent cannot be *presumed*
to establish the legitimacy of noncustomary actions or actions (which
involve risk or harm) that are not expressly authorized."[55]

Biological warfare testing over populated areas is noncustomary and
involves risks to the exposed citizens. Thus in addition to reasons of
safety and individual rights, when assessed in terms of the contractual
obligation between citizen and government, justification for such testing
fails again.

In sum, vulnerability testing in which unwitting humans are exposed
to germs should be considered inappropriate on several counts. The
claim that it is appropriate deception research disregards current ethical
standards. The argument that it is safe ignores medical and biological
evidence to the contrary. Justification on the basis of a citizen's
obligation in the context of national defense is sophistry.

Despite increased sensitivity during the past decade to the rights and
safety of human subjects, vestiges of a discredited ethos remain alive in
the form of the Army's germ warfare program. In this area contemporary
values have yet to be incorporated into national policies.

NOTES

1. S. Milgram, *Obedience to Authority* (New York: Harper & Row, 1975).

2. R. J. Levine, *Ethics and Regulation of Clinical Research* (Baltimore: Urban and
Schwarzenberg, 1981), 143.

3. S. Milgram, "Subject Reaction: The Neglected Factor in the Ethics of Experimentation," *Hastings Center Report* 7 (October 1977): 19-23.

4. T. Taylor, "Preface," in A. Mitserlich and F. Mielke, *Doctors of Infamy: The Story
of the Nazi Medical Crimes* (New York: Henry Schuman, 1949), xxv.

5. J. Katz, *Experimentation with Human Beings* (New York: Russell Sage Foundation, 1972), 305-306.

6. In 1964, the World Medical Assembly elaborated on the Nuremberg Code in a
document entitled "Declaration of Helsinki: Recommendations Guiding Medical
Doctors in Biomedical Research Involving Human Subjects." The declaration and
subsequent revisions are reprinted in Levine, *Ethics and Regulation of Clinical Research*,
pp. 287-289. The codes of American professional associations that deal with human
subject research are largely based on the Nuremberg principles, although many such

associations had not adopted formal codes until the 1970s. See L. A. Cole, *Politics and the Restraint of Science* (Totowa, NJ: Rowman and Allanheld, 1983), 119.

7. E. L. Pattullo, "Who Risks What in Social Research?" *Hastings Center Report* 10 (April 1980): 16.

8. J. H. Jones, *Bad Blood* (New York: Free Press, 1981); A. M. Brandt, "Racism and Research: The Case of the Tuskegee Syphilis Study," *Hastings Center Report* 8 (December 1978): 21-29.

9. U.S. Department of Health, Education, and Welfare, Public Health Service, *Final Report of the Tuskegee Study Ad Hoc Advisory Panel* (Washington, DC: Government Printing Office, 1973).

10. Public Law 93-348, Title II—Protection of Human Subjects of Biomedical and Behavioral Research, 1974.

11. Ibid.

12. Public Law 95-622, Title XVII—President's Commission for the Study of Ethical Problems in Medicine and Biomedical and Behavioral Research, 1978.

13. *Protecting Human Subjects*, Report by the President's Commission for the Study of Ethical Problems in Medicine and Biomedical and Behavioral Research (Washington, DC: Government Printing Office, 1982).

14. Levine, *Ethics and Regulation of Clinical Research*, pp. 69-93.

15. *Protecting Human Subjects*, pp. 26-28.

16. P. G. Brown, "Informed Consent in Social Experimentation: Some Cautionary Notes," in A. M. Rivlin and P. M. Timpane, eds., *Ethical and Legal Issues of Social Experimentation* (Washington, DC: Brookings Institution, 1975), 84.

17. F. Hatfield, "Prison Research: The View from Inside," *Hastings Center Report* 7 (February 1977): 11-12

18. P. Ramsey, "The Enforcement of Morals: Nontherapeutic Research on Children," *Hastings Center Report* 6 (August 1976): 21-30.

19. T. H. Murray, "Learning to Deceive," *Hastings Center Report* 10 (April 1980): 11-14.

20. Ibid., p. 12.

21. Ibid., p. 13.

22. Ibid., p. 14; Levine, *Ethics and Regulation of Clinical Research*, pp. 141-142.

23. Katz, *Experimentation with Human Beings*, pp. 791-792.

24. Milgram, "Subject Reaction."

25. *Protecting Human Subjects*.

26. Quotations of Mr. Capron in this and subsequent passages are from an interview conducted on June 2, 1982.

27. U.S. Department of Health and Human Services, *Rules and Regulations 45 CFR 46. Subpart A—Basic HHS Policy for Protection of Human Subject Research* (Washington, DC: Government Printing Office, 1981).

28. U.S. Senate Hearings, Subcommittee on Health and Scientific Research of the Committee on Human Resources: *Biological Testing Involving Human Subjects by the Department of Defense 1977* (Washington, DC: Government Printing Office, 1977).

29. Ibid., p. 270.

30. Ibid., p. 18.

31. United Nations Department for Disarmament Affairs, *Status of Multilateral Arms Regulation and Disarmament Agreements: Biological Weapons Convention of 1972* (New York: United Nations, 1983), 120-135.

32. S. Wright, "The Military and the New Biology," *Bulletin of the Atomic Scientists* 41 (May 1985): 11.

33. There are important distinctions between biological and chemical weapons. Biologicals are usually live agents, such as bacteria or viruses, that may continue to reproduce in the environment. Chemical agents do not reproduce. Although the possession of biological weapons is prohibited by the 1972 treaty, this does not apply to chemical weapons. The 1925 Geneva Protocol bans the use of chemical weapons, but not their possession by states.

34. Interview with Norman Covert, January 27, 1984.

35. *Assessment of Chemical and Biological Warfare Technologies*, Report prepared by the Committee on Chemical and Biological Sensor Technologies, Board on Army Science and Technology, National Research Council (Washington, DC: National Academy Press, 1984).

36. C. Piller, "DNA—Key to Biological Warfare?" *Nation* (December 10, 1983): 598.

37. J. Anderson, "Soviets Push Biological-Weapons Work," *Washington Post* (December 4, 1984): B-15.

38. L. A. Cole, "Yellow Rain or Yellow Journalism?" *Bulletin of the Atomic Scientists* 40 (August-September 1984): 36-38.

39. U.S. Department of Defense, *Soviet Military Power 1984* (Washington, DC: Government Printing Office, 1984), 73.

40. *Assessment of Chemical and Biological Warfare Technologies*.

41. Interviews with Dr. David L. Swift and Dr. F. James Primus, January 17, 1985.

42. *Assessment of Chemical and Biological Warfare Technologies*.

43. Transcript of symposium on Biological Research and Military Policy, annual meeting of the American Assocation for the Advancement of Science, Washington, D.C., May 1984.

44. J. Sasser, Letter to Caspar W. Weinberger, October 31, 1984; W. Biddle, "Army Seeks Expansion of Chemical Warfare Unit," *New York Times* (November 2, 1984): A-24.

45. Foundation on Economic Trends, press release, November 22, 1984; Foundation on Economic Trends et al. v. Caspar W. Weinberger and John D. Marsh, Civil Action no. 84, U.S. District Court for the District of Columbia, November 21.

46. W. Biddle, "Judge Forbids Army to Build Germ War Facility," *New York Times* (June 1, 1985): 24.

47. R. J. Smith, "New Army Biowarfare Lab Raises Concern," *Science* 226 (December 7, 1984): 1176.

48. Ibid., p. 1177.

49. U.S. Senate Hearings, p. 270.

50. L. A. Cole, "The Army's Secret Germ-War Testing." *Nation* (October 23, 1982): 397.

51. Capron, interview June 2, 1982.

52. L. A. Cole, "Operation Bacterium," *The Washington Monthly* (July-August 1985): 45.

53. Brown, "Informed Consent in Social Experimentation," p. 96.

54. Ibid., p. 97.

55. Ibid., p. 97, italics in original.

PART V

Policy Cases: Issues and Illustrations

10

THE POLITICS OF CRITERIA: PLANNING FOR THE REDEVELOPMENT OF TIMES SQUARE

SUSAN S. FAINSTEIN

Rutgers University

Not too long age academic theorists sought to develop a science of public policy.[1] They assumed that if a method could be developed to measure the costs and benefits of a policy initiative, then rational individuals could agree on whether or not the policy should be adopted. Attempts to introduce cost-benefit analysis into most arenas of public policy, however, inevitably founder on evident disagreements over both value criteria and measurement techniques.[2] Conflict over values arose because the maximization of one value inevitably was at the expense of another; measurement controversies derived from the difficulties both of predicting future outcomes under conditions of uncertainty and of providing weights to consequences that could only be assessed subjectively.

Disagreement on evaluative frameworks exists not primarily because of technical obstacles to a science of policy analysis but as a consequence of underlying social structural divisions. To reach consensus on the criteria by which policies should be evaluated and on the indicators by which outcomes should be measured, all groups affected by a policy must share a common interest that outweighs their particular interests. But most real policy decisions create winners and losers that are defined by their social circumstances. In order to protect their positions, groups seek to generalize their concerns by supporting the use of evaluative criteria that will favor their desired outcomes.

In the grossest terms, the conflict over criteria often boils down to a dispute over efficiency versus equity, or aggregate output versus distributional effects. Whether the subject be tax policy (should it provide incentives to investors or relief to low-income people?), transportation (efficient vehicular movement against access for low-income people), or housing (trickle down from private sector profitable investment or direct subsidy of low-income people), similar lines are drawn. Advocates of greater efficiency and increased output assume that all will benefit from growth;[3] proponents of equity criteria argue that the benefits of growth are encapsulated within the upper classes whereas the costs are disproportionately borne by those already least well off. More complicated arguments show that equity and efficiency need not be traded off directly against each other; nevertheless, growth with equity solutions are difficult to achieve because those favoring equity measures are usually relatively powerless. Nowhere are the relations among evaluative criteria, group power, and political outcomes more evident than in the controversies surrounding major plans for urban redevelopment.

THE CASE OF URBAN REDEVELOPMENT

Since the passage of the 1949 Housing and Urban Redevelopment Act, American city governments have sought to transform their central business districts so as to increase employment and enhance tax revenues. Early efforts provoked relatively little public opposition. By the 1960s, however, the consequences in terms of displacement of small businesses and low-income residences became widely known and feared. Eventually conflict became so severe as to transform sponsorship of major renewal projects from a politically appealing to a highly risky endeavor. Additionally, pressure on Congress to restrict the negative consequences for low-income people, resulting in increasingly strict relocation and public participation stipulations, made such projects less profitable. Consequently there was a hiatus in the mounting of large-scale renewal efforts.[4]

More recently, however, heightened economic activity in the cores of some metropolitan areas has once again increased the potential profitability of redevelopment. Where previously urban renewal authorities wrote down the costs of land and hoped that a developer would then use the land to create commercial space, developers are now vying for the right to acquire centrally located sites. Thus some city governments, relying principally on their own rather than federal resources, have reentered the urban renewal game. With this reinvigorated governmental intervention has come a series of familiar controversies over the distribution of costs and benefits. This chapter examines one such instance, first looking briefly at the general problems involved in evaluating redevelopment projects, then analyzing in detail a single project: New York City's plan for the redevelopment of Times Square.

WHAT MAKES A GOOD REDEVELOPMENT PROJECT?

Although at first glance the character of a successful redevelopment project seems self-evident, closer scrutiny of the question makes the definition of success ever more chimerical. The viewpoint usually expressed by promoters of development is that a net increase in city revenues and jobs within the project area is in the public interest and should be the criterion by which any project is measured. But those who argue that urban redevelopment should advance equity contend that rising property values are not a benefit, as they price neighborhoods out of reach of low-income people while delivering windfall profits to those already best off. They further argue that job creation is only a benefit if it does not result in the displacement of unskilled workers by professionals and managers, or of city residents by commuters. Thus the initially obvious neighborhood improvement resulting from the replacement of "marginal businesses" by office towers or crumbling tenements by high-rise apartments becomes less clear if the benefit criterion is amelioration of the situation of the already disadvantaged.

Other clashes of value, though perhaps less critical, also come into play and introduce measurement problems as well as further disagreement over the choice of criteria. For example, how are the aesthetics of those favoring low-rise development for its openness to light and air to be balanced against the advocates of the high rise, who claim excitement and economic efficiency as their yardsticks? Are high densities a cost or a benefit? On one hand they produce congestion on sidewalks and at transit stops; on the other they make possible more efficient use of mass transit. Should special protection be extended to certain industries at the expense of others because they offer needed services, even though they may provide a landlord with a lower return on his or her property and even though the proprietor as an individual may not be particularly deserving? But if not, is it desirable that bars, restaurants, and boutiques should drive out dry cleaners, groceries, and pharmacies, that office buildings should replace small service industries? Development proponents, when advocating the turnover of land to users who gain the most return on their investment, generally argue that doing so is consonant with the market and represents the most efficient outcome. But in fact the intervention of government in the establishment of land values through differential taxation, subsidies, and urban redevelopment schemes involving eminent domain means that a competitive market situation does not exist initially, and the triumph of certain land uses over others may simply reflect the influence of powerful actors over government rather than the most efficient solution.

All these considerations are manifest in the recent decision by the city of New York to redevelop 42nd Street, which demarcates the southern end of Times Square. The redevelopment proposal, which was approved by the city's Board of Estimate in 1984,[5] looks strikingly different depending on the observer. The proponents of economic development assert that the project will restructure land use in the area to its highest potential, thereby creating jobs, tax revenues, and economic multipliers. Other supporters foresee that it will restore the bright lights and dancing feet of yesteryear to the "crossroads of the world." For these two groups the criteria of benefit are, respectively, efficiency as measured by economic growth and superior land uses as indicated by the replacement of seemingly seedy occupants with culturally preferred ones. Opponents argue that the project threatens the viability of the last centrally located low-income residential area in Manhattan, and that it will kill the vitality of the theater district, thereby injuring one of the city's unique economic assets. Opponents not only use an equity criterion but they also claim that if efficiency were measured properly, the transformation of an entertainment area into an office district would be regarded as a cost, not a benefit.

THE 42ND STREET
REDEVELOPMENT PROJECT,
ITS SUPPORTERS, AND ITS CRITICS

Times Square is undoubtedly one of the world's most famous places. Centrally located in midtown Manhattan, illuminated at night by kinetic megasigns, site of the nation's most televised New Year's Eve celebration, it offers 24-hour-a-day activity. Stretching five blocks north from the intersections of Broadway and Seventh Avenue with 42nd Street, it is the center of legitimate theater in New York as well as its ancillary industries, including restaurants, theatrical booking agents, ticket agencies, dance studios, and costume rental establishments. Many of these theater support services rely for their continued operation on the low rents available on upper floors of nondescript buildings scattered throughout the district.

In addition to legitimate theaters, the area harbors a large number of motion picture houses. Although Times Square is notorious for spaces featuring pornographic films and live sex shows, the 42nd Street site of the redevelopment project is devoted primarily to "action movies," which display kung fu and other muscular but essentially nonsexual activities. The newer theaters on Broadway, perpendicular to the development area, show first-run films. Storefronts are occupied by bars, fast-food purveyors, bargain electronics stores, adult bookstores, videogame arcades, and miscellaneous shops. The sidewalks are shared uneasily by commuters traveling to and from the Port Authority Bus Terminal, theater- and moviegoers, patrons of the various retail establishments, three-card monte players, buyers and sellers of drugs, and loiterers. Some of the latter are (predominantly male) prostitutes; others are waiting for an opportunity to grab a purse or wallet; many are just hanging out.[6] Most patrons of the action movies and the majority of the loiterers are nonwhite.[7] A large Roman Catholic church and parochial school on 42nd Street face the bus terminal, a block away from Times Square; three other churches in the vicinity also serve the spiritual needs of the Clinton residential community, located immediately to the west.

For more than a decade, clergy, Clinton community leaders, and theater and restaurant owners have been pressing the city to take action against the unsavory uses that color most people's perceptions of Times Square. After successful rehabilitation of the western portion of 42nd Street, and a mitigation of street conditions in other parts of the area through stricter law enforcement, the city in 1981 promulgated a request for development proposals to deal with the blocks of 42nd Street within and adjacent to Times Square itself.

The most immediately striking characteristic of the winning proposal is its massiveness. The existing structures on the four corners straddling Times Square will be replaced by four office buildings totaling more than four million square feet of space. Heights of the buildings are 29,

37, 49, and 56 stories. In addition, nine of the theaters that line 42nd Street between Seventh and Eighth Avenues will be renovated, and most of them will be reconverted to legitimate theaters. A 2.4 million square foot wholesale mart will rise on the corner of Eighth Avenue; a 550-room hotel will be constructed across from the mart; and the busy Times Square subway station will be rehabilitated.

The appearance of the proposed structures is somber compared to the existing architecture of the area. Most attention has been directed to the four granite office towers, which rise up sharply, lacking setbacks and detail, varying from one another only in size. Ground-floor retailing and window displays are separated from the sidewalks by pillars supporting massive arches. The kinetic signage that gives the present Times Square its unique liveliness has disappeared. Generally the aesthetics of the buildings signify the seriousness of the business activity planned for their extensive interior spaces rather than the frenetic entertainment industry that has historically dominated the area.

The redevelopment scheme is under the auspices of a public-private partnership. On the governmental side both the New York State Urban Development Corporation (UDC) and the city's Public Development Corporation (PDC) carry out planning, staffing, and implementation functions, using UDC's powers of eminent domain and authority to override local zoning. On the private side a group of developers is responsible for various aspects of the project. In addition to putting up their own structures, they will contribute toward subway and theater renovation and pay for land acquisition costs up to a specified level. In return they will receive tax abatement of at least $650 million over a fifteen-year period.

Because the mission of the two public agencies involved is economic development, they are relatively unconcerned with such land use issues as aesthetics, densities, and impacts on surrounding areas. Basically their success criteria are number of jobs created and amount of tax revenues received. The City Planning Commission nominally bears responsibility for evaluating the proposal in terms of these other considerations, but it has not been a powerful force in the project. A group of eleven design-oriented civic groups belonging to an association called the President's Council[8] has assumed the task of monitoring the project's aesthetic and land use impacts and has expressed concerns over bulk, density, and vitality.

City council members and state assemblymen from the immediate area opposed the project. But a number of higher-level politicians including the governor, both U.S. senators, and the mayor strongly praised the scheme. Ardent supporters, when testifying at the Board of Estimate hearings, made frequent reference to the bright lights and glamor of historic Times Square, arguing that only a massive redevelopment effort could restore its former glory. Although some Clinton residents endorsed the plan, the project elicited vehement protest from community elements who felt that their conveniently located neighborhood would suffer overwhelming pressures of gentrification. Theater organizations have been split on their response to the project. Theater owners support it for its potential to alleviate surrounding blight and thus attract more patrons. On the other hand, a group called Save the Theaters, which is an offshoot of Actors Equity, opposed it, fearing its potentially deadening effects on the area and the likelihood that offices would drive out entertainment uses.

The project, as it was presented to the New York City Board of Estimate in October 1984, was the product of negotiations between the developer and city and state officials. While PDC and UDC could point to nominal consultation with community groups during the preceding years, it was only under the urgency of obtaining final political approval that any flexibility appeared. Just before the decisive Board of Estimate hearings, the sponsors of the project began to engage in frenzied negotiations with Clinton representatives and other interested community leaders. The key intermediaries in translating outside pressure into concessions were the elected officials rather than the planners, who until this point had remained obdurate. The concessions that were granted, however, were minimal and rather uncertain. Clinton was allocated $25 million over the next five years from the regular state and city budgets, to be used for low-income housing and community development purposes. Clinton representatives failed to achieve their objective of having the money come from the developers rather than regular public revenues. The final resolution also established a citizen advisory committee on design issues; whether it will succeed in seriously influencing the final outcome depends wholly on the willingness of the planners and developers to respond to it.

THE ARGUMENTS PRO AND CON

Sponsors of the proposed redevelopment stress its potential contribution to the city's economy and revenue base. The project's planners estimate that construction will produce 16,500 temporary jobs and, upon completion, 24,000 permanent jobs, as compared to 4,000 now. Contrary to assertions that if these jobs were not in Times Square, they would exist elsewhere, proponents counter that comparable space would not become available in Manhattan, tempting industries requiring large floor areas to leave the city altogether. They compare a street crowded with office workers, lined with diverse retail establishments, flanked by renovated legitimate theaters to the present corridor hosting adult bookstores, pornographic movie houses, and unattractive loiterers.

Advocates of the project argue that present uses drive out potential rehabilitators, preventing the private market from developing the area on its own. They point to the absence of new construction on the project blocks for the last fifty years as evidence of private market reluctance, despite the shortage of developable space in central Manhattan, ever to take a chance on the area without governmental intervention. To arguments that most of the movie theaters on the street are not pornographic but instead show action movies to a young, black, noncriminal clientele, they respond by asserting that nevertheless these blocks have the highest crime rate and require the most police personnel of any part of the city. Moreover, even those current uses that are not disreputable could be replaced by higher and better ones, producing enormous increases in city revenues. Indeed, the officials who negotiated the project feel they got a very good deal from the developers by obtaining for the city a share in profits as well as by making the developers responsible for site acquisition costs and subway improvements. Much publicity is given to the developers' commitments to theater restoration, although the sum of money involved is tiny as compared to the overall cost of the project and the taxes foregone.

Whereas the governmental officials involved with the project increasingly stress its economic as opposed to physical benefits, theater owners, restauranteurs, and the 42nd Street Development Corporation, which was responsible for earlier improvements on the street, enthusiastically predict a positive transformation of the theater district. They envision the spaces now showing kung fu films as once again housing hit musicals; they foresee that making the street inhospitable to loiterers will lure back suburbanites currently fearful of the district. Although, off the record, many among this group express distaste for the size and design of the office buildings, they regard these negative attributes as relatively unimportant compared to the project's benefits.

Of the groups within the President's Council, the Regional Plan

Association (RPA), which has as its purview the entire metropolitan area, was the most supportive. Basically RPA, though criticizing aspects of the plan, endorsed the concept of placing as much office development as possible in close proximity to mass transit. It thus strongly favored encouraging construction on the west side of Manhattan, which, in addition to being less congested than the east side, was well served by commuter rail and bus in addition to numerous subway lines. From RPA's regional perspective, the advantages of locating dense development where so many public transportation routes converged greatly outweighed any negative neighborhood impacts. RPA, however, like the other groups in the President's council, criticized UDC and the city for lack of responsiveness during the three-year period preceding the frantic negotiations at the Board of Estimate hearings.

Other of the civic groups, though assenting to the President's Council's limited support of the project conditional on certain modifications, individually spoke out against the project. Brendan Gill, chairman of the Landmarks Conservancy, summarized the reactions of civic groups opposing the project when, at the hearings on the draft environmental impact statement, he commented,

> We are concerned about losing Times Square as we know it: as a lively and dazzling entrance to the theater district. We have seen no evidence . . . that the addition of four million square feet of conventionally dreary office space is necessary to achieve the stated goals of the project: on the contrary it will drastically affect the character of the area, not for the better but for the worse.[9]

UDC responded to this lament by asserting that, although the size of the buildings was perhaps regrettable, the lower rents necessary to attract tenants to Times Square required construction on this scale. Informally, participants have commented that the developers could obtain bank financing only if they were able to promise rent levels substantially lower than those of new eastside buildings. Additionally the planners have argued that the height and bulk of the office buildings is mitigated by the low-rise character of the theaters on the midblock.

The civic groups mainly restricted their observations to issues of design and street life. Clinton residents, in contrast, saw the enterprise in class terms, regarding it as yet another traditional urban renewal project aimed at displacing the poor for the benefit of the wealthy. The southern portion of Clinton, which occupies the blocks directly to the west of

Times Square, houses families with incomes 50% to 83% of the Manhattan median; many have lived there for several generations; much of the labor force for the restaurants in the theater district walk to work from this neighborhood. Having already experienced a long history of gentrification and landlord harassment, many inhabitants feel that the placement of a gigantic office complex within a five-minute walk of their residences will turn the gradual erosion of their neighborhood into a landslide. Defenders of the project point to the protections offered by the city's rent-control system, the severe regulations on development within those parts of the neighborhood that constitute the Special Clinton District, the record of the city in prosecuting offending landlords, and the large number of subsidized units restricted to low-income occupants. But those residents who see homelessness as the only likely alternative to their currently affordable apartment are skeptical that these measures offer any guarantee of their right to shelter in a situation of exponentially escalating property values.

In general, many Clinton residents feel betrayed by the city. They regard the constant invocation by the project's supporters of the sleaziness of present street conditions as a cover-up by which their original demands for neighborhood improvement are cynically used to justify a tax giveaway to real estate developers. They are supported by academic critics who also question the tax benefits of the project.[10] The sizable payment in lieu of taxes that the project will be providing means that even with tax abatement for fifteen years, there will be a large net gain to the city from the area. But it may well be at the sacrifice of taxes paid elsewhere if private investors had been left to choose their own sites without government intervention.

Clinton's complaints are echoed in somewhat different form by members of the theater community, who also feel that their original call for protection of legitimate theaters is unjustifiably being used to defend the project. They point out that the sum of money allocated for theater restoration is inadequate, that no funds have been set aside for operation of the theaters, and that no guarantees are offered for their future if they fail economically. Given that 1984-1985 marked the lowest point in the last decade in terms of theater occupancy, causing the majority of theaters to be "dark" during most of the season, the addition of more empty theaters to the current stock without provisions for operation matters little. Furthermore, they worry that support industries such as costume rentals and dance studios will be forced from the area by rising rents and office conversions. Project planners have not responded to these criticisms directly; instead they point to the approval they have received from other theater people who see the key to their economic success in improved surroundings. But opponents have contended that those theater organizations which have strongly endorsed the project cannot lose—if their properties fail as legitmate theaters, they can always be converted to other, more profitable uses.

The current owners of most of the 42nd Street movie houses claim that their theaters are in fact viable as currently used and that they perform a unique entertainment function by providing inexpensive viewing in decent interior surroundings. They argue that the attempt to transform well-attended, all-day movie houses into empty legitimate theaters is discriminatory toward the present, predominantly black viewers and economically unjustifiable as well. Moreover, they profess their willingness to renovate the properties themselves, and see the transfer of ownership through eminent domain as a biased use of state power.

Even supporters of the project consider that despite assertions by the planners that the project emanates from years of public discussion, they have not been involved in the planning of it. Over the years of its formulation it has been the subject of several public hearings as well as discussions with community boards and other advisory bodies. But these interchanges have mainly amounted to public relations efforts on the part of the sponsors rather than meaningful attempts to elicit views that might change the fundamentals of the project. Consequently for those who value public participation in planning, the project falls short of their goals regardless of its other components.

WEIGHING THE ARGUMENTS

The balance sheet on the project depends on a mixture of objective and subjective assessments both of the overall values by which development projects should be assessed and of the importance allocated to specific project impacts, most of which are open to dispute in terms of either their magnitude or benefits. Certain questions, such as those concerning the final impact of the project on the city's tax base, cannot be answered with complete certainty; naturally advocates of the policy make the rosiest forecasts and detractors, the most pessimistic. Probably, however, no one would disagree that the greater the positive revenue impact, the better. Conflict then is not over whether revenue effects are an acceptable criterion but how heavily they should be weighed against other, competing criteria. Other impacts, such as a large increase in users of the area or greater architectural uniformity, are not factually contested but are viewed as blessings by some and curses by others.

Ultimately evaluation of the project's suitability depends on conceptions of the public interest and visions of alternative modes of dealing with the particular problems of Times Square. The endeavor illustrates New York City's commitment to economic development as its approach to social problems. The assumption is that the economic benefits of the project will trickle down to the broader public through job creation and expansion of city revenues. But most of the permanent jobs, and an even larger percentage of the executive-level ones, will probably go to commuters. The social pathologies evidenced on the sidewalks of 42nd Street can be reshuffled geographically through physical redevelopment but certainly cannot be vanquished in this way. The formerly taken-for-granted role of planners as the protectors of the environment has been abdicated. The project incorporates what has become the routine use of zoning code limits as bargaining chips rather than as methods of ensuring light, air, and aesthetics in an area. The office buildings exceed as-of-right floor area ratios by more than 100%. Limits have been traded away in order to attract investment to the site and to obtain contributions to subway improvements. But less ambitious development and use of regular capital budget funds for transit amelioration, though not as lucrative for the city, would contribute more to the quality of life of those who live and work in the area.

ALTERNATIVE PATHS

Would it have been possible to design a scheme for redeveloping Times Square that would have improved the physical and economic environment without producing such high densities, heavy commitment to office development, and overwhelming pressure on the adjacent residential community? In other words, was it feasible to create growth with equity? Abstractly the answer is yes. Despite the assertions of the project's planners that the only alternative to massive redevelopment is no development at all, the example of the block between Ninth and Tenth Avenues, to the west of the project site, indicates the potential for a more moderate approach. Here a more modest effort, consummated when the area was not attractive to major developers, saw the rehabilitation of abandoned commercial space into a lively row of "Off-

POLICY CASES

Broadway" theaters and restaurants. The landmark MacGraw Hill Building, though not offering the floor space supposedly required by desirable tenants, was renovated and fully rented. Across the street a subsidized housing project predominantly accommodates households involved in the performing arts.

A similar strategy addressed to the project blocks plus the additional area lying between them and Ninth Avenue would involve use of eminent domain to force out the most undesirable uses and allow the rehabilitation of present structures. Tax abatement could be used to entice the present owners to renovate their theaters without the contributions of office developers. Spot demolition could create the opportunity for some new construction. If the block closest to the existing subsidized apartment complex were used for a mixed re-sidential-commercial building, containing some low-income units, it would add much-sought residential space to Clinton and further upgrade the area. Because no influential political or administrative entity has seriously promoted such a development strategy, its virtues are unexamined and the ultimate decision boiled down to either the present project or no project at all.

Although the alternative approach suggested here could produce redevelopment without massive disruption, it would not create the kinds of huge public and private revenues promised by the existing approach. The choice to go ahead with the current strategy depended on political acceptance of the growth criterion untinctured by a commitment to equity and human scale in design.

WHOSE CRITERIA SHALL PREVAIL?

The myth that planning choices are made according to an abstract criterion of the public interest fades away in the reality of situations in which powerful actors are seeking to influence events and millions, even billions, of dollars are at stake. But neither is it true that public agencies simply respond to the behests of wealthy developers. Rather, choices are made in conformity with general criteria that provide decision rules for preferring one solution over another. These rules are themselves generated by the interplay of the narrow interests of politicians and developers, the legislative mandates given to administrative and plan-ning agencies, the mobilization of citizen groups, and the broader ideological framework within which the planning system operates.

Planning decisions are inherently political according to Lasswell's definition of politics as who gets what.[11] But they may or may not be overtly political if politics is defined by competition carried on overtly through campaigning, lobbying, and other forms of mobilization.[12] What Schattshneider called "the mobilization of bias"—that is, the tendency to accept certain frameworks of analysis or benefit criteria as givens—means that conflict may remain latent or may manifest itself over subsidiary issues rather than over the determining institutional mechanism.[13] For example, in the 42nd Street case the willingness of all parties to accept increased city revenues as a benefit criterion, although of varying weight, displaces controversy onto the factual question of the extent of revenues rather than the broader issue of whether to increase commercial development within the city at all. If, however, the New York metropolitan area were a single tax jurisdiction, then the question of whether office development occurred in Manhattan or New Jersey would be irrelevant. Thus the existing, largely unquestioned system of political jurisdictions biases the decisional process over particular projects like 42nd Street redevelopment.

The overall American system of capitalist competition and local political jurisdiction means that economic development almost necessarily becomes the dominant goal of municipal policymakers and, most of the time, is accepted unquestioningly by a public dependent on capital for its livelihood.[14] The only recent serious challenge to the reigning value hierarchy occurred in the 1960s and 1970s, when the mobilization of minority groups forced municipal governments to examine the distributive effects of urban renewal projects.[15] But in all cities, and especially in New York City after the recession and fiscal crisis of the mid-1970s, the priority of economic development, regardless of its costs to specific low-income groups, reasserted itself.

Recently, however, a new countermovement opposing real estate investment has surfaced in New York City consequent upon the resurgence of the city's economy. The rapid expansion of white-collar jobs, combined with an extremely sluggish rate of new residential construction, has put enormous pressure on the housing market and priced vacant housing out of reach of all but the affluent. Fears of displacement have caused low- and middle-income renters to oppose virtually any public or private project that improves a neighborhood, even if it has no direct displacement effects and even if it adds to the housing supply. It is assumed, not unjustly, that a neighborhood adjacent to an improving area will immediately become the object of real estate speculation, producing rising land values that ultimately will be passed through to tenants.

The growth versus equity argument has thus been resumed within a new context of opposition to private as well as public investment. Unless development ceases to be a zero-sum game in which lower-income people almost always lose, they will continue to resist the development process. Given that there is no likelihood that the system of competitive capitalism will soon end, policymakers will continue to make economic development their most important benefit criterion. Community groups that espouse equity and take their stand on opposition to all development may, given the existence of lawsuits as a vehicle for halting action, succeed in many cases in blocking development projects—as in fact could ultimately occur in Times Square. Or the obstacles to speedy development created by community opposition may force the granting of specific concessions such as the $25 million Clinton fund yet not establish any general principle of linkage between commercial development and the satisfaction of housing needs.

Opposition to individual projects alone will never change the structure that causes planning agencies continually to favor growth. Transforming development into a different game would require that new projects always be tied to specific concessions to low-income groups—for example, that the construction of commercial office space must be accompanied by contributions to a housing fund; that any new market rate residential building must contain a percentage of moderately priced units. Achieving this change in the context of development and requiring planners to take into account the needs of low-income people not just as the last beneficiaries of trickle down but as the immediate recipients of project outputs depends on the political mobilization of those groups most affected. Thus the choice of benefit criteria in urban development, if it is to change, must be political in both senses. It will necessarily determine who gets what; but in addition it will be the object of open contest rather than a paternalistic assumption by policymakers that economic development necessarily reflects the public interest.

NOTES

1. See Yehezkel Dror, *Public Policymaking Reexamined* (Scranton, PA: Chandler, 1986).

2. Frank Fischer, *Politics, Values, and Public Policy: The Problem of Methodology* (Boulder: Westview Press, 1980).

3. Paul Peterson, *City Limits* (Chicago: University of Chicago Press, 1981).

4. Susan S. Fainstein et al., *Restructuring the City* (New York: Longman, 1983), chapter 7.

5. The Board of Estimate, consisting of the mayor, the city council president, and the borough presidents, acts as the city's legislative body for all fiscal decisions.

6. William Kornblum and Vernon Boggs, "Redevelopment and the Night Frontier," *City Almanac* 18 (Summer 1986): 16-18.

7. New York Landmarks Conservancy, statement by Brendan Gill, Chairman, for the public hearing of March 26, 1984 on the 42nd Street Redevelopment Project.

8. Members are the New York chapters of the American Institute of Architects, the American Planning Association, and the American Society of Landscape Architects; the Architectural; the League; Cultural Assistance Center; the Municipal Art Society; the Landmarks Conservancy; the Parks Council; the Public Art Fund; the Regional Plan Association; and the Women's City Club of New York.

9. New York Landmarks Conservancy statement.

10. John Mollenkopf, "The 42nd Street Development Project and the Public Interest," *City Almanac* 18 (Summer 1985): 12-13.

11. Harold Lasswell, *Who Gets What, When, How* (New York: Whittlesey House, 1936).

12. Robert Dahl, *Modern Political Analysis* (Englewood Cliffs, NJ: Prentice-Hall, 1963).

13. E. E. Schattschneider, *The Semi-Sovereign People* (New York: Holt, Rinehart & Winston, 1960).

14. Harvey Molotch, "The City as Growth Machine," in H. Hahn and C. Levine, eds., *Urban Politics: Past, Present, and Future* (New York: Longman, 1980), 129-150.

15. Norman Fainstein and Susan Fainstein, *Urban Political Movements* (Englewood Cliffs, NJ: Prentice-Hall, 1974).

11

THE SYMBOLIC SIDE OF
POLICY ANALYSIS: INTERPRETING
POLICY CHANGE IN A HEALTH DEPARTMENT

STEVEN MAYNARD-MOODY
DONALD D. STULL

University of Kansas

POLICY AS AN EXPRESSIVE ACT

POLICIES ARE MORE THAN CAUSAL ARGUMENTS

Policy research methods derive from assumptions about public policy.[1] The prevailing view is that policies are causal arguments and successful policies efficiently deliver objective outcomes. While criticizing the narrow positivist base of policy analysis, Cook recently restated this assumption: "Every social program is implicitly or explicitly undergirded by theoretical postulates about factors that will ameliorate a social problem, whether it is poor academic achievement, underemployment, or prison recidivism."[2]

Although no one suggests that legislators and bureaucrats are disciples of scientific reasoning, government policies are, on the surface at least, designed to shape individual or collective behavior. "People typically think of government as a rational device for achieving their wants and see their own political opinions and actions as the epitome of

Palumbo, Mel Dubnick, and the editors of this volume.*

Authors' Note: *Support for this research was provided by grant number 85-404 from the General Research Fund of the University of Kansas. We are grateful for the openness and patience of the many individuals we interviewed and the thoughtful critiques of Dennis Palumbo, Mel Dubnick, and the editors of this volume.*

reasoned behavior."[3] Advocates promise that the death penalty will deter violent crime, threatening advertisements will reduce drunk driving, and tax cuts will spur economic growth. Detractors counter with alternative approaches to produce similar results. Amid the debate the policy analyst applies for grant support to examine these competing hypotheses.

The view that public policies are causal arguments implies that experimental designs are preferred. The strength of experiments, quasi-experiments, and the use of statistical controls is their power in rejecting false claims about causal relationships. Curiously even critics of the experimental approach accept the assumption that policies are primarily instrumental. Patton, Cronbach et al., and Guba and Lincoln argue that qualitative or ethnographic research provides a more useful, valid, and detailed picture of the effects of policies.[4] They do not advocate qualitative methods as a means of understanding the noninstrumental side of policy.[5] Rather, "qualitative techniques [add] to the list of possible causal methods."[6]

Policies have tangible results, and examining effects, whether through experiments or in-depth interviews, is an essential component of policy analysis. But policies have an expressive as well as an instrumental side: They say as well as do things, they communicate values and intentions, and they distribute symbolic rewards as well as alter behavior. Returning to the previous examples, anti-drunk driving ads, though ignored by drunks, reinforce values of sobriety and satisfy the demands of organized interest groups. Similarly executions and tax cuts express toughness on criminals and devotion to free enterprise though neither demonstratively discourages crime nor encourages investment.

These expressive dimensions of policy are central to understanding government actions but are left out of current discussions of policy analysis. This problem extends to the academic field of political science: "Although there are exceptions, the modern perspective in political science has generally given primacy to outcomes and either ignored symbolic actions or seen symbols as part of manipulative efforts to control outcomes, rather than the other way around."[7]

MEANINGS OF THE EXPRESSIVE DIMENSION

Strategic

The expressive side of policy can take several forms. These forms are not exclusive; a single policy can include them all. The first is strategic.

Many policies are designed specifically to send a message that we are serious about a problem. They are intentionally expressive. For example, the recent increases in defense spending broadcast resolve as well as build military muscle. Critics, who demonstrate that spending does not purchase more defense, have overlooked this central point.

The strategic uses of policy can be overt or covert. The president and advocates of defense spending have publicly repeated the need to "send a message to Moscow." In other cases the expressive side of policy masks intentions. David Stockman, former head of the Office of Management and Budget, claimed that the massive tax cuts of the first year of the Reagan administration were presented as an economic stimulant to disguise the purpose of cutting social programs. Tax cuts were, in Stockman's term, a "trojan horse"; they clothed policy in a misleading expressive context.[8]

For policy analysts the strategic uses of expressive policies create difficulties. Such uses are instrumental in the sense that they are consciously designed, but the means of achieving results is symbolic. Furthermore, the policy analyst must carefully identify the strategic uses of expressive disguises, what spys call "disinformation."

Symbolic Rewards

Second, governments distribute symbolic rewards. Policies communicate to individuals and groups the rightness of their causes, even if the policies do little to remedy problems. They reward individuals and groups with legitimacy and attention. Mothers mad about drunk driving press politicians to do something and are satisfied, in part, by ineffectual media campaigns. These ads do, however, reiterate that drunk driving is wrong, and this message is a primary outcome of policies aimed at drunk driving.

The importance of political language and symbolic rewards has long been recognized as central to politics. Few disagree with Edelman's observations that support for policies does not depend entirely on performance and that "political language is . . . not simply an instrument for describing events but itself a part of events, shaping their meaning and helping to shape the political roles officials and the general public play."[9] The problem is that policy analysts, when exploring policy options or evaluating policy outcomes, ignore symbolic results and thereby overlook a central feature of policy.

Value Statements

Third, public policy expresses values and beliefs that may have little to do with encouraging certain outcomes. At times these beliefs are obvious, such as the effort to remove the study of evolution from the classroom. Often beliefs are obscured by rational arguments.[10] The norm of rational discourse requires policymakers to describe and defend decisions in terms of effects.[11]

In other issues public policies balance value conflicts. For example, the values of punishment, remediation, and cost-effectiveness pull corrections policy between the polls of "conscience and convenience."[12] Successful policies, such as community corrections, encompass these value conflicts as well as produce results.[13] The policymaking process involves framing issues so that conflicting views and values are brought together. Consensus building is central to policymaking, and articulating values is at least as important as tangible results in understanding public policy. Policies are cultural as well as causal statements: They are ingredients in the expressive glue that holds societies together, especially diverse societies such as our own.

ADMINISTRATIVE REORGANIZATIONS AS POLICY

In the preceding sections we argued that public policies are expressive as well as causal statements, and that the preoccupation of policy analysts with instrumental outcomes presents a one-dimensional picture of public policy. In the following sections, we will present an analysis of the expressive side of the reorganization of a state regulatory agency. Although all public policies are a mix of expressive and instrumental elements, some, such as administrative reorganizations, are more completely expressive and therefore provide exemplary cases for analysis.

Findings from previous research suggest the expressive nature of reorganizations. First, reorganizations are common at all levels of government. Second, the history of reorganization is "a history of rhetoric."[14] Reorganizations are opportunities to repeat publicly commitments to greater economy, efficiency, and responsiveness, the dominant values of public bureaucracies. Third, empirical studies of the impact of structural changes on economy, efficiency, and responsiveness have found few tangible results. Reorganizations are therefore paradoxical;

they are repeated over and over but do not produce the promised
objective outcomes. As will be shown, they provide the context for
reinforcing certain values and legitimizing the authority of certain
groups.

Although not often considered public policy in the same way as are
programs such as community corrections programs, the structure of
public agencies is an essential form of policy. The existence and
responsibilities of agencies and their various divisions for the most part
are mandated by law. Changing structure often requires new legislation.
Moreover, the organizational status of a particular social problem
reflects its importance to both policymakers and constituents. The
creation of the Department of Education during the Carter administration and the efforts to dismantle it during the Reagan administration
effect education policy more than any individual program.

Reorganizations alter the access and decision structure that determine to a large extent which policies are considered important and how
policies are implemented. It is now widely recognized that the manner in
which policies are implemented largely determines their nature. Reorganizations alter the context within which laws and policies become
programs. Like budgets, they do not define the details of specific
policies; rather, they change the relative salience of certain issues and
define who participates in decisions. Such institutional factors are
central to forming and implementing policy. As March and Olsen
conclude, "the organization of political life makes a difference."[15]

METHODS

INTERPRETING THE EXPRESSIVE SIDE OF POLICY

The site of the present study of administrative reorganization was the
Kansas Department of Health and Environment (KDHE), a major state
cabinet agency. The work of KDHE is primarily regulatory, and the
focus of the present research is the 1983 reorganization. Previous
reorganizations, especially one in 1974, were also examined in order to
isolate general characteristics of reorganizations from those unique to
the 1983 enactment.

Understanding the expressive dimension of reorganization presents
several challenges. The first is that reorganization, like any policy,
communicates different messages to different groups. Second, analysis
involves identifying patterns of interpretation rather than measuring

behavioral change. Third, meanings, even more than behavior, are mutually created. The most skillful strategic use of the expressive side of policy depends on the interpretations of the audience for impact. Nevertheless, administrative policy, like any form of communication, does not say all things; the potential meanings are few.

Analysis of the expressive dimension of policy moves from observables, such as statements and actions, to interpretations of meaning. Because expressive phenomena rarely lend themselves to quantification, the standards of evidence and argument are ambiguous. Nonetheless, the approach is empirical.[16] Quantification does not translate subjective perceptions into objective characteristics, but it does provide a set of shared and overt decision rules for inferences. Empirical interpretation parallels the data collection and inference of statistical social science but lacks its clear and agreed standards of proof. Like statistical inferences, interpretive inferences are judgments about unseen patterns based on observations.[17]

The process of empirical interpretation begins with traits and proceeds through two levels of interpretation. Interpretation requires (1) the interplay of the observable characteristics in the form of words, actions, and artifacts; (2) the various explanations of these characteristics by relevant actors; and (3) a search for a theoretically useful understanding of these various interpretations. Traditionally policy analysts have shunned theory and preferred practical answers to policymakers' questions. Nevertheless, interpretation requires the explicit reference to social theory and breaks down false distinctions between applied and academic research.

For policy the traits include history, legal mandates, administrative rulings, statements by sponsors and opponents, and the actions of implementers and clients. The specific traits of the reorganization of KDHE were described based on: (1) one- to two-hour taped interviews with key informants; (2) collecting memoranda, letters, and other documents; and (3) the careful review of annual and biannual reports dating from the founding of the agency in 1885. Interviews were open-ended and recorded the informants' reconstructions and interpretations of current and historical events. A list of standard questions and topics was followed to increase comparability of responses.

Key informants included all of the top management, selected individuals representing all sections and levels of the agency, from the agency head to the clerk typist, and a few persons from outside the agency. Informants were selected on the basis of their position and history within the agency and upon the recommendation of other informants. To increase external validity, informants were deliberately selected for their heterogeneous viewpoints. Interviewing ended when no new perspectives were provided.

Various actors in the policy environment offer differing perceptions and understanding of the words and deeds we call policy. The first level of interpretation ascertains the meaning of the traits to the various actors in the system and was based on the informant interviews. Interviews were transcribed verbatim and examined for themes.

This first level of analysis is described by linguists and anthropologists as "emic" interpretation.[18] Emic meaning is the interpretation given by members of a group, the natives, and may seem foolish, incomplete, and rationalized to outside observers. Nevertheless, first-order empirical interpretations require researchers to inhibit their own judgments about meanings and to gather, sort, and organize the interpretations of the actors within the social system.

Second-order interpretations require inference beyond observations and interview transcripts. Guided by theory about individuals, organizations, and political systems, the policy analyst describes reasonable latent functions. Latent functions refer to the underlying purpose and value structure of a policy; they inform us about the nature of the particular society and about social behavior in general. Latent functions are a form of "etic" interpretation that is meaningful to outside observers, such as policy analysts, but not necessarily meaningful to the actors in the system.[19] This characteristic of much social science theory may explain, in part, the limited use of social science by decision makers. Latent functions are "disciplined abstractions."[20] They are abstract in that they describe unobservable patterns, yet they are disciplined by their base in empirical observations. As with statistical science, the strongest discipline for ideas is the active and open search for disconfirming evidence.

Most social events can be understood from a variety of theoretical perspectives. In interpreting the expressive side of administrative reorganization, we turned to theories of organizational power and subcultures. The primary characteristics of power relationships in bureaucratic organizations are stability over time and the absence of overt conflicts.[21] Power is highly institutionalized, and shifts in assumptions are rare and disruptive. As Zucker observed, "For highly institutionalized acts, it is sufficient for one person to tell another that this is how things are done."[22] The institutionalization of power becomes part of the shared understanding of organizational members,[23] with organizational subcultures playing a central role in maintaining, communicating, and altering such assumptions.

Schein writes that group culture is a set of shared and transmitted assumptions that form in response to the basic problems of "1) survival in and adoption to the external environment and 2) integration of its internal processes to insure the capacity to survive and adapt."[24] The group's shared assumptions grow out of joint problem solving, but with time these assumptions shape how problems are perceived and what solutions are considered. In this way institutionalized assumptions have a strong influence on the manner in which policies are implemented. Reorganizations may not increase efficiency, but, as will be described, they are powerful status dramas that communicate to members the basic assumptions about organizational power and the nature of policy.

THE CASE OF KDHE

TRAITS

Our analysis of the symbolic side of the reorganization of KDHE follows the three steps outlined: We begin with traits and discuss two levels of interpretation. The traits of the 1983 reorganization of KDHE fall into three categories: (1) the public language used to promote and condemn the reorganization, (2) changes in structural relationships and personnel, and (3) history.

Public Language

The 1983 reorganization, like most, promised to increase efficiency and improve responsiveness to elected officials and citizens. The rhetorics of efficiency and responsiveness are common to administrative reorganizations. Proponents of KDHE's reorganization argued for "maximum accountability to the [secretary] as the representative of the people." Opponents decried the interference of "political hacks" over "technically qualified personnel."

The conflicting language of efficiency, responsiveness, and expertise justified a range of opinions and shaped the debate surrounding the reorganization. The reorganization was a clash of rationales, each symbolically emphasizing different values. One function of the reorganization was the balancing of these inconsistent values. In the case of

KDHE, the values of technical competence had traditionally eclipsed those of responsiveness, and the reorganization provided an opportunity to find a new compromise between the need for expertise and accountability.[25]

A New Organizational Chart

The reorganization also changed the organizational chart. Although organization scholars have long understood that the formal hierarchy provides only faint clues to organizational behavior, the organizational chart is an important organizational symbol. Most departmental reports dating from KDHE's founding began by displaying the organigram. Organization members take seriously the status, power, and authority implications of hierarchical positions.

Moreover, during reorganizations considerable group time and effort is invested in the minor changes in the organizational chart, even though no one interviewed suggested that these changes altered the day-to-day operations of the agency. Two offices that existed previously as support services became divisions headed by political appointees. Within the divisions of Health and Environment 18 bureaus were reduced to 8. This reduction was, except in one case, based on consolidating bureaus under new bureau managers. Nevertheless, nearly all of the original 18 bureaus remained as intact programs with a new layer of midmanagement separating division from program directors. The basic work of KDHE remained unchanged. Renewed emphasis on following the chain of command and formal procedures accompanied the streamlined organization chart.

The reorganization opened up all management positions, and position descriptions were rewritten to emphasize managerial, not technical, skills. Individuals who had held key administrative positions, some for many years, were encouraged to reapply but none was guaranteed his or her old job. In the end three of the four division directors were new or very recent employees. The bureau manager positions were filled with a mixture of insiders and outsiders, but no one who was strongly identified with previous administrations retained a position of authority. Many of the old guard, who were later referred to as "the malcontents," were given jobs with little formal authority. Thus under the guise of impersonal alterations of the organizational chart and promotions based solely on qualifications, a coup was staged.

End of an Era

Although reorganizations were common throughout KDHE's 100-year history, the 1983 reorganization was unique. Previous reorganizations involved minor adjustments to structure as the department grew or took on new tasks. Reorganizations prior to 1983 left the same group in control of the agency and the established organizational assumptions intact. From 1904 to 1983, the department was dominated by a subculture with roots back to the department's founder.

Although not the board's first secretary, Dr. S. J. Crumbine was the founder of the modern department. Secretary from 1904 to 1923, Crumbine's primary legacy was an organizational philosophy and approach to solving the state's public health problems. Organizational norms stressed freedom from political interference, the innate power of science, and a commitment to do whatever was needed without regard for the political consequences. His highly visible public health pamphlets repeated such slogans as "Dare to do it different." He armed troops of Boy Scouts with fly swatters ("Are you a swatter or a quitter?") and had the sidewalks of the capital paved with bricks admonishing "Don't spit on the sidewalk." He published lists of companies that sold adulterated and spoiled food and examined drugs and remedies in his labs.

In 1974, a major structural reorganization occurred. The old board system was abolished and the department became a cabinet-level agency within the executive branch of state government. No longer did the appointed Board of Health insulate the agency from politics. Ironically, this profound change in organizational structure was hardly felt within the agency. This was partly because the first secretary of the reorganized department was a long-term employee with strong allegiance to the organization's core values.

Over the next decade, growing concern about environmental pollution and the regulation of nursing homes brought the department into increasing conflict with legislators and interest groups. In 1983, the governor appointed a secretary, who, for the first time in the department's history, was an outsider to both the agency and its dominant subculture. Secretary Barbara Sabol had held top-level positions in state and federal bureaucracies and placed a high priority on relations with elected officials. Within months of taking office, the new secretary ordered a major reorganization.

FIRST-ORDER INTERPRETATIONS:
THE MEANING TO MEMBERS

Although our informants generally agreed on the events that transpired during the reorganization, their interpretations of the meanings of events and actions differed markedly along subcultural lines. One of the primary findings was that the interpretation of events clustered into two identifiable groups. These groups were not defined by status within the organization; both included a range from management to clerk-typists. What distinguished the groups was their assumptions about the organization, its work, and core values.

Especially instructive were the two groups' views, summarized in Table 11.1, of the reasons for the reorganization. The incoming Sabol subculture saw KDHE as a stale, overly bureaucratic organization run by people promoted beyond their capability and concerned only with defending their organizational turf. The outgoing Crumbine subculture saw the reorganization as a ruse. They complained that highly skilled, committed employees were replaced by "pure bureaucrats" and saw the structural changes as adding needless layers of midmanagement. Each denounced the other as bureaucratic; each attached different meaning to the epithet.

In addition, informants from the two subcultures differed in their interpretations of the reasons for and meanings of the new hiring process. These differences are illustrated in Table 11.2. Both groups recognized the emphasis of administrative over technical skills, but the Sabol subculture pointed to the value of trained administrators in management jobs whereas the Crumbine subculture lamented the downgrading of experience and expertise. Both defended their views as consistent with merit promotion while expressing radically different definitions of merit. In reorganizations, as with all policy changes, finding that different groups attach different meanings to the same concept underscores the importance of examining first-order interpretations. There are no universal definitions of "merit," "efficiency," "fairness," or whatever the guiding values of a particular policy. Each must be understood in context.

Thus the new leaders differ greatly from the old in both membership and values. It is important to stress that the differences in values exist even though both groups paid public homage to efficiency and responsiveness. The differences lie in what they meant by those terms. The incoming subculture views responsiveness to elected officials as a

TABLE 11.1

Subculture Differences on the Reasons for Reorganization

Reasons for Reorganization	
Sabol Subculture	*Crumbine Subculture*
"I think some programs were probably stale. . . .Maybe they had been around for 20 years making decisions, but weren't being responsive to the secretary's needs."	"It was given the name of 're-organization,' but I think it was just a ruse to get rid of people that they wanted out of there."
"What happened prior to the reorganization was a lot of dissatisfaction, and I think there was a looseness to the work structure of the department that did not provide you with much understanding."	"I see no point in what she's done. . . . She comes in, she wants her own people, she terminates the bureau directors, makes them apply for the jobs that they were in under new titles, then most of them she doesn't keep. I don't see that it's streamlined. I don't see that we're any more efficient."
"I think we have for the most part a fine crew of bureau directors now, whereas before we had some people who were prime examples of the 'Peter Principle.' They had just absolutely no right being in the position they were in. It was just completely above and beyond their capability."	"I was appalled by the whole thing . . . because I saw some very great people, I thought, really tromped in the dirt, just ahead of retirement."
"[The reorganization has] given those people in the programs a new direction that is healthy and it's a new administrative outlook. The people in the programs, the administration, have been more responsive to the programs rather than responsive to building turf."	"They just wanted to clean shop and have all their own people in there. . . . And here you come in with a . . . pure bureaucrat [referring to the secretary]."
"From a management standpoint, there was no doubt that it was top heavy."	

central value and defines sound policy in terms of legislative intent. To the old guard relations with politicians are a necessary evil. For them good policies pursue the technically correct response to the situation regardless of the political consequences and are, in their view, responsive to the long-term interests of citizens.

The new leaders have different views of management efficiency as well. Budgets and standard operating procedures became sacrosanct, and all internal communication strictly adhered to the "chain of

TABLE 11.2
Subculture Differences over the Hiring Process

Hiring Process	
Sabol Subculture	*Crumbine Subculture*
"I think it's great because I've always felt that administrators who were trained as administrators do top-notch jobs."	"[The new administration] rewrote the job descriptions [and] took away a lot of the education and experience requirements.... They had no intention of hiring the guys that were in those positions.... And they had credentials.... They had professional qualifications that won't quit."
"And we never really had a pure administrator, somebody that keeps things right on, and keeps the paper work going and doesn't become personally involved with the projects . . . ."	"The [old guard] had been here 30 or 40 years and have the technical training."
"I honestly feel that if all the 'old people' who had applied for jobs performed as well in interviews as the 'new people,' they would have been chosen."	"We've been here longer than they have. We know the ropes a little better than they do."
	"I thought they would base [hiring] on the merits and the credibility of the people and choose the best person, but evidently it isn't that way."
	"The only thing I can think he did is like the old spoils system."

command." This view differs sharply from the Crumbine subculture, whose members boasted of using money for important but not budgeted projects. Working relationships and communication lines were informal; they took pride in the lack of formal procedures within the agency. For the Crumbine subculture cutting red tape and bypassing the chain of command defined efficiency. Quotations from informants in Table 11.3 illustrate these subcultural differences.

The two groups also differ in their career paths. The new leaders have advanced by moving from job to job and agency to agency, whereas the Crumbine subculture members worked their way up through the ranks of KDHE. The new group identifies with other administrators in state

TABLE 11.3
Subculture Differences in Management Philosophy

Management Philosophy	
Sabol Subculture	*Crumbine Subculture*
"[The chain of command] is formal from the standpoint that the section directors come to me and I go to the division director and the division director goes to the secretary. I rarely see the secretary; it's been about six months. . . . Under the old system . . . I saw [the secretary] four or five times a week. . . . I would just as soon keep it the way I have it now and that way I don't have to respond to two bosses."	"Someone was telling me that he now had five different layers to go through before he got a decision. Now that is ironic, indeed! We set out to simplify and now are really stuck on dead center."
"I think that what you have to do is just follow the hierarchy and act the way that you expect an employee to act."	"I used to know all the executive staff comfortably enough that we called each other by our first names, but I would never call Secretary Sabol 'Barbara,' and I would never call Dr. Jones 'Sam,' whereas [the previous division director] we called 'Jim.' This is a difference. . . . Also I would never, ever speak my mind to either of them."

and national government; the reference for the displaced leaders is their profession. Thus the most significant outcome of the 1983 reorganization was the dramatic shift in sanctioned values that accompanied the overthrow of one subculture by another.

SECOND-ORDER INTERPRETATIONS: REORGANIZATION AS A STATUS DRAMA

In the previous section we saw how members of the two subcultures attached quite different meanings to the reorganization. Is there a reasonable explanation for these differences? Can we interpret these differences to gain insight into reorganization as a policy? As suggested earlier, these events gain meaning when interpreted in terms of the relationship of organizational power and subcultures.

The 1983 reorganization was characterized by a series of events that dramatized the new ideology of the incoming leaders and their overt rejection of the agency's established policies and procedures. The reorganization proved an opportunity to act out, as in a morality play, the competing values of the two subcultures. For example, during meetings to discuss the reorganization, members identified with the Crumbine subculture were expected to denounce their past publicly. As one member put it: "What happened with those who were here before, if you tried to get on board [after the reorganization] was to make a finding that everything that went before was incompetent."

In contrast, previous reorganizations dramatized a different message. Earlier reorganizations, especially one in 1974, involved changes in structure, but the same group remained in control of the redesigned organization. Previous reorganizations reinforced the stature of the established subculture; they told members that despite adjustments in form, the same group remained in control and the core assumptions remained intact.

These brief examples indicate that although most reorganizations involve adjustments in structure and changes in policies and personnel, their impact varies according to the message inherent in the reorganization. The differing messages that are sent through similar traits are thus central to understanding the role of reorganizations in defining shared assumptions of members. The 1983 reorganization challenged and replaced the Crumbine subculture by making clear that old assumptions, established procedures, and the existing informal structure of the organization were no longer operative. Basic assumptions about institutionalized power were reorganized. This was done by altering the informal structure of access, information flow, and influence. It opened up the organization so that the entrenched dominant subculture could be replaced by a new one.

The latent functions of the 1983 reorganization were thus in sharp contrast to previous reorganizations, which have served to affirm the values and behaviors of the dominant Crumbine subculture. Previous reorganizations had served to shore up the status and authority of the established subculture by fine tuning the formal structure. The informal structure was left in place and the norms of the dominant subculture were reinforced.[26]

By probing beneath the surface instrumental outcomes of reorganizations to uncover the meanings of the process, we discover the powerful expressive latent functions. It then becomes apparent why the 1983 reorganization of the KDHE was so traumatic whereas previous reorganizations, although more instrumentally substantive, were, as one informant put it, "hardly noticed by anyone outside the executive wing." Affirmative reorganizations, such as the one in 1974, build a sense of stability and security by reinforcing the existing social order. Denial reorganizations, such as the one in 1983, seek to overturn the established order and thereby bring about uncertainty and insecurity. It is not surprising that although they have little instrumental impact, they are keenly felt within the organization.

IMPLICATIONS FOR POLICY ANALYSIS

We have argued that administrative policy is both instrumental and expressive and presented an example of the empirical interpretation of the expressive side of policy. Most previous evaluations of administrative reorganizations looked for improvements in efficiency and responsiveness and found few instrumental effects.[27] We explored the expressive elements and found that reorganizations communicate to policy implementers the changing status of different groups and assumptions about their work.

These messages alter the manner in which policy is implemented. For example, the 1983 reorganization of KDHE indirectly yet forcefully underscored the need to work more closely with the governor's office and state legislators and less with regulated industries. Such a shift in emphasis has a greater impact on policy than any individual health program or environmental regulation.

What are the implications of this point of view for policy analysis? Focusing on the intended and unintended effects of policy remains an important contribution, but at minimum policy analysts need to recognize that their assumption that social policies are causal statements is incomplete. Clearly policy analysis, whether highly quantitative or completely qualitative, that focuses exclusively on instrumental effects presents an incomplete picture.

In addition, the expressive or communicative aspects of policy remain central to the policymaker's art. Observers of the tenuous relationship between policy analysts and policymakers find that each inhabits a different conceptual world. The assumption that policies are exclusively designed to have identifiable impacts is a major source of this misunderstanding.

This analysis also suggests a different form of triangulation. Previous calls for multiple methods assume that social phenomena are unitary. The use of various imperfect research methods provides a valid picture from converging results.[28] But phenomena as complex as social policies are not singular.[29] They encompass, at minimum, two distinct dimensions: the instrumental and the expressive. Interpretive policy analysis strives to decode the messages delivered by policies and to present a more complete picture of policy. This picture does not discount instrumental effects; it broadens understanding to include the expression of social values.

NOTES

1. This chapter is not about all policies, although it has implications for all policies. It concerns administrative policy, not decisions on oil leases, dams, or weapon systems.

2. T. Cook, "Postpositivist Critical Multiplism," in R. L. Shotland and M. Mark, eds., *Social Science and Social Policy* (Beverly Hills, CA: Sage, 1985), p. 30.

3. M. Edelman, *Political Language: Words that Succeed and Policies that Fail* (New York: Academic Press, 1977), 4.

4. M. Q. Patton, *Utilization-Focused Evaluation* (Beverly Hills, CA: Sage, 1978); L. Cronbach, S. Ambron, S. Dornbusch, R. Hess, R. Hornik, D. Phillips, D. Walker, and S. Weiner, *Toward Reform of Program Evaluation* (San Francisco, CA: Jossey-Bass, 1980); E. Guba and Y. Lincoln, *Effective Evaluation* (San Francisco, CA: Jossey Bass, 1981).

5. Advocates of qualitative policy analysis, however, present a more complicated view of causal relationships. Guba recently argued that policies, causes, and effects are socially constructed and cannot be abstracted from their social context. Such a view is compatible with the observation that social policies are expressive as well as instrumental. See E. Guba, "What Can Happen as a Result of a Policy?" *Policy Studies Review* 5 (1985): 11-16.

6. Cook, "Positivist Critical Multiplism," p. 34.

7. J. March and J. Olsen, "The New Institutionalism: Organizational Factors in Political Life," *American Political Science Review* 78 (1984): 738.

8. W. Greider, "The Education of David Stockman," *Atlantic Monthly* (December 1981): 27-54.

9. Edelman, *Political Language*, p. 4. See also M. Edelman, *The Symbolic Uses of Politics* (Urbana: University of Illinois Press, 1964).

10. S. Maynard-Moody, "The Fetal Research Dispute," in D. Nelkin, ed., *Controversy: Politics of Technical Decisions, 2nd ed.* (Beverly Hills, CA: Sage, 1984).

11. M. Feldman and J. March, "Information as Signal and Symbol," *Administrative Science Quarterly,* 26 (1981): 171-186.

12. D. Rothman, *Conscience and Convenience: The Asylum and Its Alternatives in Progressive America* (Boston: Little, Brown, 1980).

13. D. Palumbo, S. Maynard-Moody, and P. Wright, "Measuring Degrees of Successful Implementation: Achieving Policy Versus Statutory Goals," *Evaluation Review* 8 (1984): 45-74.

14. J. March and J. Olsen, "What Administrative Reorganization Tells Us about Governing," *American Political Science Review* 77 (1983): 282. This paper provides a thorough review of the reorganization literature and stresses their symbolic nature.

15. March and Olsen, "New Institutionalism," p. 747.

16. M. Harris, *Cultural Materialism: The Struggle for a Science of Culture* (New York: Random House, 1979), chapter 1.

17. C. Taylor, "Interpretation and the Sciences of Man," in P. Rabinow and W. Sullivan, eds., *Interpretive Social Science: A Reader* (Berkeley: University of California Press, 1975), 25.

18. K. L. Pike, *Language in Relation to a Unified Theory of the Structure of Human Behavior, 2nd ed.* (The Hague: Mouton, 1967); Harris, *Cultural Maternalism.*

19. Pike, *Language and Relation,* Harris, *Cultural Materialism.*

20. J. Lofland, *Doing Social Life: The Qualitative Study of Human Interaction in Natrual Settings* (New York: John Wiley, 1976).

21. J. Pfeffer, *Power in Organizations* (Marshfield, MA: Pitman, 1981), 299.

22. L. Zucker, "The Role of Institutionalization in Cultural Persistence,"*American Sociological Review* 42 (1977): 726.

23. R. Brown, "Bureaucracy as Praxis: Toward a Political Phenomenology of Formal Organizations," *Administrative Science Quarterly* 23 (1978): 365-382.

24. E. Schein, *Organizational Culture and Leadership* (San Francisco: Jossey-Bass, 1985), 51.

25. For a more detailed discussion see S. Maynard-Moody, D. Stull, and J. Mitchell, "Technocrats versus Bureaucrats: The Ritual of Reorganization" (Paper presented at the Annual Meeting of the American Anthropological Association, Denver, November 1984).

26. For a fuller discussion of prior reorganizations see S. Maynard-Moody, D. Stull, and J. Mitchell, "Reorganization as Status Drama: Building, Maintaining and Displacing Dominant Subcultures" (Paper presented at the Annual Meeting of the American Political Science Association, New Orleans, LA, August 1985).

27. A recent evaluation of the 1983 reorganization of KDHE followed this standard approach and found few improvements. See R. Green, C. Lask, and C. Winegarner, *Performance Audit Report: Reorganization of the Division of Environment* (Topeka, KS: Legislative Post Audit, 1985).

28. E. Webb, D. Campbell, R. Schwartz, and L. Sechrest, *Unobtrusive Measures: Nonreactive Research in the Social Sciences* (Chicago: Rand McNally, 1972), 3.

29. L. Greene and C. McClintock, "Triangulation in Evaluation: Design and Analysis Issues," *Evaluation Review* 9 (1985) 523-545.

12

ECONOMIC THEORY IN PRACTICE: WHITE HOUSE OVERSIGHT OF OSHA HEALTH STANDARDS

CHARLES NOBLE
Rutgers University

Prior to the 1973-1975 recession, economists and corporate executives were almost alone in urging cost-benefit and cost-effectiveness tests for health, safety, and environmental regulations. Today, politicians and administrators holding otherwise quite divergent political points of view have joined their ranks. A broad and growing consensus supports the use of decision-making methods that balance the goals of social regulation against the economic values of growth and efficiency. Reformers still continue to press for the aggressive implementation of protective legislation. But their ranks have been thinned by high rates of inflation and unemployment, and their influence has been diluted by this rising tide of opposition of protective legislation passed in the halcyon days of the Great Society.

How has this change in perspective affected the course of protective policy? Clearly cost-benefit and cost-effectiveness tests for health and safety rules have lowered the costs of social regulation. According to the Reagan administration's Task Force on Regulatory Relief, the applica-

Author's Note: *This chapter draws on my book,* Liberalism at Work: The Rise and Fall of OSHA *(Philadelphia: Temple University Press, 1986).*

tion of these review procedures to just three agencies' rules—the Department of Transportation, the Environmental Protection Agency and the Occupational Safety and Health Administration—between 1981 and 1983 led to savings of $6.4 billion in one-time capital costs and $2.4 billion in annual recurring costs.[1]

But in the long-run economic review has had another, often ignored impact that may prove more important to the course of public policy than short-term cost reductions. Economic analysis of health and safety regulation is shaping the way policymakers interpret the social rights and responsibilities that are the legal foundations of the modern regulatory state. In particular, by introducing economic values into the regulatory process, economic review has colored the way in which policymakers frame the two basic decisions that must be made when regulating health and safety. First, what level of risk should people assume in the ordinary course of their lives and work? Second, how should protection—or risk reduction—be distributed among individuals?

This article considers this precedent-setting dimension of economic review by considering how cost-benefit and cost-effectiveness analyses have shaped the debate over health standard setting by the Occupational Safety and Health Administration (OSHA). The first section frames the discussion by explicating two different ways of thinking about protection within the liberal tradition: one based on notions of universal rights and equity, the other on economic values—most importantly, the value of efficiency. In the second and third sections I suggest that the rights created in the Occupational Safety and Health Act (OSH Act) contradict the economic perspective outlined earlier. The fourth section examines how the White House review programs have attempted to resolve this contradiction by imposing the economist's notion of efficiency through administrative means.

The last section considers the implications of the White House review program for democratic policymaking in America and suggests that it poses a serious challenge to those who support democratic control of social policy and citizen participation in the exercise of public authority. It is, of course, difficult to generalize in this way from a single example. But I have chosen OSHA because many of the most important issues are apparent in this case. Critics and advocates of economic review have been forced to confront, and their debates help to illuminate, these issues. And the lessons of this case are generally applicable, as the following discussion will make clear.

EQUITY, EFFICIENCY, AND
PROTECTIVE POLICY

There is no objectively correct way to allocate protection among individuals at risk in society. Competing traditions of political and economic thought offer competing standards. Radical critics of capitalism argue that work should be designed to promote political and economic self-determination by workers as a class. In contrast, market conservatives seek to maximize individual economic freedom and labor productivity. But even within the liberal tradition of political economy, policymakers are often faced with hard choices because liberalism offers two alternative standards—one political and the other economic—for evaluating protective policies.

To be sure, there are important homologies between liberal political and economic theory. Both argue that the self-interested action of individuals will produce the good society. Both presume that that action will occur in a capitalist economic system. Both privilege and seek to preserve as large a role as possible for the private sphere. But there are equally important differences between liberal political and economic theory. These are reflected in conflicts between modes of analysis that stress the norms of equity and those that stress the norms of efficiency.

Liberal notions of equity are based in a philosophical reading of the just relationship between the citizen and the positive state. At minimum, the liberal view of equity requires formal political equality: Each citizen should enjoy the same political rights as every other citizen. More broadly, equity is sometimes taken to mean that public officials have an obligation to compensate individuals for the harm suffered from socioeconomic inequalities that derive from differences in their initial endowments of wealth or inherited social status. Affirmative action programs, for example, implement this view.

In contrast, the liberal norm of efficiency—derived from the neoclassical microeconomic theory of resource allocation—argues that private and public decision makers should allocate scarce resources to their most economically productive uses. This is accomplished by satisfying certain marginal equalities. For example, firms should produce a particular commodity until the marginal revenues from its sale equal the marginal costs of its production. Similarly, workers should sell their labor to employers until the marginal benefits of work (i.e., wage increments) equal its marginal costs (i.e., foregone leisure).

Traditionally this view has been applied to the private market decisions of firms, consumers, and employees. But it can also be used to evaluate the supply of public goods. Applied directly to regulation this view suggests that policymakers choose programs that deliver the greatest net benefits; that program goals be established which result in the equalization of marginal costs and benefits; and that policies be cost-effective—that is, equalize the marginal costs of protection across programs.

Additionally, wherever possible benefits should be calculated by using the values that individuals place on them when they act in markets. For example, the value that policymakers place on health and safety at work should be based on the trade-offs that workers themselves make between wages and safety. Costs, in turn, should be calculated by aggregating the market prices of the resources consumed, and opportunities foregone, due to government programs. If these rules are followed, policymakers will choose policies that are "optimal" from an economic point of view.

In the best of all possible worlds, public policies would promote equity and efficiency simultaneously. This is sometimes possible. There are redistributive programs that also promote the more efficient use of the factors of production. By more fully utilizing existing productive capacity, public policies that stimulate high employment can benefit the unemployed and increase the overall productivity of labor and capital. But there are also instances in which equity and efficiency are competing ends. In such cases policymakers must choose between maximizing one or the other.

The most obvious examples occur when social policies produce benefits in ways that contradict the least-cost principle of production. Public works projects that hire workers at union wages, for example, may provide jobs and create infrastructure inefficiently. But the more complex and less understood examples occur when policymakers *distribute* public benefits in ways that violate the efficiency criteria of the neoclassical market model. Many social regulatory statutes do this in several ways.

First, social regulatory legislation often requires agencies to achieve levels of protection that do not correspond to what individuals would choose in markets. Rather, administrative rules are substituted for market processes. Consequently, the mandated level of risk reduction departs significantly from what consumers, workers, or residents would select if they had to trade wages or other opportunities or resources for protection. Second, many protective statutes disregard least-cost principles of production in setting rules for distributing protection. The American welfare state has tended to promote equal protection, and social regulation follows suit. Thus liberal policies seek to treat individuals equally. But different individuals face different kinds of hazards at work and in their communities. As a result, hazard abatement for one group may entail a considerably larger resource commitment than hazard abatement for another.

For example, it is much more expensive to provide clean air to someone who lives in an industrial city than to a resident of a sparsely populated rural area. In the latter situation, the environment is likely to be comparatively unpolluted; fewer safequards will be necessary than in a crowded urban area; those that are required are likely to be far less costly than those that are required to protect city dwellers. Because it is less costly to save lives in rural areas than in cities, this case presents the policymaker with a choice between maximizing efficiency or equity. If the amount of resources that can be devoted to air pollution control is limited, economic principles argue that policymakers should first save lives in rural areas. Equity argues, however, that residents in both areas be afforded the same level of protection. Policymakers should accept the fact that they will have to spend more money to save lives in cities than in rural areas. In other words, they must disregard least-cost principles in producing and distributing clean air.

THE OCCUPATIONAL SAFETY
AND HEALTH ACT

Nowhere is the conflict between the norms of equity and efficiency more apparent than in the political struggle to interpret and implement the Occupational Safety and Health Act of 1970. The OSH Act challenges neoclassical market principles by creating a universal, state-enforced right to protection. In doing so it divorces the allocation of risk and protection from individual choice in labor markets and orders administrators to equalize risk among workers. In combination, these provisions create a substantive, generic entitlement to workplace health and safety that counterposes liberal norms of equity to the efficiency criteria of the market place.

The suspension of the market in health and safety and the obligation to equalize risk are required by several of the act's provisions. The act's stated purpose is "to assure so far as possible *every* working man and woman in the Nation safe and healthful working conditions" ([Sec 2(b)], italics added). To accomplish this the act requires that each employer "furnish to each of his employees employment and a place of employment which are free from recognized hazards that are causing or are likely to cause death or serious physical harm to his employees." (Sec 5(a)(1)). To enforce these rights, the Secretary of Labor is required, when issuing standards that deal with toxic materials or "harmful physical agents," to

> set the standard which most adequately assures, to the extent feasible, on the basis of the best available evidence, that *no* employee will suffer material impairment of health or functional capacity even if such employee has regular exposure to the hazard dealt with by such standard for the period of his working life. [Sec 6(b)(5), italics added].

The blanket protection afforded workers by Section 6(b)(5) is exceptional. No other social regulatory statute so clearly precludes a regulatory agency from weighing economic effects before taking action. Some sections of the Clean Air and Clean Water Acts require pollution to be reduced to the lowest achievable level. But the Clean Water Act requires state water quality standards to consider the impact of regulation on the availability of water for industrial uses as well as the cost of technology and the age of existing equipment and facilities. The Clean Air Act requires that emission control and fuel standards be accompanied by cost-benefit analyses. In fact, most statutes require agencies to take multiple factors—including costs—into account. The National Environmental Protection and Toxic Substances Control Acts require consideration of the technical, economic, and social impacts of agency actions. The Consumer Product Safety Act and the federal pesticide law force the Consumer Products Safety Commission and the EPA, respectively, to weigh the costs of regulation against the benefits of protection.

Understandably, the precise meaning of Section 6(b)(5) of the OSH Act has become the subject of intense controversy in and out of the courts. Many critics of the act have argued that Congress did not mean to protect workers in this way; most often they have tried to temper the act's provisions by reading some sort of cost-benefit test into the reference to feasibility. But none of the provisions of the act requires OSHA to take costs into account. Its language and history are relatively inhospitable to economic review. The term "feasibility" occurs only once in the entire act, in the Sec. 6(b)(5) reference to permanent health standards. Nowhere are "economic" feasibility, the general cost issue, or balancing mentioned.

The legislative history is clear on this point. The act's cost provisions were contested by industry and labor. The steel and chemical industries lobbied Congress to require that OSHA standards consider costs. The unions, however, objected on the grounds that such a provision would allow employers to appeal every standard and enforcement action. The Democrats agreed with organized labor, and the industry proposal was rejected in committee. In fact, the bill lacked any reference to feasibility until the very last moment of legislative deliberations. Only then did Senator Jacob Javits (R-N.Y.) succeed in amending the health standards section to acknowledge the cost issue. But his reference to feasibility is much vaguer than industry wanted, and business lobbyists recognized this.[2]

The bill's legislative proponents and opponents also understood the limited purchase of the term. According to Rep. Carl Perkins, Chair of the House Labor Committee, the bill as written provided a "congressionally recognized right to every man and woman who works to perform that work in the safest and healthiest conditions that can be provided."[3] Republican opponents agreed. Sen. Peter Dominick (R-Colo.) was the author of several industry-oriented amendments that were defeated on the Senate floor. His comments, though hyperbolic, reflected industry and Republican anxiety about the legislation:

> It could be read to require the Secretary to ban all occupations in which there remains some risk of injury, impaired health, or life expectancy.... The present criteria could, if literally applied, close every business in this nation.[4]

The courts have not gone this far in interpreting the act's provisions. Judicial review has made room for some kinds of economic analysis. In 1974 the Court of Appeals resolved a controversy over the asbestos standard by holding that the act's feasibility clause required that the agency consider the economic consequences of Sec. 6(b)(5) health standards. In *IUD* v. *Hodgson*, that court ruled that although OSHA standards could put individual firms out of business and cut into the profits of all firms in a particular line of business, a standard was economically infeasible when it threatened the very existence of an entire industry. According to the court, common usage suggested that "a standard that is prohibitively expensive is not 'feasible.'"[5]

The Supreme Court cleared the way for other forms of economic analysis in the 1980 benzene case when it ruled that OSHA had to provide quantifiable evidence of the benefits of health standards. In this case the Court imposed a "substantial evidence" test on agency rules based in the Act's Sec. 3(8) definition of a standard. According to that section, standards had to be "reasonably necessary or appropriate." Thus, the Court held, OSHA had to demonstrate that its preferred exposure level was more "necessary or appropriate" than the alternatives that it rejected. In other words, it had to demonstrate that a standard eliminated a "significant risk."[6]

But although the asbestos and benzene cases legitimated some kinds of economic review, the Supreme Court rejected cost-benefit analysis of health standards in the 1981 cotton dust case. In this case the Court returned to the phrasing in Sec. 6(b)(5) and held that it contained a general congressional decision about the appropriate relationship between costs and benefits. Congress, the Court ruled, understood that worker protection would be costly and might reduce profits. But the legislature had decided that in the case of health standards practicability was the only limiting criteria. Standards that met the "significant risk" doctrine promulgated by the Court in the benzene case, did not threaten entire industries, and were "capable of being done" were "feasible."[7]

ECONOMISTS AGAINST OSHA

According to the neoclassical economist's notion of efficiency, this approach to workplace safety and health is irrational. Neoclassical economic values argue for individual choice between protection and other resource commitments and against the equalization of risk among workers in diverse settings. Otherwise, society will fail to maximize the total net benefits of the resources devoted to health and safety. Concretely, this means two things.

First, considering that efficiency is served if individuals are allowed to choose the level of safety and health that they want and are willing to pay for, policymakers should, wherever possible, rely on market mechanisms to allocate protection. Specifically, policy should not prevent workers from choosing among competing jobs based on their own preferences for safety or wages. Employers, it is argued, provide a mix of jobs with different safety and wage characteristics. Risky jobs carry risk premiums—that is, wage supplements to compensate workers for being exposed to more hazardous work. These wage offers, in turn, reflect the true costs of providing safety in different plants, industries, and occupations as well as availability of labor. Thus workers who choose safer jobs "buy" protection at cost by foregoing compensatory wage increases. As a result, the level of safety supplied is determined by the interplay of supply and demand. Thus it is optimal from an economic point of view.

In contrast, as Robert Smith, one of the leading academic critics of OSHA, argues, the OSH Act "force(s) more safety and health on society than workers would choose for themselves if they had to pay the costs of safety and health directly." In economic terms "the safety and health mandate of the Occupational Safety and Health Act of 1970 is inconsistent with the goal of promoting the general welfare."[8]

If market mechanisms do not function and government standards are necessary to protect workers, the neoclassical view argues that policy-makers should use economic criteria to set standards. This entails two procedures. First, the economic costs and benefits of standards should determine the levels and kinds of protection provided. Standards should be imposed only where the net benefits exceed the net costs, and standards should in all cases be cost-effective. W. Kip Viscusi, Professor of Business Administration at Duke University and a consultant to OSHA during the Reagan administration, clearly states this case. If OSHA must set standards, the agency should make decisions in the following way:

> First, the government should select the policy that provides the greatest excess of benefits over its costs and, since one alternative is to do nothing, it should not adopt any policy whose costs exceed its benefits. Second, to obtain the highest net gains from policies the scale of the programs should be set at levels where the incremental benefits just equal the incremental costs; further expansion or reduction in the policy will produce lower net benefits overall. Third, all policies should be cost-effective, that is, the cost imposed per unit of benefit should not be greater than for other policies.[9]

In addition, wherever possible administrators should use workers' "willingness to pay" as revealed in risk premiums to value the benefits of standards. If risk premiums do not provide reliable information, policymakers should rely on other measures of how workers value protection, including survey research, to calculate benefits.

Some policy analysts stop short of suggesting that cost-benefit tests actually determine the level of protection sought by OSHA. Richard

Zeckhauser and Albert Nichols of the Kennedy School of Government endorse economic review because it would

> force OSHA to examine the consequences of its standards more closely. . . . It would highlight inconsistencies in different areas; it might show, for example, that at current levels of stringency one standard costs $5 million at the margin per expected life saved, while another could be tightened at a cost of only $5,000 per expected life, thereby yielding 1,000 times the OSH gain for its cost impositions. In such a case, by loosening the first standard and tightening the second, it would be possible both to increase longevity and to free resources for other uses.[10]

But, as Zeckhauser and Nichols argue, this would lead OSHA to focus its standard setting on areas in which it could achieve "the greatest health gains for whatever resource costs they entail."[11] In practice, then, their version of cost-effectiveness would lead to the disaggregation of the OSH Act's rights to protection. Risk would remain unevenly distributed among workers.

WHITE HOUSE REVIEW OF
OSHA HEALTH STANDARDS

As it has been conceived and practiced, the White House review of OSHA's health standards has attempted to implement the economists' view of protective legislation. Lodged in various agencies within the Executive Office of the President (EOP), the reviewers have not always been successful. But they have been insistent. In Ronald Reagan's first term they succeeded in winning their point, and economic review played an important part in shaping the way in which policymakers defined the rights granted by the OSH Act.

The White House preview program began in earnest under President Gerald Ford in 1974, in the midst of what was then the most serious economic recession since the Great Depression. Ford sought to increase presidential control over regulation as part of his "Whip Inflation Now" program. Subsequently, the White House's oversight capacity increased steadily, and a centralized institutional apparatus was created within the EOP for analyzing the economic effects of regulation and making periodic interventions into agency rule-making. Executive orders have required executive agencies and departments to assess the economic consequences of proposed actions, keep reviewing bodies abreast of their plans to regulate industry, and justify their proposals to the reviewers.

OSHA became an early and favorite target for White House review. Under Ford the Council on Wage and Price Stability (CWPS) intervened seven times in OSHA standards cases. It issued three reports on a proposed noise standard and one report each on rules for coke oven emissions, agricultural sanitation, arsenic, and deep sea diving. During the Carter years, CWPS and/or the Regulatory Analysis Review Group (RARG) intervened nine times into OSHA rulemaking. They issued two reports on lead and one each on sulfur dioxide, benzene, cotton dust, acrylonitrile, the cancer policy, pesticides, and electrical safety.

Under Reagan, White House oversight was further centralized and economic review became stricter. The Presidential Task Force on Regulatory Relief revoked OSHA's walkaround pay standard, delayed the implementation of the lead standard, delayed and then ordered the revision of the proposed hearing conservation rule, and ordered a reconsideration of the cotton dust standard. Thorne Auchter, the Reagan-appointed head of OSHA, tried to anticipate OMB's objections. But even his mild forays into standard setting drew fire from the reviewers who intervened to block or revise several major standards proposals after 1981, including a revised and weakened labeling standard and a proposed ethyl dibromide standard.

In addition, Reagan's Executive Order 12291 made cost-benefit tests mandatory for all of OSHA's nonhealth standards.[12] In situations in which the agency was blocked by the Supreme Court from doing cost-benefit analyses, OSHA developed a fourfold test that established other, equally strict criteria. Sect. 6(b)(5) health rules had to (1) target substances that could be demonstrated to pose a "significant risk' to workers, (2) substantially reduce that risk, (3) adopt the most technologically and economically feasible approach, and (4) be cost-effective. Not only was the agency limited to health standards that clearly reduced obvious hazards, it had to choose the *most* feasible— that is, the least costly—control technology available.

In practice these review procedures did more than reduce the costs of standards. They introduced neoclassical economic theory into OSHA standard setting, as White House review of two standards demonstrates.

THE COKE OVEN STANDARD[13]

In 1975, OSHA proposed to reduce the permissible exposure limit (PEL) for workers exposed to coke oven emissions. Coke is a byproduct of coal and is used as fuel in steelmaking and in foundries, and as a reducing agent in blast furnaces. The materials produced during the distillation of coal are known to cause cancer of the lungs, skin, and urinary system. In the mid-1970s, approximately 22,100 workers were believed to be at risk from this hazard. When it proposed to reduce the PEL, the agency submitted an inflation impact statement (IIS) to OMB in conformance with the requirements of Ford's executive order. The IIS estimated that the coke oven standard would cost between $218 million and $241 million per year and save up to 240 lives yearly.

In 1976, CWPS challenged OSHA's analysis of the standard's costs and benefits as well as the logic underlying its decision to regulate at all. Although OSHA had refused to do a cost-benefit analysis, CWPS's did one for it. Using OSHA's own figures, CPWS calculated that OSHA proposed to "spend' between $9 million and $48 million to save the life of a worker at risk. CWPS also supplied its own figures and did a second analysis along the same lines. It lowered OSHA's estimate of the number of lives that would be saved yearly as well as its cost estimate. Based on these new figures CWPS calculated that the true costs of protection in this case were between $4.5 million and $158 million per life. This was, CWPS suggested, excessive. It recommended that OSHA consider regulating risks in "other occupations with both higher relative risks and much larger absolute numbers" of workers at risk, thereby taking advantage of "the potential of saving more lives at lower costs."

OSHA rejected CWPS's recommendations. In justifying its decision, it cited the act and its policy of limiting economic review to the determination of abatement periods and the satisfaction of a court-imposed requirement that OSHA standards not endanger the viability of entire industries. Nonetheless, the coke oven case is an important landmark in the development of economic review. The reviewers were not content to check OSHA's estimates; they did not argue that the steel industry would be imperiled by the standard; they did not maintain that the macroeconomy would be weakened. Rather, CWPS used economic review to argue for the disaggregation of the right to protection and against the equalization of risk. Efficiency considerations, CWPS maintained, argued for leaving the affected steelworkers unprotected and protecting workers in other industries in which morbidity rates were high and the costs of protection low.

Actually, CWPS used the equity issue against OSHA. It agreed that "the question of equity must be considered." However, CWPS's interpretation of the concept was based not on the language and history of the act but on an economists' reading of the problem of protection:

There are many other occupations ... that present us with the potential of saving more lives at lower costs. This is important because the nation's resources that may be devoted to saving lives are limited. The total number of lives saved can be maximized only if the expenditures devoted toward saving lives are made in such a way so as to be equalized at the margin.[14]

THE LABELING STANDARD[15]

Reagan's 1981 Executive Order required all executive agencies to satisfy cost-benefit tests. Specifically, the benefits of regulatory actions had to outweigh their costs; agencies had to select only those regulatory objectives that maximized the net benefits to society; and agencies had to choose control methods that involved the least net cost to society. The Supreme Court's ruling in the cotton dust case precluded cost-benefit tests for OSHA health standards, but the administration was not prevented from doing cost-benefit analyses of nonhealth standards. Consequently economic review was used in the development of the labeling standard, and this case illustrates how cost-benefit analysis affects the interpretation of rights and responsibilities in the OSH Act.

This controversy began in the last days of the Carter administration when OSHA proposed a rule requiring employers and chemical manufacturers to identify chemical hazards in the workplace and to make this information available to workers. In keeping with the administration's Regulatory Relief program, Auchter immediately withdrew this proposal for reconsideration. In this case, however, there was strong employer support for some sort of agency action. Supported by unions, environmentalists, and public interest groups, the "right to know" movement was proving successful in passing state and local labeling laws; many of these were quite stringent. After 1980, the chemical industry and other affected employers shifted their position on federal regulation and, instead of opposing it, sought sympathetic federal action as a means of preempting more hostile state and local regulation.

In response, Reagan's OSHA proposed a revised rule that substantially limited coverage and augmented employer rights to withhold trade secrets. In keeping with the executive order, the agency submitted a cost-benefit analysis that calculated the rule's benefits to be $5.2 billion versus compliance costs of $2.6 billion (both in present, i.e., discounted future, values). The rule, OSHA claimed, would save medical costs and augment labor productivity because better-informed employees would have fewer injuries and illnesses. Moreover, it would serve the public interest in two ways: State protection would lead to uneven coverage whereas OSHA's rule would provide uniform protection. In addition, the labeling standard would provide workers with more information, an important but undersupplied public good.

OMB rejected OSHA's logic, its figures, its conclusion, and the rule. According to OMB, OSHA grossly overestimated the benefits of labeling by making a number of faulty assumptions. It incorrectly assumed that compliance with the standard would change worker behavior and reduce the rate of job-related illnesses and injuries by 20% over a 20-year period. This, OMB declared, was far too optimistic; there was no hard evidence that labels and warnings really did lead people to change their behavior. In addition, OSHA overstated the rule's benefits. It overestimated the number of job-related illnesses and, at the same time, exaggerated the rate of introduction of new chemicals into the workplace and the rate of inflation in medical costs.

Equally damning to OMB, OSHA's claim that more information and uniform standards were in the public interest failed to speak to the economic values of the review process. The first was misguided; the second, tangential to the issue at hand. From an economic point of view a federal standard was actually a positive disability. "By increasing smaller companies' overhead costs," OMB argued, the standard "would put them at a competitive disadvantage relative to companies that already have such programs." To OMB, the survival of small business was as important as worker protection. Information, in turn, could not be treated as a general public good. While "some value should be ascribed to knowledge even if it does not improve safety," OMB admitted, "this knowledge should not be considered a 'right' in isolation from cost considerations."

Having dispensed with OSHA's interpretation of the act, OMB adjusted the benefit figures according to its own assumptions. The standard's real benefits, it calculated, were $85 million dollars—one eightieth of OSHA's original estimate.

In response to these criticisms, OSHA shifted its strategy. Armed with a third cost-benefit analysis that spoke only to the economic issues, OSHA appealed OMB's decision to the Presidential Task Force. This new study, conducted by Viscusi for OMB and OSHA, estimated the rule's benefits to be $2.85 billion, or $285 million more than the estimated costs. Viscusi agreed with OMB that OSHA had incorrectly calculated the rule's benefits by monetizing future medical cost savings and productivity increases due to lower accident and illness rates. But

Viscusi also disagreed with OMB's benefit estimates. Unlike OMB, Viscusi assumed that workers would respond to increased information by acting more safely. Moreover, he argued that the value of a standard should be calculated by using the "willingness to pay" approach that estimated benefits based on individual workers' preferences for accident reduction. Using this method Viscusi concluded that OSHA's standard passed the cost-benefit test.

In the end the Task Force sided with OSHA—powerful industrial interests wanted the revised labeling standard, and Auchter was able to use their support in his effort to secure the support of Task Force head Vice-president George Bush. But the controversy over the labeling standard illustrates two key aspects of the review process. First, it indicates the inherent ambiguity of the method. Three competing cost-benefit tests were used. Each began from different assumptions and reached very different conclusions about the need for and desirability of a rule in this area. Even OMB had to acknowledge that unavoidable uncertainty about health, safety, and worker behavior had forced the agency to speculate about the effects of its rule.

More important, this controversy illustrates how policymakers who sought an efficient standard used economic assumptions to reach conclusions that bore little or no relation to the spirit of the OSH Act itself. Each cost-benefit analysis diluted the legislative right to protection. OSHA's original cost-benefit test was used to justify a comparatively weak rule that would have preempted stronger state and local efforts. In turn, OMB's critique of OSHA's cost-benefit analysis was used to discount worker rights to information and uniform protection despite the act's emphasis on worker participation and federal coverage. Finally, by using a "willingness to pay" approach to calculate benefits, OSHA's second cost-benefit test reintroduced market principles into the allocation of protection among workers.

ASSESSING ECONOMIC REVIEW

The economists' critique of blanket protection is not unreasonable. Clearly, in a world of scarce resources and many hazards, it is important to set priorities among competing goals. Agencies should take care that the resources they devote to protection are used intelligently and not wasted on trying to provide unrealistically high levels of protection. It is also true that the OSH Act neither requires OSHA to establish priorities nor emphasizes the efficient use of resources. In this context it makes sense that economic review has been recommended as one solution, albeit an imperfect one, to a real defect in the social regulatory policymaking process.

But there are two major problems with economic review, and these are sufficiently severe to recommend against it. The first follows from the way in which efficiency criteria shape decision making about the distribution of protection. Standards and enforcement programs that do not seek to equalize risk subvert the OSH Act's universal right to healthly work and disaggregate worker protection. Both cost-benefit and cost-effectiveness analyses have been used in just this fashion. Indeed, as cost considerations have played an increasingly larger role in setting PELs, OSHA health standards have begun to vary widely in the degree of protection afforded affected workers. The arsenic standard, set during the Carter administration, assumes a risk of eight cancer cases for each 1,000 workers over a lifetime of exposure. In contrast, the proposed revision in the benzene standard, revised to take the Supreme Court's "substantial evidence" ruling into account, envisions between 44 and 152 cases of cancer per 1,000 workers.[16] Moreover, this variation in risk follows directly from the emphasis on cost-effectiveness.

Equally disturbing, economic review imposes this approach to the allocation of risk and protection from above, under the guise of value-neutral decision making, rather than through reasoned debate and democratic deliberation. To the extent that the oversight process works effectively, general legislative decisions about worker protection are countermanded by White House economic advisors accountable only to the president. Thus it not only alters the criteria used to make policy, White House regulatory oversight shifts the balance of power and authority between the executive and the legislature.

Because White House oversight centralizes decision making in the executive branch and augments the power of economic advisors and agencies such as the CEA and OMB, it also diminishes the role that affected constituents can play in the determination of regulatory policy. Organized labor, for example, has proven relatively successful at influencing congressional committees and regulatory agencies and less effective at lobbying EOP agencies. Thus to the extent that oversight shifts the locus of decision making from traditional subgovernments to the White House, it diminishes the unions' ability to promote workers' interests in protection.

The antidemocratic implications of economic review are especially clear in the case of the OSH Act because the reviewers' recommendation to equalize the marginal costs and benefits of protection rather than equalize risk directly contradict the provisions of the law. Some of OSHA's critics recognize this and its political implications. To their credit, Zeckhauser and Nichols acknowledge that cost-effective health standard setting is incompatible with the OSH Act and suggest that Congress amend the legislation.[17] But many other critics of OSHA are not equally forthcoming.

Some economists sidestep this issue by redefining the idea of democratic control. They suggest that policies that allow workers the freedom to choose between safe work and higher wages promote democracy. This view equates market choice with liberty and liberty with democracy: Individuals who buy occupational safety and health or opt for well-paid but risky jobs are freer than those who are constrained by standards that impose a uniform level of protection on all workers. Viscusi, for example, argues that "uniform standards do not enlarge worker choices; they deprive workers of the opportunity to select the job most appropriate to their own risk preferences."[18]

Similarly, some economists argue that cost-benefit tests that use "worker willingness to pay" as a means of valuing the benefits of regulation provide a democratic method of determining which hazards to control because they reflect individual choices between protection and other resource uses. Thus deregulation maximizes both democracy and economic welfare. In this way the problem of protection is redefined and the conflict between equity and efficiency eliminated. The efficient solution is also the fair one.

But this redefinition of democratic control is fundamentally flawed. The equation of individual choice in markets with liberty, and liberty with democracy is by no means obvious or consensual. To the contrary, it substitutes a market model of individual choice for a political model of public choice. In doing so it replaces one kind of decision-making mechanism with another, despite the majority's clear preference for collective decision-making mechanisms in cases such as health and safety, where markets often fail to provide important public goods and discourage the kind of informed choice that makes for democratic policy.

Equally important, the market model incorrectly assumes that individual choices in labor markets are truly free. But several factors shape workers' trade-offs between safer and better paying jobs, including their income and wealth position. Given that a worker's initial market position will shape how he or she shall values health and safety, standards and policies based on the market model distribute protection

according to preexisting market inequalities. All other things being
equal, poor people are likely to suffer in the process. Zeckhauser and
Nichols acknowledge that the poor will assume greater risks in
competitive markets. But they conclude that this may be necessary if
government seeks to set standards efficiently.[19]

In the end the distributional decision remains a political one, and we
necessarily confront the conflict between the two liberal notions of the
good society—one arguing for universal rights; the other, for economic
efficiency. Taken to their logical conclusions, these ideas offer competing
visions of the just society and radically different policy prescriptions.
Society may decide, as Congress did in 1970, that democratic values
require the kind of effort envisioned by the architects of the OSH Act.
Within these parameters, policy makers can use efficiency criteria to
assess alternative compliance techniques. Economic review can be used
to raise questions about the desirability of reducing risk in situations in
which protection is very costly.

But economic review cannot decide these issues in a neutral fashion.
The economists' observation that resources are scarce does not provide
a rule for determining the level of resources to be devoted to health and
safety. It only suggests that society will have to forego other social goals
if it wishes to pursue this one and that the inefficient use of resources in
one program decreases the resources available for other programs. Once
we recognize the political issues at stake here, however, economic review
does not provide a compelling argument against the equalization of risk
among workers.

Of course, liberal notions of equity also have limited applicability.
Abstract universal rights are not appropriate guides to action in all
settings. A host of compensatory programs from affirmative action to
public assistance require that individuals in diverse situations be treated
differently. Health and safety protection may be another case in which
legislators decide to establish rules that distribute the benefits of the
welfare state unequally. But democratic values still argue for public
participation in making this decision and against a centralized review
process legitimated only by the norms of economic efficiency.

NOTES

1. Presidential Task Force on Regulatory Relief, *Reagan Administration Regulatory
Achievements,* August 11, 1983.

2. Personal interviews with John J. Sheehan, United Steelworkers of America, June 8, 1983; Leo Teplow, American Iron and Steel Institute, February 11, 1983; Anthony Obadal, United States Chamber of Commerce, February 11, 1983 and July 26, 1983.

3. *Legislative History of the Occupational Safety and Health Act of 1970* (Washington, DC: U.S. Congress, Senate Committee on Labor and Public Walfare. Subcommittee on Labor, 1971), 986.

4. Ibid., 367.

5. Industrial Union Department v. Hodgson, 499 F.2d 487 (D.C. Cir. 1974).

6. American Petroleum Inst. v. OSHA 581 F.2d 493 (5th Cir. 1978), aff'd sub. nom. Industrial Union Dept v. American Petroleum Inst. 448 U.S. 607 (1980).

7. AFL-CIO v. Marshall, 617 F.2d 636 (D.C. Cir. 1979, aff'd sub. nom. American Textile Mfrs. Inst. v. Donovan, 452 U.S. 490 (1981).

8. Robert S. Smith, *The Occupational Safety and Health Act* (Washington, DC: American Enterprise Institute, 1976), 3.

9. W. Kip Viscusi, *Risk by Choice* (Cambridge, MA: Harvard University Press, 1983), 80-81.

10. Richard Zeckhauser and Albert Nichols, "The Occupational Safety and Health Administration—An Overview," in *Study on Federal Regulation* (S. DOC. No. 13, 95th Cong. Ist Sess., Vol. VI, 103-248, 1978), 226.

11. Zeckhauser and Nichols, *OSHA*, p. 167.

12. *Federal Register*, 46, 33. Title 3. E.0. 12291 (February 19, 1981).

13. This discussion is based on "Council on Wage and Price Stability Testimony on Coke Oven Emissions Inflation Impact Statement," *Occupational Safety and Health Reporter*, (May 1, 1976): 1798-1800.

14. Ibid., p. 1799.

15. This discussion is based on "Pressure from VP, Study Confirming Benefits Pushed OMB to Issue OSHA Rule," *Inside O.M.B.* 7 (March 28, 1982): 1ff.

16. Philip Shabecoff, "Tangled Rules on Toxic Hazards Hamper Efforts to Protect Public," *New York Times* (November 27, 1985): Al, 2ff.

17. Zeckhauser and Nichols, *OSHA*, p. 167.

18. Viscusi, *Risk by Choice*, p. 80.

19. Zeckhauser and Nichols, *OSHA*, p. 163.

NAME INDEX

SUBJECT INDEX

ABOUT THE AUTHORS

Douglas J. Amy is Assistant Professor in the Department of Politics at Mount Holyoke College. His primary research interests include ethics and public policy, environmental politics, and democratic theory. He is the author of *The Politics of Environmental Mediation* (forthcoming, Columbia University Press).

Charles W. Anderson is Hawkins Professor of Political Science at the University of Wisconsin—Madison. He has done research on and has taught about the problems of Latin America and Third World development, the common policy problems of industrial nations, and, most recently, the political-economic implications of contemporary liberal theory. He is the author or editor of seven books, and his current project is entitled *Pragmatic Liberalism*.

John Byrne is Director of the Center for Energy and Urban Policy Research and Associate Professor of Urban Affairs and Public Policy at the University of Delaware. He has published articles and books on regulatory policy, cost-benefit analysis, technology policy, and urban political economy. He is editor or coeditor of four books, including *Energy and Cities* and *Energy Policy Studies*.

Leonard A. Cole, a political scientist, is an Adjunct Professor at the New School for Social Research. His publications include *Blacks in Power: A Comparative Study of Black and White Elected Officials* (Princeton University Press) and *Politics and the Restraint of Science* (Rowman and Allanheld). He is completing a book entitled *Secret Clouds*, about the Army's biological warfare tests over populated areas.

Susan S. Fainstein is Professor of Urban Planning and Policy Development at Rutgers University. She is coauthor of *Restructuring the City* (Longman, 1983), coeditor of *Urban Policy under Capitalism* (Sage, 1982), and has written a number of other books and articles on urban political economy and public policy.

Frank Fischer is Associate Professor of Political Science at Rutgers University in Newark. He is the author of *Politics, Values, and Public Policy: The Problem of Methodology* (Westview Press) and coeditor of *Critical Studies in Organization and Bureaucracy* (Temple University Press). Currently he is completing a book on technocratic politics.

John Forester is Associate Professor in the Department of City and Regional Planning at Cornell University. Interested in the politics and ethics of professional practice, he has recently edited *Critical Theory and Public Life* (MIT Press, 1985) and coedited *Policy-Making, Communication, and Social Learning: Essays of Sir Geoffrey Vickers* (Transaction, 1987).

Bruce Jennings is Associate for Policy Studies at the Hastings Center in Hastings-on-Hudson, New York. His recent publications include *Ethics, the Social Sciences, and Policy Analysis* and *The Ethics of Legislative Life*. He is currently at work on a study of ethics and professionalism in the field of public administration.

Timothy W. Luke is Associate Professor of Political Science at Virginia Polytechnic Institute and State University in Blacksburg, Virginia. His research focuses on modern social theory, comparative politics, and international political economy. He is the author of *Ideology and Soviet Industrialization* (Greenwood Press).

Steven Maynard-Moody is Assistant Professor of Public Administration in the Division of Government and Director of the Policy Analysis Program in the Institute for Public Policy and Business Research at the University of Kansas. His publications have appeared in numerous journals, including *Public Administration Review, Administration and Society,* and *Administrative Science Quarterly*. Currently he is coauthoring a book on the process of policy innovation.

Charles Noble is Associate Professor of Political Science at California State University, Long Beach. He writes on American politics, public policy, and political economy and is author of *Liberalism at Work: The Rise and Fall of OSHA* (Temple University Press).

Donald D. Stull is a research associate in the Institute for Public Policy and Business Research and Associate Professor of Anthropology at the University of Kansas. His recent publications focus primarily on current American Indian affairs and policy. He is the coeditor of the forthcoming book, *Collaborative Research and Social Change: Applied Anthropology in Action* (Westview Press).

Rosemarie Tong is Associate Professor of Philosophy at Williams College. She is the author of two books: *Women, Sex, and the Law* and *Ethics in Policy Analysis*. Currently she is authoring *Contemporary Feminist Thought* and coauthoring *Genetic and Reproductive Technology: A Scientific and Philosophical Overview*.

NOTES

NOTES

NOTES